9⁹⁵

D0966050

SALESWOMAN
A guide to career success

SALESWOMAN

A guide to career success

BARBARA A. PLETCHER

President
Creative Sales Careers, Inc.

DOW JONES-IRWIN
Homewood, Illinois 60430

ISBN 0-87094-166-6
Library of Congress Catalog Card No. 78-059222

Printed in the United States of America

1 2 3 4 5 6 7 8 9 0 K 5 4 3 2 1 0 9 8

Preface

This book was written for the woman who wants a career in professional selling. I firmly believe that a career in sales is the best path to business success. This book contains four separate sections linked by the common theme of how to achieve a fulfilling and rewarding career.

Chapters 1 through 3 explain what you need to know about yourself and the profession of selling in order to select the sales job that's right for you. Chapters 4 and 5 deal with the realities facing women in a business environment. I have tried to describe very realistically what you can expect. I have also made every effort to coach you rather than prescribe to you how to deal with the situations you will encounter.

Chapters 6 through 10 are the meat of this book. They represent the best advice of sales professionals on how to sell effectively and how to consistently outperform your peers and your competition, both male *and* female. Chapters 11 and 12 discuss how to realize your goals of more responsibility, authority, and money; in other words, how to get promoted.

Many people have helped me in my efforts to answer these questions. I want to thank all of the saleswomen, salesmen, and sales managers who have been willing to share their experiences and feelings. I truly appreciate the efforts of those who read the manuscript and provided helpful guidance. Ruth Cleary, Linda Ebbets, Bill Faught, Joan Fischer, Joyce Perkins, Dale Pletcher, and Jerny Rieves all made important contributions. David Pletcher has not only served as my proofreader but has given me great hope for the future.

July 1978   Barbara A. Pletcher

Contents

1 Do you have what it takes? 1
2 Turning roadblocks into building blocks 22
3 Your first sale: Landing the right job 39
4 Be assertive, not aggressive 65
5 Whoever said the world is fair? 84
6 The first step to successful selling: Preparation 101
7 Help your customer buy 118
8 Follow-up and follow-through 137
9 Use your time: Don't kill it 152
10 Vive la différence: Special concerns of women in sales . . . 172
11 Helping your sales manager help you 192
12 You, too, can have role models and sponsors 212
    Index 225

1 Do you have what it takes?

Do you have what it takes to be a successful saleswoman? This may appear to be a simple question, but don't answer yet. If you have what it takes, some outstanding opportunities await you. If you have never before considered a career in professional sales, it might be because of the stereotype salesperson personified by Professor Harold Hill in Meredith Willson's musical *The Music Man.*

STEREOTYPES FLOURISH

Most people think of salespeople as retail clerks, door-to-door peddlers, and the person who sold them a house or car. While all of those people are salespersons, they are not professional salespersons any more than the

Florida land dealers, the freezer plan promoters, or the characters in books, TV, and movies are the true representatives of a professional sales career.

Can you think of any reason why the writer of a 30-minute situation comedy should accurately portray professional salespeople? Just as a political cartoonist emphasizes unique features or memorable qualities, a writer gets into your mind through the nearest entrance by building on stereotypes. Therefore, we are bombarded with hard-driving business*men* who can't cope without a pitcher of martinis, and sales*men* who are patterned after Willy Loman in *Death of a Salesman*. These characterizations are no more reflective of reality than is the pervasive image of the dumb blonde or the horse-kissing cowboy.

The stereotype dictates that salesmen are cigar-smoking, back-slapping men who chase farmers' daughters. You know that the stereotyped treatment of women, blacks, and other ethnic groups is a disservice. Should you believe the fictional accounts of salespeople are any more accurate? But you know some women and you know some blacks. Therefore, you have some ammunition to resist these stereotypes. Do you know any professional salespeople? Most people are willing to accept the idea that salespeople are some composite of the Music Man, a snake oil dealer, and a horse trader. If that were the case, the conclusion would be that a sales career would only attract those with a callous disregard for the welfare of others. This is not true.

WHAT IS PROFESSIONAL SELLING?

Professional selling is a challenging career which offers capable women continuing opportunities to serve the needs of their buyers while benefiting themselves. Professional sales bears little resemblance to routine over-the-counter retail sales or high-pressure fast-buck operations. *Professional sales involves the active investigation of the customers' needs to determine the best ways to satisfy those needs on a continuing basis. The professional saleswoman serves as a helpful liaison between her company and her customers. In fact, sales positions are often classified according to the type of customer being served.*

Retail salespeople deal with people who buy products and services for their own use or for use by their families and friends. There are professional and nonprofessional positions in retail sales. When you buy a car, toothpaste, a shirt, or a package vacation trip, you are dealing with a nonprofessional retail salesperson. At the retail level, professional sales positions are associated with intangible and highly individualized products such as stock, insurance, and even real estate. Many women in real estate, for example, have high earnings and advance rapidly. Women have been concentrated in nonprofessional retail sales. While this is considered selling for the statistical purposes of the government, it is not the position to which the term *Saleswoman* refers.

Trade salespeople sell to the firms which sell to customers at the retail level. The person who checks with the supermarket manager to assure an adequate supply and attractive display of laundry detergent is in trade sales. If you think about the number of products in the average supermarket and the number of stores in the country, you will realize that there are many sales positions supplying supermarkets alone. Now consider all the other stores. Someone is selling pencils to the dimestores, toy plastic trucks to the discount stores, and stereos to the appliance stores. Trade sales are also referred to as consumer product sales. Essentially these are sales of finished products which will be resold in the same form.

The responsibilities and rewards in trade sales vary widely. Some trade sales are essentially delivery routes. Some people make a lot of money on these delivery routes. Other trade sales positions require sophisticated approaches to knowledgeable buyers who will be placing very large orders or making decisions of continued importance. Someone helps major department and discount stores decide to carry a particular product. These are major business decisions and require a responsible performance.

The third type of selling is *industrial selling*. This involves selling products and services to buyers for use in producing other goods and services or maintaining businesses. Someone sells steel to the Ford Motor Company, and someone else sells sodium silicate to Proctor and Gamble. As you move away from selling to the general public to selling to businesses, the average dollar amount of the sale increases. As the responsibility increases, the rewards tend to increase.

Women in sales have been clustered in the lower paying positions just as they have been in the lower paying positions in most other businesses. The situation has been changing recently. Many companies are actively recruiting women as sales representatives. A Research Institute of America study revealed that only 15 percent of the nation's 500 largest manufacturing firms had women in their sales ranks in 1972. That figure increased to 38 percent in 1975. This, of course, does not mean that 38 percent of the industrial sales representatives are women. It means that 190 of the 500 firms surveyed had at least one woman in a sales position. There are tremendous opportunities for capable women in professional sales. But before you decide if you have what it takes to be a successful saleswoman, think about what it could mean to you. The business world has certain defined patterns and practices. You must recognize that structure and you must take active control of your career if you want to succeed.

WHERE DO YOU WANT TO GO?

Each of us is making this trip through life just once. If you are going to make the most of your trip, you must be certain that you are spending your life doing those things which will bring you the greatest personal rewards. While there may be little value in change simply for the sake of change, a periodic reexamination of the course of your life can be beneficial. You will either recognize that you are making the most of your potential and be even more satisfied with your situation, or you will find that you have drifted into patterns of behavior which are not contributing to the attainment of your personal goals.

All of us operate under constraints. Some people bow to those constraints and are buffeted about much like tumbleweeds on the desert. Others fight the constraints and waste their energies shouting into the wind. The person who recognizes the constraints and deliberately plots a course among the obstacles to a predetermined goal is the person who makes the most of the trip. Will you spend your life or enjoy it? It's up to you.

There is an old saying: "If you don't know where you're going, any road will do." Increasingly women are recognizing that there are preferred destinations. Women are aspiring to managerial positions that just a few years ago seemed unattainable, but while many women can recognize the desired end, they continue to start down the wrong path. If you go to the station and get on the wrong bus it doesn't matter how much you pay for your ticket or how long you stay on the bus. You'll never get to your preferred destination. How would you behave if you actually got on the wrong bus? Would you change your preferred destination? Would you get off and sit on the curb? What if you couldn't get a transfer? Would you invest in another ticket? How is life any different? Do you know where you are going? It's a long trip and it's your responsibility to get on the right bus. Most people are reluctant to change. They have invested time in a particular career and feel that they should stay to see if that investment will pay off. They are reluctant to admit an undesirable outcome even when the signs are quite clear. You can't do a single thing about your yesterdays; you can only work on your tomorrows. If your tomorrows justify change, you shouldn't delay on the basis of your yesterdays.

Are you satisfied that you are headed in the right direction? Try to think of your position ten years from now. Perhaps you're in a situation you can endure from day to day, but think about the next ten years. If you don't like what you see, you owe it to yourself to change. Should you ask the people you work with if your present career is right for you? What kind of answers would you expect? Maybe they selected that career with care and are pleased with it. If they are harboring secret doubts, they aren't likely to share them with you. They don't wish to appear foolish, frivolous, or weak. Even when circumstances have changed dramatically, people tend to cling to and defend past decisions. If the information and constraints have changed, changing your course is a sign of strength, not weakness. Only you can define what is right for you, but you must operate within the realities of the existing business system. Some of those realities have had a significant impact on the career choices of women.

STAFF OR LINE

Women in business have taken and continue to take the staff rather than the line route. Women in marketing are highly concentrated in marketing research, advertising departments, and in retailing staff functions. Some of these women are among the most successful people in their chosen fields and have accomplished a high level of professionalism. Unfortunately, many women are encouraged into staff positions even though their talents and ambitions would indicate that they are more suited for line responsibilities. Tradition or some other force deflects them from investigating alternatives such as sales.

The purpose of this book is to uncover the realities of professional selling as a possible route to success for women. While the advantages and opportunities can be great, they are not without costs. Before investigating professional selling as a career option, let's take a closer look at the nature of staff positions.

WHAT IS A STAFF POSITION?

Staff positions are created to support the main operations of the organization. They are basically service-oriented activities. Staff people assume the administrative responsibilities such as record keeping, personnel, and marketing research. Staff units within the organization relieve the operating units of duties for which they are not technically prepared or which would interfere with their main duties. Staff responsibilities range from highly technical research and design activities to clerical duties. Some staff positions are highly rewarding both psychologically and monetarily. Others aren't.

Staff positions have certain characteristics which are both the source of advantages and the root of disadvantages. First, in order to support the operating units, staff people must be available on a regular basis. Second, staff accomplishments contribute to the effectiveness of operating units, but the extent of an individual's contribution is often difficult to measure. Third, staff duties tend to be quite specialized. These three characteristics, regularity, contribution, and specialization, have interesting implications.

REGULARITY

Staff positions usually involve set working hours, such as the normal 9 to 5 pattern. This can be both a benefit and a drawback. Because women have been concentrated in staff areas, this type of work has been the focus of attention of many groups interested in the equalization of opportunity. One of the points raised is that many otherwise highly employable women cannot work because the 9 to 5 schedule conflicts with other responsibilities. If there could be some flexibility in time schedules, many women could assume higher paying and more rewarding positions. Unfortunately, although some serious efforts have been made, the very nature of staff responsibilities conflicts with this adjustment. Because staff duties support operating units, people who perform these duties are most often expected to maintain regular and predictable schedules. They are expected to be available to the operating units they support.

To some people time regularity represents an advantage. It means that they know exactly when they are expected to work, exactly what time they will arrive home each day, and exactly when they can plan their vacations. They can be quite certain that there will be few work interruptions in their nonwork schedules.

CONTRIBUTIONS

Staff positions often lack defined scales of productivity phrased in terms of the major mission of the organization. For example, a word-processing center can generate x pages of reports for a division of General Motors, but how does that translate into numbers of cars sold? A research unit may generate 12 viable new product ideas, but it will be a long time and many steps later before the first dollar of profit is seen. Today on some college campus a recruiter assigned to the personnel staff of some corporation may have persuaded a young job applicant to take the entry-level position which will eventually lead to the president's office. How can that recruiter's contribution be measured today? Many staff contributions pay off in the future. This can't be measured directly, so substitute measures are used. What measures are there? In some cases the scales used bear some resemblance to productivity. A recruiter's rewards may be based on the number of interviews and a researcher's on the number of projects completed. It is extremely difficult to incorporate a factor to account for the quality of the applicants or the usefulness of the research findings.

Some of the measures used have no relationship to productivity whatsoever. Rewards may be based on attendance, seniority, appearances, politics, or a host of other quantifiable or subjective measures. Obviously those people who fall at the extremes, the very very productive and the very very lazy, tend to get what they deserve. But for others, there is the potential for differences of opinion or

8

confusion with regard to reward and promotion. If there is no obvious standard, your employer could be using one standard and you could be using another.

There may also be a problem if you need to feel that you personally have accomplished something. In staff positions you can often only reach the final accomplishment through someone else. Michael Korda points this out in his book *Male Chauvinism.*

> How many women are in a position to present their work as their own in American business rather than handing it to some man at some stage in its path up the decision-making process at which point it tends to become "his" if only because without him it cannot move any further toward implementation.[1]

Even if others do not intend to annex your efforts, it is difficult to keep your eye on your individual contribution. Out of the Far East comes the story of the elephant and the ant who were traversing an arid section of land together. The ant looked back at the trail of dust and commented, "We sure are raising a lot of dust, aren't we?" In many staff positions it can be difficult to tell whether you are the elephant or the ant. Are you really accomplishing a lot or are you along for the ride? Then, of course, there is always the chance that someone else is taking credit for your dust.

There are two real dangers associated with the difficulty in measuring contribution. One is related to time and the other is related to money. For years women have been encouraged to accept substitutes for money. There are endless examples of elderly never-married school teachers who, after a lifetime of subsidizing the school system by accepting a less-than-fair salary, turned around and willed all their money to the school. The secrets of the joys of money have been kept from generations of women.

Money is more than something to exchange for the things you need. Money is a way of keeping score. Just as the women athletes have been playing for lower stakes, the women in business have been operating under different standards than those for men. Two practices have kept women from appreciating their situation. One is that men and women alike are reluctant to discuss money issues. People will relate intimate details of their social lives or discuss their visits to the analyst before they will disclose their salary. Ask yourself

---

[1] Michael Korda, *Male Chauvinism: How It Works* (New York: Random House, 1973), p. 20.

who tends to lose from the nondisclosure of monetary reward information. If you are at the lower end and don't know it, you are hardly in a position to bring about adjustments.

The second practice that has kept women from appreciating money is incomparable comparisons. While specific income information is very difficult to obtain, aggregate figures are available broken down by sex. This provides an opportunity for intrasex comparisons. A woman who is earning more than $15,000 a year can soothe her feelings with the knowledge that she is earning more than about 99 percent of all working women. The fact that she is undercompensated in comparison to all other people with her credentials and experience can be ignored. In the absence of clearly defined measures of productivity and individual contribution, it is difficult to establish equitable measures of compensation. In those areas dominated by females, the solution has often been to err on the low side.

The money problem certainly extends outside the work environment, but so does the time question. Staff responsibilities can cause you to lose a sense of the value of your time. You have contracted to be in a certain place doing a certain type of work over a certain period of time. For that, you are entitled to a certain reward. If you complete the work ahead of schedule, you may be praised. If you are late, there are probably any number of scapegoats. Either way, the basic reward structure remains unchanged.

Indeed, some of the rewards, as they are structured, may be counterproductive. Devotion is difficult to measure, but its mirror image, sacrifice, is more easily observed. During a recent interview with a major bank, a woman was surprised to observe the attention paid to voluntary overtime. She met with several men, and each one stressed the fact that he was always in the office early and always left late. Each man related this to the excitement he felt for his job, the enormity of the task he faced, or the fact that more work could be accomplished during these extra hours because there were no calls. But she observed that none of the men seemed anxious to conclude the interview, and in only one instance was the interview interrupted by a call. Only one man was working when she entered his office, and each of these men was able to fit her into his schedule despite the fact that the interview schedule had not been established in advance. Clearly each of these men had some less than fully utilized hours during the regular working day. The answer seemed to be that there was strong peer pressure to demonstrate devotion through voluntary overtime.

Parkinson said a great deal in a few words: "Work expands so as to fill the time available for its completion."[2] In staff positions the pressure is sometimes toward filling the time rather than fully utilizing the time. This absence of time pressure may be desirable. In the early days of management study there were many studies of the time-and-motion variety. There was an effort to discover the one best and most efficient way to accomplish any particular task. Then people were supposed to become little machines and work efficiently in an effort to beat the clock. People were paid strictly on the basis of units of output. This was supposed to lead to efficient utilization of human resources, but it didn't work. It didn't take long to discover that neither the human system nor the business system could endure these inhuman practices.

In all things there must be a balance. The danger inherent in work that pays on the basis of time and lacks indicators of productivity is that people develop attitudes that time is something to be used up rather than something to use as a resource. These attitudes may carry over to the hours spent off the job. You have 168 hours per week and 52 weeks per year. Each hour can be used or wasted.

SPECIALIZATION

You may believe that you can attain security and rewards if you can learn to do some very necessary things better than other people are able to do them. One way to do this is to become a specialist. A specialist is a person who has concentrated on a fairly narrow range of activities and developed special skills in those areas. Staff people are very likely to become specialists. They perform the same functions for a number of people or operating units and are appreciated for their depth of skills in a limited area. While this may make them indispensable to the organization, their indispensability is tied to that particular specialty.

If you are an expert market researcher, you are valuable to the organization only so long as you continue to function as a market researcher. The time and attention you devote to acquiring expert status in one area may even be at the expense of your development of a broader understanding of the mission of the organization. You may be aware enough to work toward the broad understanding

---

[2] C. Northcote Parkinson, *Parkinson's Law, and Other Studies in Administration* (Boston: Houghton Mifflin Company, 1957), p. 2.

required for advancement into higher level managerial positions, but most of the people responsible for your advancement will have difficulty believing that you can do so. Perceived expertise in a particular function and perceived lack of broad-based experience can combine to limit the upward mobility of the staff people.

WHAT IS A LINE POSITION?

What about the other side? How do line positions differ? Line positions are those which place you on the front, where you are fighting the battles for the organization. Line positions involve activities directly associated with the major functions of the organization. While titles may vary depending on the industry, in marketing organizations the entry level line position is normally sales. From sales a person may proceed to sales management or marketing management. Women are notably absent from line entry positions in most industries. It is no accident that this is associated with a shortage of women in line marketing management positions. As G. E. Rickus, director of the Sales Manpower Foundation, puts it, "Most company presidents have come up through the sales field. I think women are missing the boat in shying away from certain product areas."

Line positions differ dramatically from staff positions in some ways which can afford outstanding opportunities to women. While all business positions demand some degree of time regularity, sales positions are unusually flexible. Line personnel are usually held accountable for their individual contribution. Salespeople, in particular, operate in an environment which fosters a generalist approach.

TIME FLEXIBILITY

As a professional salesperson you represent the company to current and potential customers. This requires three types of activities. Professional salespeople interact with customers, interact with people within their own companies, and make records of these interactions. In effect, you are running your own minibusiness. You have your own accounts or customers. As far as they are concerned, you are responsible for their satisfaction or dissatisfaction. While you can call upon others in your organization for help, you bear the responsibility. Consequently you are allowed a great deal of flexibility to plan your own schedule. While you may be subject to some guidelines as to the number of contacts to make or may be expected to provide the office with your itinerary, your schedule is your responsibility. It is assumed that you realize that your rewards will be based on your productivity and that you will attempt to schedule your time effectively.

As a saleswoman you are free to schedule your own day within certain environmental constraints. The most obvious constraint is the availability of customers. If your customers keep normal working hours, you will no doubt have to schedule meetings within the 9 to 5 timeframe. If your office runs on a normal workday and you need to interact with staff people to get information or to file reports, you will schedule these activities during the normal workweek. If you are selling in an industry which is subject to cycles, you may be especially busy during certain periods of the year. Within these constraints you can construct your personal schedule. If the morning was never your favorite time, you can schedule appointments in the afternoon. You could work feverishly Monday through Thursday and make every weekend a three-day holiday. If you have children in school you could schedule all outside appointments in the morning and early afternoon in order to be home before the children get home from school. You could plan to complete necessary paperwork in the afternoons while your children play.

No career offers total time flexibility. There are even times when time flexibility is a disadvantage. You may encounter out-of-town travel during which you are, in effect, working 24 hours a day. You may be called upon to work what would normally be considered overtime, but without overtime pay. You may be required to entertain during evening hours. Flexibility works both ways. Generally, however, as long as you continue to produce sales at some expected level, you will have considerable freedom to arrange your days and weeks to suit your requirements or preferences. Your performance is not measured according to the substitute measure of time on the job since suitable measures of productivity are available.

ACCOUNTABILITY

Salespeople are hired to sell, and sales can be measured. The profitable sale of the company's products or services is the end result and objective of all of the preceding efforts of the organization. Sales represents a direct and relevant measure of productivity.

1. Do you have what it takes?

As a salesperson, your compensation is related to your productivity as measured in sales dollars. If you work effectively and sell more, you earn more. If you sell less, you earn less. Risk and opportunity are closely related. If your compensation is based on commission, you must balance the risk that you won't earn enough money against the opportunity to receive superior rewards for superior performance. Are you willing to trade security for opportunity? Most people prefer the security of a situation in which their contribution is subject to less direct measures. They may complain when they feel that their superior performance goes unrewarded, but they seldom complain when their performance is inadequate and the paycheck is unchanged.

In sales your paycheck will change from month to month as it reflects your recent performance. If you have done well, you will earn more. If you have had a bad month, you will earn less. Are you willing to bet on your own performance? It's not as precarious as it may sound. Most sales compensation plans allow either for a draw, a loan against your expected future commissions, or a base salary to which commissions are added.

Perhaps the most important benefit of working in a variable income situation, in which you are compensated in direct relationship to your contribution, is that it will lead you to accept the concept of expansible income. In fixed income situations, the amount of money you receive is constant over a period of time and is controlled by some external force. Unless you change jobs or lose your job, you know exactly how much money you will have to work with over that time period. If you want to maintain or improve the quality of your existence, you must make those dollars go further. You must save your money. You must spend your money wisely. Thrift is a virtue.

Expansible income requires a different pattern of thought. If you can earn more or earn less depending on what you do, you can actually give yourself a raise. You can *take* a raise. You can make a list of the things you want and then you can tell yourself, "I am going to go out there and make that sale and buy myself that new watch." Your task changes from trying to make the most of a fixed amount of money to trying to make the money to get what you want out of life.

The idea of expansible income can have far-reaching effects on your attitudes. Not only do you begin to view your work in terms of the satisfactions it provides, but you begin to value your life in a different manner. When you are compensated on the basis of time rather than performance during that time, the task is to get through that time. The objective of most office workers is to traverse the time period between 9 and 5 as smoothly as possible.

Of course, working does help to make that time pass more quickly. That attitude can easily carry over to nonworking hours. The object may then be to pass the time between dinner and bedtime. You could easily pass your entire life away. When you are compensated on the results you get out of your efforts, your attitude changes. Time is not something to be passed, but something to be used. If you work more efficiently you earn more for your time. You determine how much your time is worth, and this attitude can easily carry over to nonworking hours. If every hour you spend at leisure or every hour you waste could have been spent expanding your income, you begin to be more conscious of the cost of your leisure. If it costs a lot, you want to be sure that you get a lot out of it. You demand more of your nonworking hours. People with fixed incomes can afford to spend a part of their time at unrewarding tasks because it helps them to pass the time, an underlying objective. They have no value attached to those hours since there is no way for them to "sell" those hours. They have filled the hours for which they have a contract. With an expansible income you can look at an unrewarding task and decide whether to do it or to spend the time expanding income in order to pay to have the unrewarding task done by someone else. Moreover, additional effort devoted to your career may not only pay off in dollars, but may pay off in terms of opportunity for advancement within the organization.

A GENERALIST APPROACH

In order to adequately represent the company and its products to customers, you must be familiar with many aspects of the organization and its functions. A substantial segment of any sales training course involves familiarizing you with the firm, its policies, its history, its competitors, its customers, its objectives, and its problems. As you deal with customers this information is constantly being updated. All of these factors are important to successful selling, but the outcome of this training is to automatically guide you into a generalist position.

At the lower levels of any organization, technical skills are more important than general understanding. You have a specific task to accomplish and are supposed to know how to do it and do it well. As you move up it is less important that you can do specific tasks well and more important that you can understand what has to be done and why. You hire others to actually do the tasks. Professional selling is considered to be excellent training for later management positions because salespeople are required to understand so many elements of the business.

From a very practical standpoint, sales provides more opportunity to advance into a management position because you develop your own personal track record. Your performance and contribution to the firm can be documented. Michael Korda puts it bluntly,

> Even to have been a salesman is a badge of courage in business—proof that one has been out on the road, known the harsh realities of selling a product, been exposed to the tough world of moving merchandise. Like battle scars, sales experience, however lowly, is regarded with esteem.[3]

There are basic differences between staff positions and sales positions. Staff positions tend to have inflexible time requirements and offer little opportunity for direct measurement of your contribution to the organization. Your value to the organization is a function of your specialized skills. Sales positions, on the other hand, are characterized by more flexible hours and compensation which is directly related to your productivity. You have the opportunity to develop a generalized approach which may lead to advancement in the management ranks. Your risks are greater, but so are your opportunities. Do you have what it takes to make the most of those opportunities?

Researchers have conscientiously attempted to develop an accurate picture of the qualities associated with success. No one wins when a person is ill-suited to the job. There must be a good fit. Your needs and your employer's needs are best met when your skills and character traits match the requirements of the job. Turnover is costly for everyone. It's often thought that a salesperson simply needs to be able to get along with people. Actually, salespeople also have to be able to get along without people. While a staff position provides a stable work group, salespeople generally see lots of people but work alone. It takes something else to be a success in sales.

---

[3] Korda, *Male Chauvinism*, p. 71.

In the 30s, life insurance sales managers estimated that a new salesperson had a 50-50 chance of surviving on the job for three years. After almost 30 years of study in an attempt to develop selection procedures which would reduce turnover, that figure remained at 50 percent. When research fails to turn up a solution, it is common practice to do more research.

Mayer and Greenburg did just that and reported the results of their 7-year field study in a classic *Harvard Business Review* article in 1964. They identified two factors which have since been widely accepted as the determinants of success in sales: Empathy and Ego Drive.

EMPATHY

What is empathy? Empathy is your ability to understand another person's position and feelings. Now that doesn't mean that you have to be sympathetic and like the other person's position, agree with that person, or feel the same way. It simply means that you can, for a few moments, see the situation from another's point of view. You can develop a rapport. It is only by understanding how the other person is feeling that you can interpret what you are selling in terms of that person's needs. People are some combination of heredity and environment. No one enters any social or business interaction with a clear head. People come from different social, educational, or business backgrounds. Each person is subject to distractions, thoughts of unfinished business, biases, prejudices, and fears. The sales approach which was tremendously successful with the last customer may fall flat with the present customer. The empathetic person is able to adjust to a situation by reading the cues and being sensitive to the verbal and nonverbal communications.

Adjusting to the situation does not mean giving in or letting others take advantage of you. It simply means that you try to read the signals so that you can be prepared to take the most advantageous action.

Think back over your experiences in auto showrooms. Have you ever had an insensitive salesperson dwell on styling while your major concern was economy? Perhaps you hinted that your decision would be based on gas mileage, yet the salesperson, wrapped up in personal needs, prattled on about color options and chrome accessories. You may not have bought the car even though it was economical. The essential communication link was missing. The successful salesperson is the one who realizes that the product is intended for the customer's use; therefore, it is the customer's needs that must be understood and satisfied.

EGO DRIVE

Ego drive has been described as the need to make the sale, the need to succeed, or the need to win. It is the internal force that gets you up and keeps you going. You should be your own strongest motivator. Some people have goals and strive toward them. Others drift. Still others flail about aimlessly. If you strive toward your goals, you are high on the ego drive scale. You have a need to accomplish your goals simply to satisfy yourself.

High ego drive is a combination of high energy and self-direction. Think of the carrot and the stick. Some people generate energy to continue in order to get a bite of the carrot, to satisfy some need for reward. Other people move because of fear of punishment. If you are high in ego drive you are able to keep those carrots in mind. You not only seek material rewards, but you enjoy success in itself. Some people strive toward their goals, and others sit and wait. As a striver you are far more likely to achieve success in selling or in any other demanding career.

EMPATHY AND EGO DRIVE INTERACT

Empathy and ego drive are interactive in the successful saleswoman. The diagram on page 19 indicates the nature of the relationship. Imagine that you had a dual thermometer. You could hold it under your tongue and get a readout on both ego drive and empathy. Where would you be on the diagram? Think about it! There are four extreme personality types.

Doormats

Doormats are low on both ego drive and empathy. Their self-esteem is so low that they don't even expect a fair share. They don't bother to ask for it. Doormats actually invite others to use and abuse them. While they may believe that they are being thoughtful, generous, and considerate, they are actually forcing an unbalanced interpersonal relationship on others. Consistent interaction with a doormat can turn a normal person into a selfish person.

A doormat's approach to interpersonal relationships is really rigid and insensitive. A doormat has developed a fixed approach and fails to adjust to new situations. If you honestly place yourself in the lower left-hand corner among the doormats, your chances of success in sales are probably low unless you can improve your readings on the thermometer. But take heart! If you were destined to be low on ego drive and empathy forever, you'd never have gotten this far in this book.

Servants

More likely you see yourself as higher on empathy than on ego drive. The traditional socialization process has conditioned women to be sensitive to the needs of others and not to be self-satisfiers. It might be an extension of some primeval "might makes right" wisdom. If you're not the biggest or strongest you had better pay attention to the cues if you're going to avoid the axe. Whatever the underlying factors, the socialization process has been well documented in sociological studies of women. If you have a high degree of empathy but are low on ego drive you end up in one-sided relationships. The objective of the interaction becomes serving the other person's needs without due regard for your own needs. In selling terms, this means that the customers would love to have you around. You would show concern for their needs and help them to sort out their problems. But the only sales you would make are those that someone would give you. In your lack of appreciation of yourself you might fail to ask for the order. You would probably be unable to bring yourself to expect equal satisfaction out of the transaction. Servants are givers but are sometimes taken. Again, if you have placed yourself in this category, do not despair. It's not as difficult as you might think to develop your self-appreciation, a key element in ego drive.

Bulldozers

There are too many people who have no difficulty appreciating themselves but seem to have some problem understanding when others do not see every situation just as they do. Unfortunately these people can survive quite well as long as others fail to assert themselves. A few years back Burger King ran a commercial on the theme

EXHIBIT 1-1

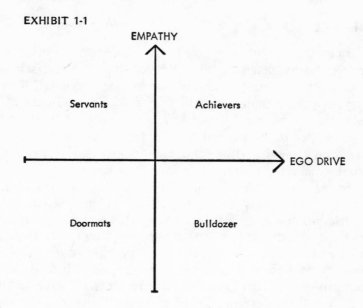

"have it your way." In one scene, a woman who was dissatisfied with the tickets for a show was intimidated with "If you don't take 'em, lady, somebody else will." Surely there are many high ego drive/low empathy salespeople who have made comfortable livings because they were the only source of supply. They have learned to depend on intimidation as a weapon. To the extent that people of this type experience success, they see little need for change.

Achievers

Being high on both ego drive and empathy allows a person to interact with others in a balanced manner. Because achievers are able to think about the needs of others without sacrificing their own self-interest, they tend to make good salespeople.

The closer you can get to the upper right-hand corner of the diagram, the more likely you are to succeed in selling. Not only must you be able to understand what other people need, but you must be able to understand and appreciate that the transaction must satisfy your own needs. It's sensible to expect that the needs of the buyer and seller be in balance. Any sale is an exchange. When it's over, each party should feel better off for having made the deal.

WHERE ARE YOU?

Think carefully about the point you picked for yourself on the ego drive/empathy diagram. Why did you position yourself at that point? Could it be that you have underestimated yourself? There are pressures on you to underestimate your ego drive and empathy. Up to this time, the business world has been reluctant to accept high ego drive/high empathy women. Women high in ego drive were afraid to let anyone know it. If they did, they risked being labeled aggressive, troublemakers, or worse. In short, they were a threat.

Women who were high in empathy and showed their ability to understand the feelings of others risked being labeled political. Empathetic women have also been subjected to strong pressures to convert their empathy into sympathy—to not only understand others but to agree with them. In many cases they have found it necessary to at least feign agreement since those other people have usually had a better position in the power structure. If they gave in, it was assumed that they were unable to make objective decisions. They might be downgraded for letting their emotions interfere with their work. In short, the business world has neither encouraged nor rewarded high ego drive and empathy in women. You may have those qualities but may have underrated them as a result of the continuing pressures on you to take a less assertive approach.

Negative reinforcements on women's ego drive are so common that we have come to accept them as normal. All of the propaganda on becoming a good wife in the traditional sense leeches away the life fluids of ego drive. How many girls have read *Little Women* by Louisa May Alcott? In one passage the oldest daughter who had recently married comes home because she and her husband have had an argument. The mother gives her, and coincidently the impressionable reader, some well-intended advice. The daughter is cautioned to deliberately lose the first argument. In this way she can feed her husband's ego and smooth out her life. In fact she smooths out her life by accepting a no-risk position. She climbs into the high empathy/low ego drive trap. She assumes a servant role. She lines up with the other women who get dressed up and made up in hopes of pleasing someone who will then ask them to dance. Don't misunderstand. There's nothing wrong with good grooming nor did the daughter need to establish her position by persisting and winning the argument, but she should never have been advised to throw the fight. Have you ever played ping-pong with someone far more skilled than yourself and realized that this other person was letting you win? That's not too satisfying to either person, even in a game. Imagine the kind of damage this can cause in real life. The argument should have been settled on the basis of the merits of the *positions* of the participants.

Think about the information that nutritionists have been trying to provide on sugar. They point out that the average American's consumption of sugar has been increasing over the years to the point where sugar is associated with health problems. Why do we consume that amount of sugar? It's because we've become accustomed to it. Researchers have found that baby food has much more sugar than necessary. Babies are apparently just as happy without it. But parents often taste the baby food, and if it doesn't meet their standards of good taste, they reject it without consulting the babies. Because parents introduce excessive sugar into the babies' diets, they develop an excessive appetite for it.

You and all the other babies, male and female, started out with a "normal" appetite for success. What happened to your appetite? If you received a balanced diet of ego stimulators and satisfiers, you were both lucky and unusual. The social system has been set up to starve your ego appetite until, as an adult, it will be atrophied. Think of it as a balloon. If someone blew it up a little once in a while, it retained its ability to function. If it was drained, the sides may have become stuck together.

How did your environment suck the air out of your balloon? Were you ever encouraged to throw the game? Did well-meaning advisors caution you that you wouldn't be popular if you showed how smart you were? Were you ever told that winning isn't important, it's how you play the game? Were you coached in the techniques of stroking the male ego? Did you learn that it's "lady-like" to be patient until someone else has decided to give you some reward? Were you carefully taught to suppress your wanting behavior and to be satisfied? If any of these things apply, yours was a normal childhood.

You must carefully evaluate the possibility that you have been selling yourself short, that you have denied even to yourself that you have ego drive and empathy. While your ego drive and empathy might be a little rusty, remember that today is the first day of the rest of your life. It is easy to sit back and blame external forces for a lack of success. It is easy, but it is hardly progressive or productive. If you have what it takes, it's up to you to seek out the opportunities to succeed.

2 Turning roadblocks into building blocks

Risk and opportunity are closely related. Many people fail to achieve their potential because they are unwilling to assume the risk. They would prefer to stay within the established patterns of behavior where they are comfortable. They know what is expected of them and what they can expect of others. As people look up the road toward success, they can see many roadblocks. Some people succeed despite the roadblocks, and some fall short of their goals. What makes the difference?

To some extent the difference lies in the strength of your desire to reach the goal. If you want something badly enough you may overcome barriers which would otherwise appear insurmountable. There is some difference in personality types. Some people perceive any barrier as a challenge and attempt to overcome it even if they do not particularly desire whatever is to be found on the other side. Perhaps more important, however, is preparation. If you are able to anticipate the roadblocks you will encounter, you will be able to plan the most efficient course. You may either develop a means to overcome the roadblock or plot a detour.

There are both real and imagined roadblocks. Some people construct roadblocks to serve as excuses to avoid change. After all, change is risky. Think about jumping into a swimming pool. Even if the water is the right temperature, at first it will be a shock. It will seem cold. After a few moments you will again be comfortable. Undertaking the change necessary to move toward a new goal or begin a new career is very much like jumping into that pool. While it may seem uncomfortable at first, you will soon begin to feel more comfortable. If you are convinced that the benefits are worth the effort, you can start to define the roadblocks that lie in your path and plan to overcome them one by one.

The first important factor in overcoming the roadblocks in your path is to recognize that you are responsible for you. A few years back there was a TV commercial for a liquid body shampoo. A young woman peeked out from behind a shower curtain and declared, "After all, if I don't take care of my body, who will?" While the product was apparently less than successful, the message is terribly important. All too often women use real or imagined roadblocks as an excuse for a lack of action. They seem to say, "If I try, something might get in my way. Therefore I won't try and then I won't fail. I will wait until someone makes it easy for me. If someone else removes all the barriers, then I will move in that direction." You cannot expect someone else to remove the barriers in your path. You are responsible for you. If you wait for someone else to provide a favorable climate or to help you along the way, you may wait the rest of your life. Ask yourself the simple question: "Who has the most to gain from my success?" That is the person you should count on to put the effort into achieving your success. That person is you.

Of course, it is one thing to convince yourself that change is justified or even possible, but it is an altogether different matter to define the direction of that change and to develop plans to accomplish it. What are the actual mechanisms you can use to increase your levels of ego drive and empathy, the two qualities often related to success in sales?

No one has developed a foolproof scale for measuring ego drive and empathy. It seems fairly obvious that some people have more of either, or both, of these qualities than other people. Some people are low on both and are called doormats. Those low on ego drive but high on empathy are inclined toward servant behavior. Bulldozers are people who are low on empathy but high on ego drive. Achievers are high on both qualities. As a saleswoman, you should be able to understand the needs and attitudes of customers and be sufficiently goal-oriented to persevere to achieve your own goals.

It is certainly not easy to develop your potential in either the ego drive or the empathy area. To this point you have probably been subjected to a continuous stream of socialization experiences which have worked against the development of these qualities, especially ego drive. But you still have the potential. Your success in developing these qualities depends on the same factors as does success in any venture. First, it depends on the desirability of the goal. The more you want something, the more likely it is that you will devote the necessary energy to achieving it. Second, it depends on your technical competence. Do you know how? Your energies must be directed. Finally, your success depends on your faith in yourself. If you believe that you can succeed, you are far more likely to try.

Actually, those requirements of success may be taken in reverse order. If you believe that you can succeed you may be more willing to develop the skills required. Once a goal seems more attainable because you feel confident in your skills to achieve it, it may appear even more desirable. Before we consider some of the mechanisms which you can use to become more skillful in exercising your ego drive and empathy, let us consider some of the internal and external forces which may be interfering with your success image.

SUCCESS IMAGE INHIBITORS

If you could start over on a clean slate or operate within a vacuum, the situation would be far less complex. You have had a variety of experiences and have been influenced by many people. These experiences and influences have caused you to develop a self-image. Your self-image is very important to your attitude toward success. Your self-image is really a defined psychological space. It is somewhat like a little mental shell into which you have crawled or were pushed. There are pressures to keep you in this shell. Other people can understand you if you stay in the shell. Their world and yours is easier to deal with because you both have expectations as to your behavior. While human behavior is certainly complex, life becomes more predictable when people stay in their shells.

Your self-image is made up of several parts. You are constantly trying to bring these parts into balance. Think of the standard magician's act in which the assistant steps into a vertical four-part compartment. Various parts of her body show through small openings in each of the four boxes. The magician then proceeds to separate the four boxes creating the illusion that the woman has indeed been divided into four parts. Finally, of course, when the four boxes are stacked vertically in the proper order, the whole assistant emerges.

When the parts of your self-image are out of balance, you are no more comfortable than you imagine the magician's assistant to be in her separated condition. Therefore you may devote a great deal of energy to keeping those parts in balance. What are these parts? One part is your preferred-other image. This is the way you wish others would see you. Your preferred-other image may or may not be in line with your perceived-other image, the way you believe others see you. Your perceived-other image results from the feedback you have been receiving from others during your lifetime. If you have been complimented on your accomplishments and encouraged to try, you will believe that others believe you to be a competent individual. If you have been discouraged and stifled, you will believe that others do not see you as an able person. There is another segment which may surface on occasion—your actual-other image—some way which others actually see you. Finally, of course, there is your self-self image, the way you see yourself. (See Exhibit 2-1.)

If you are more comfortable when these image segments are in balance, you will work toward achieving or maintaining this balance. Which of these segments are you more able to control? Assume that you had your image segments in line. Then for some reason your perceived-other image gets out of line. Suppose someone who was

EXHIBIT 2-1. SELF-IMAGE SEGMENTS

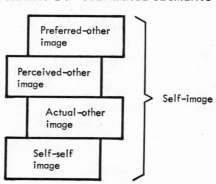

significant to you made some comment regarding your abilities or performance. Is it easier to change your perceived-other image back into line with the others or to adjust your self-self image and your preferred-other image and hope your actual-other image falls in line? Usually you have more control over your self-self image and your preferred-other image and can bring them into line with the perceived-other image. If the comment was positive, your total self-image is improved. On the other hand, if the comment was unkind or unpleasant, your total self-image deteriorates. If it happens often enough you may come to believe that you are incapable of success. You may be allowing other people to define your potential for success. (See Exhibit 2-2.)

EXHIBIT 2-2.
SELF-IMAGE
ADJUSTMENT

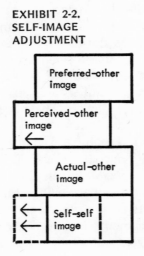

Actually, some people are inclined toward contributing to the deterioration of their own self-image. See if you recognize the following sequence—the image spiral. Imagine a woman left alone on a rainy Sunday night with nothing but TV reruns of grade B movies. In such a circumstance she may be prone to reflection. What kind of thoughts emerge? Each of us is painfully capable of recalling a number of embarrassing events in our lives. This woman may recall the horrible feeling she felt when she forgot her lines in the senior play. She may recall how inadequate she felt when she went out for her first job interview. If she runs short on embarrassing events she could reflect on some physical shortcoming such as the relative size of this or that. A few moments spent on performance shortcomings such as a fear of public speaking is always good for a few units of depression. Before long she can shrivel her self-image to a mere fraction of its rightful magnitude.

At the same time she has, no doubt, subjected herself to the parallel exercise of developing a composite superhuman. Having been carefully socialized she has been taught, "If you can't say anything nice, don't say anything." Taking this advice to heart, she carefully ignores the shortcomings of others. It is amazing that while we can concentrate on our own shortcomings and carefully attempt to conceal them from others, we seldom stop to realize that they are just as carefully concealing their shortcomings from us. She has probably noticed someone among her friends who dresses impeccably and is always the object of admiration in a fashion sense. Someone else seems to be able to come up with the ideas which are always accepted. Perhaps another person is noted for being particularly creative. Another friend seems to express herself so well. The story goes on and on. Before long she has created a composite superhuman image to which she compares her own depressed self-image. She hasn't got a chance. Her self-image spirals downward.

Is there hope for our friend? Of course there is, just as there is hope for you if you are subject to the image spiral. What goes down can come up. The first step is to begin to develop a list of your strengths. Weaknesses are all too easy to recall. You should carefully compose a list of your strengths—things in which you take pride. While a résumé is a start, it is a poor substitute for a pride list. The purpose of a résumé is to record those events and accomplishments which others will value. A pride list is a personal accounting of the accomplishments which are important to you. These may have no significance to any other person. Perhaps you handled a particularly difficult social situation well. Maybe you finally spoke up for your rights at the office. Your first step is to record those situations in which you felt good about yourself. Keep it on a 3 x 5 card in your wallet if you can. When you are subjected to unpleasant comments or events, you can bring it out and fortify your self-image. Your second step must be to recognize the total humanness of other people. You don't have to concentrate on their weaknesses or snicker and laugh at your friends. You only have to realize that each of their strengths is probably balanced off by some less than strong characteristic.

All people have strengths and weaknesses. These two steps will allow you to compare apples to apples while in the past you may have been comparing apples to oranges. The comparison is bound to show you in a better light. Your image may indeed spiral upward to its rightful level. You may begin to think of yourself as capable of actions which you had previously avoided.

It is really quite difficult to undertake a self-assessment of your capabilities. Brenda, the younger sister on the television show "Rhoda," commented on this idea. She said that her psychiatrist said that people are the only animals who make themselves sick trying to be something they aren't. You never see a turkey trying to be an eagle. More important, you never see an eagle trying to be a turkey. Among human beings there are examples of people who have the potential to achieve at the eagle level who seem satisfied, or indeed determined, to underachieve. Unfortunately, the socialization process increases the likelihood that women will be among these under-achievers. There are both direct and indirect social influences which would lead an otherwise capable woman to believe that she was not suited for a position in sales.

On the indirect side, you may not have any encouragement. There is probably little in your family, social, or educational experience which would direct you into a sales career. While there may be little initial encouragement for a man to pursue this career, he may at least be spared the discouragement. More important, a man has the advantage of established role models. He can read articles in business periodicals and pick up examples of men who have been successful in sales before moving into responsible management positions. He can read his textbooks and be reminded that business and especially sales is a male-dominated environment. There is a good chance that he can scan his family, friends, and acquaintances and come up with a few examples of men who have been reasonably successful in a sales position. A woman is seldom exposed to a role model in sales either in the literature or among personal contacts.

On the direct side, you may well be discouraged from pursuing a sales career. Imagine two types of people—Jealous Jabbers and Cautious Creepers—with different approaches but similarly negative effects. Jealous Jabbers are convinced that the rewards available are limited and will be divided among us. If you are successful, there is less left over for them. Instead of competing with themselves against previously established personal goals, these people compete against you. This is the type of person who would deliberately block your progress. Unfortunately, some people can only measure themselves against other people. There are some people who would interfere with the possible success of others in order to maintain their own feeling of superiority. While Jealous Jabbers can be dangerous, you can minimize their impact by recognizing them for what they are and either avoiding them or ignoring them. It is simply better to avoid discussing your plans with a person of this type. While they have a tendency to pry, the less they know, the less damage they can do.

The other type may be more damaging because the approach is positive while the effect is negative. Cautious Creepers mean well. They have your best interests at heart. They just do not know what is in your best interest. Cautious Creepers are the people who encourage you not to venture from the norm. They want you to follow established patterns of safe behavior. They are uncomfortable with the unknown and the untried. If you suggest to a Cautious Creeper that you would like to enter a traditionally male career such as sales, the Cautious Creeper will respond with the advice, "Don't do that; you'll be sorry." They seem to operate under a philosophy of nothing ventured, nothing lost. They mean well when they seek to impose their risk-avoidance patterns on you. Cautious Creepers are potentially damaging because due to their sincere interest in you, you tend to seek out their advice and to give credit to their opinions.

Perhaps there are other types of people lurking in your environment ready to pounce on your ambitions and dampen your aspirations. While you could seek to identify each of them and define a strategy to minimize their negative impact, the process would consume time and energy which could best be devoted to developing ego drive and empathy potential. There is a simple approach which is generally applicable. The Incubation Approach can be very important to you as you are considering a nontraditional course of action. Very simply, the idea is to protect your plans from possible infection by outside interests. You keep your plans to yourself until they are strong enough to withstand outside pressure. There may be several people in your environment who will have difficulty understanding that you have determined that you are responsible for yourself. They may prefer to think that they are responsible for you. While they will be willing to help you to make your decisions, you will have to live with the consequences of those decisions.

Your self-image is terribly important to your success. In most cases people lack the capacity or interest to adequately evaluate your level of competence. They evaluate you on the basis of their perceptions of your perceptions of your competence and potential. If you believe that you can achieve success in sales, they will be inclined to agree with you. You cannot expect to depend on outside sources of positive influence. You must make the effort to enhance your own self-image and to protect yourself from the outsiders who will try to discourage you. A success attitude can make it even easier to develop the qualities which lead to success in sales.

DEVELOPING EGO DRIVE AND EMPATHY

Ego drive and empathy both represent patterns of behavior for which you develop a taste just as you would develop a taste for a new food. If you try something new and it is pleasant, you will try it again. If you concentrate on your ego drive and empathy behaviors, you may find that they hold the potential for satisfaction. At first some of the elements may seem strange and you will need to rely on some crutches. If these behaviors eventually lead you to a more comfortable situation, they will become a part of your automatic behavior system.

In that empathy is more commonly stressed in the traditional female socialization process, let's consider that quality first. Empathy is not a blind acceptance of someone else's ideas or propositions. Empathy is your ability to be aware of the feelings of other people. If you are engaged in an interpersonal activity, your ability to perceive the feelings of the other person will affect the likelihood that the interaction will result in your satisfaction. As a saleswoman, you are required to accomplish your objectives through other people. You are successful if those other people are inspired to purchase your products. There may be a number of explanations for a purchase decision, but it is logical that one of these reasons is because the purchaser believes that the product will be satisfying. You can only present your product in terms of the buyer's needs if you understand what those needs are from the buyer's point of view. You can only calm the buyer's fears and settle the buyer's objections if you attempt to understand the buyer's feelings. In selling, empathy is that quality which allows you to present your product most effectively by adjusting your presentation to the buying situation. While that may make sense, the real question is "How can I develop empathy?"

One very successful senior executive is noted for having advised his new salespeople, "Make the buyer feel like the most important person in the world." It is simple advice, but it has great merit. Many people engage in interpersonal interaction with some hope of feeding their own egos. If two people approach the situation each with this as one of their objectives, neither may be satisfied. If you look upon the actual interaction as but one phase of the whole process, you may recognize that by sensitively filling the other person's ego needs for a few moments you can achieve greater satisfaction at a later date. Instead of listening to yourself, you may be able to listen to the other person. Instead of being concerned about winning individual battles, you can concentrate on the war. The mechanism to accomplish this rests on self-questioning. Before a planned encounter with a customer, you should ask yourself two questions: "Where is this buyer coming from?" and "Where am I going?" During the interaction you should continually ask yourself, "How will my intended comment make this person feel or react?" and, "Will that move me toward my objective?" Perhaps you have heard the distinction between checkers and chess. The checkers player is supposedly thinking only of the next move. The chess player is considering a series of moves or looking ahead to consider the impact of a present action on possible future action. As an empathetic person you are not only acting in the present but are considering the effect of those actions on the reactions of others. Sensitivity to the other person's feelings provides a basis for action.

Consider the basic communications model. In any communication there is a sender, a receiver, some message, and some vehicle through which that message is communicated. It seems very simple, but the difficulties arise when the sender's intended message must be encoded or translated into a form suitable for sending to the receiver. When President Jimmy Carter spoke in Poland, a mistranslation changed a friendly greeting into an offensive, suggestive comment. Do the sentences you speak always accurately express your thoughts or are you sometimes unable to properly encode your message? Then, of course, the message also must be decoded and again the possibility of misinterpretation exists. Finally, the basic communications model acknowledges the possibility of noise or interference. There are many possible disruptions of the communications process. Sometimes people hear what they expected to hear regardless of what you said. Their perception of the person sending the message may either increase or decrease its impact. Finally there is the element of feedback, an important factor in empathy. Feedback is the response of the receiver to the perceived message of the sender. It is the receiver's reaction to the message, not necessarily as it was intended or sent but as it was received. It is by carefully attending to feedback that the sender can be prepared to understand the receiver's position. (See Exhibit 2-3.)

EXHIBIT 2-3. THE COMMUNICATIONS MODEL

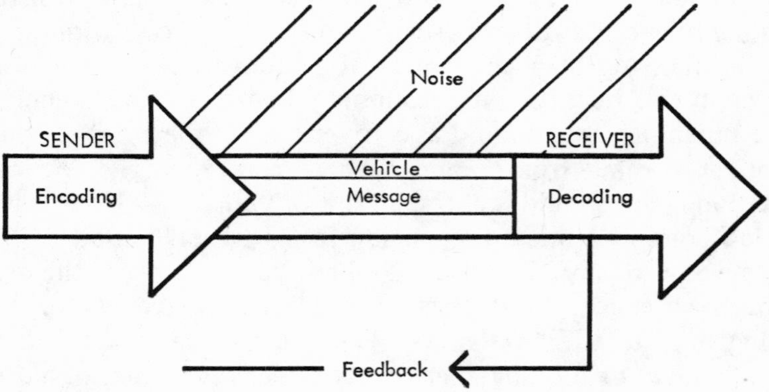

Acquiring empathy requires the adoption of an analytical orientation toward interpersonal interaction. For most people interpersonal interactions are a one-step occurrence in time. It happens and it passes. If you are interested in developing empathy, the interpersonal process expands to three steps. The first step is planning, the second is the actual interaction, and the third step is the evaluation. (See Exhibit 2-4.)

While continuing evaluation of your interpersonal effectiveness is the key, you cannot evaluate your performance without preestablished objectives. Unless you specify what you intend to accomplish before the interaction occurs, you can hardly determine how effective you were in achieving your objectives.

EXHIBIT 2-4. THE INTERPERSONAL EVALUATION PROCESS

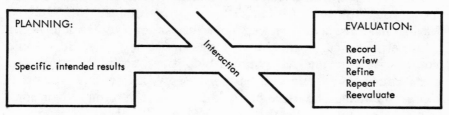

The first step is to think about an impending interpersonal situation and to specify exactly what you would prefer to be the outcome of that interaction. It might be a sales call on a possible new customer. Try to make a list of the results you would like to achieve. It might include determining some things about the customer, such as current source of supply, average order size, and reasons for considering another supplier. You might also intend to acquaint the customer with your product and your firm. You may have decided that the call would be a success if you could get the customer to agree to sample your product. Having listed your intended results, you will be more able to keep them in mind while you interact.

After the meeting (the second step) you are ready for the evaluation step, the critical step most people fail to take. First, attempt to *record* the critical elements of the interaction. Your purpose is to make a list of the types of feedback you received to key statements in your presentation. When you said, "Tell me, why are you considering switching suppliers?" your customer reacted with, "I'd really rather not say." To your question "Can you tell me about how many units you would be ordering next year?" the answer was "That all depends." When you paid your competition a mild compliment: "The XYZ Company has been a tough competitor over the years," your customer nodded in agreement. Your list need not be complete but should include those communications which were significant to the accomplishment of your preestablished objectives. Go over your list and *review* each communication. Review means to take another look. Take another look and decide how effective each communication was in moving you toward your preferred results. Did it contribute or detract from your effort? Had you anticipated your customer's reaction? Was your question about reasons for switching suppliers an invasion on your buyer's privacy? Think about the impact of your messages.

How can you improve? How often have you thought of a comment you wish you had made and then promptly forgotten it? Having recorded and reviewed your interaction, you should *refine* your performance. Imagine that it was an act in a play. How would you rewrite your lines? If you could do it over again, there might be parts you would retain and parts you would throw out. The other characters in the play have personalities. You can rethink their lines, but you cannot rewrite them out of line with their characters. If your interaction was successful, if you accomplished your objectives, you must ask yourself why. What did you do right? You will want to remember it so that you can try it again. If your interaction was less than successful, you must again ask yourself why. What could you have done better? While the same situation may never reoccur, there will probably be other situations with similar elements. What would have happened if instead of saying, "Tell me, why would you consider switching suppliers?" you had said, "Most buyers are interested in reliability and price, but do you have any special areas in which you feel your needs could be better met?" The second question is less likely to make the buyer feel that a response is a betrayal of previous suppliers. Maybe the way you said something was all right, but your timing was off. The question on expected orders might have been answered if you had asked it later in the discussion.

If you feel that you have identified some communication technique which worked well, you may want to look for an opportunity to *repeat* it. There are some techniques and phrases that work better than others. While the delivery may be personalized, the principles remain intact. For example, the mild compliment for your competitor may be just the thing to put your buyer at ease. Instead of implying "You dummy, why did you ever order from the XYZ Company?" it implies "There are probably some good reasons why you have dealt with XYZ, but there are better reasons to deal with me." There is little reason to put your buyer on the defensive. As you practice this process you will begin to recognize common elements in situations. You may even develop names for situations. When you encounter a familiar situation, you may have some tested technique to draw upon. Each time you repeat a behavior you must *reevaluate* it in an attempt to measure its effectiveness in various situations.

This approach may seem mechanical, but it can be extremely valuable. Its real value lies in its use as a tool to encourage you to become more aware of your interpersonal effectiveness. If you analyze your performances you are in a much better position to improve. The more success you experience, the more agreeable the process will become. Eventually it will become automatic. You will continually assess the impact of your actions on others and act accordingly.

To this point it has been assumed that you wish to be successful. While it would make little sense for you to read this book otherwise, wanting to be successful and striving toward success are two different things. You may want to be successful but still lack the ego drive that you need to succeed. You may feel uncomfortable admitting to yourself or others that you have certain expectations of reward. Women are typically taught to wait until something is offered to them rather than to go out and seek that which they feel they deserve. They are taught to allow others to determine both the nature and the extent of their rewards. How do you develop that important "I'm somebody too!" attitude? You will be working against two forces. One is yourself, and the other is the collection of people who also subscribe to the idea that you will be satisfied with less.

Many women have no choice. They truly need the money and have to go in there and fight. Even so there is a big difference between optimizing and satisficing. Optimizing is making the very best out of your situation. Satisficing is achieving at a satisfactory level. Where do you get that little edge that converts you from a satisficer to an optimizer? How do you put ego drive in motion?

There are basically two choices. You can seek outside energy or you can act as your own cheerleader. Note carefully that this says seek outside energy. It is already clear that you cannot afford to wait for outside energy to come to you. Self-confidence and a success orientation are contagious. If you surround yourself with people who believe in themselves and what they are doing, have ambitions and aspirations, you will soon catch on. Ben Franklin once said that the world is made up of those who are immovable, those who can be moved, and those who are movers. Since you will tend to work up to the expectations and standards of your associates, one of the ways to encourage yourself to a higher level of drive is to associate with those who are movers. Disassociate yourself from those who are forever seeking the easy way out, who are satisfied to muddle through life with little or nothing to take pride in as they go along.

While they may be fun or available, they will have a depressing effect on your ego drive.

An interesting exercise which may help you is the Support Assessment Scale. Set up a scale from one to ten. (See Exhibit 2-5.) Label one end Underminers and the other end Supporters. Supporters are those who sincerely help you to enjoy your accomplishments. They try to understand your plans and to help you to evaluate your progress. They are genuinely pleased for you when you have a right

EXHIBIT 2-5. SUPPORT ASSESSMENT SCALE

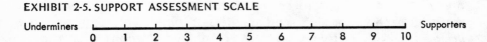

to be proud of yourself. Sometimes they may play the important role of devil's advocate. Given a chance, they will encourage you to reach out toward your goals. Underminers are those who don't care, who make you feel uncomfortable about your accomplishments, or who seek to dissuade you from attempting to achieve without really thinking about your plans or your welfare.

Begin to place the people you know along the scale. If you aren't certain of the position a particular person should be assigned, go ahead and test that person. Give that person a chance to react to a plan or to an accomplishment of yours, even if you have to make one up. Was the reaction positive? How positive? Was the reaction thoughtful? Some people who are indiscriminantly enthusiastic are mistaken for supporters. With this information in hand you can adjust your level of disclosure to the individual's position on the scale. When you need support, seek out the advice or comments of those who are high on your support scale. Your objective is to build a cluster of thoughtful supportive people from whom to draw energy. You may serve the same need for them in return.

While outsiders may be supportive, real ego drive springs from within you. It is circular in nature. Success breeds a need to succeed. How do you break into the cycle? You can either develop a feeling of success or cultivate the need to succeed. Several means of overcoming the barrier of a poor self-image have already been discussed. Having reached the take-off level, you must become your own cheerleader. You are responsible for you. You can be the force behind attempts which will lead to the necessary success experiences. You may have to use every technique you can imagine to stir yourself to action and to avoid depression. Some people respond to visual reminders. They plaster their walls with inspirational sayings. If you are avoiding some task and look up only to see a poster reading "Do it now," it might just provide the edge you need. When pondering some action, visual reminders such as "What is the worst thing that can happen?" could be the turning point. When you are tempted to give up you may be spurred on by the phrase "No one should be rewarded for sitting around being capable of achievement." Visual reminders such as "Time is money" or "Today is the first day of the rest of your life" have inspired all kinds of people.

Some people surround themselves with reminders of what they want. Pictures of sports cars, vacation paradises, slim bodies, and other desired material things or states of being are not uncommon. They actually serve as reminders of the need to succeed. Taken a bit further they can actually be effective in stimulating ego drive. By themselves they may be exciting, but coupled with a plan of accomplishment, they become a reason for action.

Some desired objects seem very far away until you sit down and draw up a plan to approach them. You need a list of the things you are going to have to do in order to achieve your objectives. The trick is to break each task into a number of small steps. Once your list of small steps between your current situation and your desired situation is completed, you can move along one step at a time until you reach your goal. Reaching one goal can give you the courage and energy to strike out for others. Success breeds success.

Allow yourself the luxury of basking in your successes. You should learn to take pride in your accomplishments. Since a lot of your experiences would deny this, you may have to lean on a crutch in order to develop the ability to appreciate yourself. You have probably been taught that you "shouldn't blow your own horn." Have you heard people speak with disdain of someone who "almost breaks her arm patting herself on the back"? You should be your own most dependable stroker. You cannot depend on others. Why not congratulate yourself? You might set up some reward to give yourself whenever you have accomplished something which is significant to you. Buy yourself a present. Treat yourself to your favorite pasttime. If you acknowledge your successes, you will remember them longer and hunger more for them. Hunger for success is the essence of ego drive.

You can be your own worst enemy or you can be your own best friend. You can change your self-image from a burden to a powerful and positive force on your behavior. You can make the most of your potential for ego drive and empathy. You can develop your sensitivity to the needs of other people and at the same time appreciate your own needs and strive toward their satisfaction. There is a space for you to accomplish up to your potential. The question is whether or not you will claim that space.

3   Your first sale: Landing the right job

Certainly there is a lot of material available to you on job search and interviewing. You have probably already had some experience in looking for a job. One of the unnerving features of seeking employment is that you never know if you have uncovered the best position. You may be stopping just short of the really important opportunity. Wouldn't it be terrific if all of the opportunities presented themselves simultaneously so that you could thoroughly evaluate the offers before choosing one? We all know that that isn't the case, but the thought does point to one of the most important characteristics of an effective job search. Effective job seeking is a deliberate and concentrated effort.

All the good intentions in the world will hardly make up for a lack of action. Now that you have convinced yourself that definite opportunities exist in the area of sales, plan a deliberate and concentrated attack which will enable you to most effectively present your case to the people who can offer you the greatest opportunities. Your attack must be deliberate if you are to satisfy yourself that the position you finally select is the one which best matches your needs. Your efforts must be concentrated so that you have the greatest number of opportunities from which to choose at the time the decision is reached. If you allow yourself to dawdle in your job search, you may find that you will have to decide whether or not to reject an acceptable offer while waiting for a superior offer to materialize. Another danger is that you will run out of steam.

The job search process is indeed a sales job. You must proceed through all of the steps you would follow in selling any other product. Just as in selling any other product, unless both the buyer and seller are satisfied with the transaction, neither wins. While both the buyer and the seller need to make the transaction, it is usually your responsibility to search out the buyer, that is, the potential employer. This chapter will present the job search in terms of the normal sales pattern. The steps to be followed are presented in Exhibit 3-1.

EXHIBIT 3-1. STEPS IN THE SELLING PROCESS

1. Prospecting—identifying and qualifying potential buyers.
2. Assessing needs—identifying needs from the buyer's viewpoint.
3. Assessing competition—measuring the buyer's options.
4. Preparing the sales presentation—developing a communications tool to present the selling points of your product.
5. Making the sales presentation—communicating with and listening to the buyer to stress benefits and answer objections.
6. Following through—closing or asking for the order.

Some people have probably stumbled across exactly the position they wanted by sheer accident. There are people who assume the gravity approach to job hunting; a job will fall in their lap. It could happen. It's more likely that you will find what you are looking for if you follow the deliberate method described in the following sections.

PROSPECTING

Don't you wish you could choose a new job from the largest possible number of opportunities? Just think how comforting it would be to have a list of all the possible positions. If you were going to buy a house you could go to a real estate office which participated in the multiple listing system and review the listings of the houses on the market. No such multiple job listing system exists. There are no complete or even partially complete lists of available positions. It's your responsibility to generate your own list. The more complete that list is, the less likely you will miss the opportunity for which you are best suited. Building that list is a two stage process. The first stage is prospecting, uncovering the possible job openings. The second stage is qualifying those openings. Qualifying is a screening process through which obviously unacceptable or unattainable positions are dropped from the list.

Uncovering job openings puts you in the role of a detective. Baretta interviews all the witnesses, examines all the clues, ponders relationships, pursues details, and checks out every single lead which might be the key to the case. One of the outstanding characteristics of the successful detectives, real or fictional, is persistence. This same persistence will pay dividends in the prospecting process. You simply have to remember that the benefactor from all this activity is yourself.

Many people take the easiest route to an adequate position. They are willing to settle for the first position which meets some minimal set of standards. Some people stay in unsatisfactory positions because they are unwilling to search for a better opportunity. Some people sit and wait for others to recognize their potential and to offer a position unsolicited. There may be some ego satisfaction in being recruited for a position as opposed to asking for the job, but you may spend the rest of your life waiting.

The task of prospecting job leads is sometimes approached in a half-hearted manner because the job seeker is reluctant to admit the need to others. This kind of behavior is often evident in the political arena. A notable politician will hint of interest in a political office but if asked directly will deny that interest. After all, if you throw your hat in the ring and no one picks it up, it can be embarrassing. Think about the opportunities which people have missed because the fear of temporary embarrassment caused them to be reluctant to express interest. Unfortunately, many people operate under the "nothing ventured, nothing lost" philosophy. In job prospecting that is hardly appropriate.

You are already aware of some places to start your search for job openings. The most common, of course, is the local newspaper. There are some characteristics of selling positions that you should consider when using newspapers. Depending on the geography of your area, the newspapers to which you should refer will vary. Some positions are very localized and others require travel. Where travel is required, it often makes little difference to the employer where you live as long as you can cover the territory. A position of interest to you may be advertised in a newspaper in a major metropolitan area as much as 100 miles away. If you live in a mid-size community, do not overlook the local newspapers of neighboring major cities.

Old newspapers can be very helpful too. Part of your prospecting effort will involve direct contact with sales organizations which are not currently advertising positions. Reference to an old newspaper can provide you with names and addresses of people within organizations which have had openings in the past and will no doubt have openings in the future. Your unsolicited letter will have a much better chance if it is addressed to an appropriate individual. Printed ads can be an important source of information.

The classified section of your regional edition of *The Wall Street Journal* is one of your best sources. This is the only national daily newspaper published in the United States. Other periodicals such as *Advertising Age, Marketing News,* and *Sales and Marketing Management* regularly publish classified job advertisements.

One of the problems encountered in using print sources is the blind advertisement. There are probably several logical explanations for a company placing an advertisement without identifying itself. One is that current employees might feel insecure with the idea that the company is advertising for new employees. In one-of-a-kind positions, such as vice president of marketing, this argument would have some merit. Another explanation is that the image of the company might interfere with the candidate's ability to objectively evaluate the nature of the position. Underlying all these explanations, however, is the desire on the part of the persons responsible for the recruiting function to reserve the right to prescreen applicants. It becomes a device whereby the company is protected from responding to or processing all applicants. While there may be some very defensible behaviors involved, it remains a highly discrimination-prone mechanism. This in no way means that you should avoid responding to blind advertisements, but you should recognize that the possibility exists that your inquiry will go unanswered.

There are some publications which are specifically focused on individuals who are likely to be interested in new positions. Major firms take out full-page display ads in publications such as *MBA* magazine or *Business World.* These publications are focused on graduating college students and provide information on fairly standardized opportunities with major employers. Even if you do not fall in this category, you might gain some better understanding of job opportunities by checking these magazines.

If you are a college graduate, you can return to your school's career planning facility for help in locating positions. It's true that placement offices and dormitory cafeterias often vie for the criticism of the student body. While it is not possible to generalize on dorm food, the problems that students perceive at the placement centers are sometimes a function of the students' lack of preparation to undertake the job search process. These facilities remain an important source of information. Many companies make conscientious efforts to provide information to these centers and to send interviewers to talk to job seekers.

The free enterprise equivalent of the placement center is the employment agency. You could find a suitable position in this manner, but there are some very important considerations. You must remember that the employment counselor at the agency gets rewarded on the basis of placement. The idea is to place the most people with the least problem. While these people must stay on the job for a certain period in order to justify the fee, the job need not be the optimal job for that person; it must be acceptable. If you are changing careers, you must be careful that the employment counselor understands your determination to make that change. There will be strong pressure on you to continue in the type of work in which you have experience. Remember, that person gets paid if you are placed. It is usually easier to place you in another position just like your last. It is your responsibility to make your expectations clear and to stick to those expectations.

Another characteristic of employment services and their sophisticated cousins, executive search firms, is that they work from specifications supplied by the employers. The reason employers list their positions with agencies is because they do not want to be involved in processing unqualified applicants. They expect the agency to send them only those persons who meet the requirements specified, whether or not the person has other interesting qualities. Agencies are extremely reluctant to present you to an employer unless you fit those specifications. To do so may well cause them to be dropped from that company's list of acceptable agencies. They are not willing to risk their relationships with their client companies just because you feel strongly that you are qualified to pursue a different career path.

Each of the sources discussed to this point is reasonably impersonal. You can read ads, contact your alma mater, or visit agencies without disturbing any interpersonal relationships. There is low personal commitment. Some of the other sources are potentially more fruitful but involve personal contacts.

Among the more important sources of job leads are personal friends, acquaintances, relatives, and friends of friends. For ages men have made use of these kinds of contacts. A man is likely to call an old football buddy who has achieved some level of success and ask for help. Sit down and think of everybody you know who might know anybody who can get you on the inside track for a job. A college roommate's father might have a decision-making position. Call upon your relatives to search their address books for names of possible contacts. This is not the time to be shy. Think of it as a compliment to the person you are contacting. In effect you are saying that you believe that person has some worthwhile information and has conducted his or her professional life or career in a way which has generated the respect and confidence of others. You are in no way obligating that person. If someone has no information or does not wish to assist you, it is not that difficult to say no. On the other hand, from your point of view, what is the worst thing that can happen? Some people will tell you that they don't want to or can't help you. How much can that really hurt you?

In seeking out leads from individuals, keep some of the same thoughts in mind as when dealing with agencies. It is important that you make it clear that you want a job with certain characteristics and that you have particular qualities. There is a balance between defining the job too narrowly and turning up no leads or leaving the question wide open. If you say, "Do you know of any job openings I might be interested in?" you haven't helped your contact to understand that you're interested in a professional selling position. You might end up with interviews for secretarial positions. Most people do not associate women with sales positions. They may even know of such a position but be reluctant to mention it to you on the assumption that you wouldn't be interested. Be specific: "I'm interested in a sales job. Do you know of any?" If your contact suggests a lead be sure to ask, "Can I use your name?" Having a reference can be helpful, but to use someone's name without permission is a serious breech of etiquette.

Even if the people you contact can provide no hard job leads, they may be able to help you to widen your circle of contacts. One easy way to accomplish this is through professional organizations. Normally people will concentrate on jobs, so it will be your responsibility to bring up the idea. "Do you belong to any professional organizations such as Sales and Marketing Executives International or the American Marketing Association? Could I attend the next meeting with you?" Another avenue is to consult your telephone directory for professional organizations in your area. Take yourself to a meeting. There is an important organization which is often ignored. If you are already employed in a staff capacity, there is always a possibility that your firm would be able to transfer you to a sales position. Many organizations, large and small, have discovered that their under-utilized women represent excellent candidates for sales positions. In making this point to management, you might stress that you are already familiar with the organization, its people, its mission, and perhaps its customers. They should have ample evidence of your work habits and relevant qualities. There is no reason to deny your present employer the opportunity to bid for your services.

As you continue the process of generating leads, you can progress to the stage of qualifying those leads. Your objective is to eliminate those leads which are not likely to result in an appropriate opportunity and retain those that do. There are two types of mistakes you can make. If you set your standards too high or make your requirements too rigid, you will delete from your list some leads which do hold potential. If you are too lax, you will retain leads which hold no potential and are a waste of your time. Of the two errors, it is better to retain some leads which turn out to be dead ends than to eliminate worthwhile leads.

As you develop your system for qualifying leads, consider the situation facing the person responsible for recruiting salespeople. In most cases, this is not this person's principal responsibility. Most salespeople are hired by sales managers who are themselves former salespeople who have now assumed managerial responsibilities. They usually have little if any formal training in personnel matters and are trying to accomplish this in addition to their day-to-day responsibilities. Since there are no hard and fast measures of success in sales, they normally have some favorite substitutes. Some depend heavily on evidence of determination or independence, such as having worked to support yourself through school. Others would like to base their decisions on "gut feelings," but the imposition of affirmative action plans in most major corporations has forced at least partial establishment of standards. Now this person is forced to sit down and describe the position and the type of candidate desired for an ad or job opening statement. Often a rather fuzzy idea of what is needed becomes unnecessarily concrete. The need to know a little about the business might suddenly be transformed into "three years' experience required." Mechanical aptitude may become an engineering degree. The question you must ask yourself is whether or not you must meet each of the requirements as specified or whether you can convince the employer that your qualifications are adequate. Each situation will be different, and your qualifying skills will improve with practice but there are some ideas to keep in mind.

Usually the experience requirement is at least flexible if not to be ignored. You can develop some argument for parallel experience and, with a suitable personal presentation, overcome this barrier. An otherwise acceptable position should not be eliminated from consideration on the basis of an experience requirement. Educational requirements can be a bit more firm, but before striking a lead from your list you might inquire if the firm ever deviates from that standard.

The principal reason to eliminate potential positions from your list is that they fail to measure up to your standards. Perhaps the income potential fails to meet your expectations. You may have some deep-seated aversion to an industry. For example, if marijuana should be legalized there would be many people who would be uncomfortable selling it to others. The point is that you should not eliminate leads on the basis of the employers' expectations of you as much as on the basis of your expectations of the employer. Obviously the more leads you have generated, the more choosey you can be about the ones you will vigorously pursue.

ASSESSING THE EMPLOYERS' NEEDS

Ask yourself why people are hired. Are they hired because they need a job? Are they hired because they are in the right place at the right time? Are they hired because they have managed to present their credentials in a positive and convincing manner? While there is some reason to answer yes to all these questions, the real truth is that you will be hired if, in the judgment of the person charged with the responsibility for the decision to hire, you will be able to do the job. While you should be conscientiously seeking a position which is exactly what you want, most employers are seeking an employee who will be adequate. Of course, given a group of people to choose from they would like to choose the optimal person. Employers do strive to stimulate the interest of potential employees and to generate the highest possible number of candidates from which to choose. But when the chips are on the table, they often ask the question "who will fit in here and do the job I need done?"

Now we get down to the truth. The person who is hired is the one who does the best job of convincing the employer that he or she can fit in and do the job that needs to be done with the least problems and hassle. Many employers view the recruiting-hiring cycle as a disruption of activities, something which needs to be completed in order to get on with the business at hand. No employer wants personnel problems. Employers want to build a team of people who will work together and get the job done. If you want to be hired for a job, the first thing you have to do is to decide exactly what that employer wants. Then you can build a presentation which will convince that employer that you are the person who is best suited to that job. You need to convince that employer that the firm will be better off for having hired you. It really doesn't matter to the employer that this is the very best job for you. That doesn't mean that the employer doesn't want you to be happy in your work. No employer wants unhappy employees. That causes immediate morale problems and eventual turnover problems. But you have to recognize an employer's main concern is legitimate self-interest. Your task is to discover how to satisfy that interest.

The total needs package of any employer is made up of two parts. Every employer has needs in common with every other employer and has needs specific to the firm or industry. The needs that are held in common are both logical and well-documented. To name just a few: Employers seek honesty, energy, enthusiasm, career orientation, common sense, loyalty, and competence. In the area of sales we've established that both empathy and ego drive are desired qualities. There are some requirements which vary from firm to firm and industry to industry. Some industries, for example, require mechanical aptitude while other industries require artistic talents. The individual who sells space in a publication or time on a radio station is called upon to demonstrate an array of talents quite unlike those of the individual who sells fabricated steel products. How do you determine what talents and qualities are required by a particular employer? Beyond the clues offered in the ad or by the person who fed you the lead, job applicants seldom seek out this pertinent information. While the sources are few, it is possible to develop some understanding.

The best way to understand is to be able to candidly discuss the industry and the company with someone in a position similar to the one in which you are interested. While professional organizations may offer some opportunity for that, such contacts are not always available. The next best course is to try to learn something about the industry. A trip to your public library can sometimes turn up information. Don't look for books. Seek out a helpful librarian, the *Readers' Guide to Business Periodicals, The Wall Street Journal Index*, and the Annual Report and Pamphlet files. These are the places where you will find leads to practical, up-to-date information on the industries and specific companies.

Depending on the industry in which you are interested, you may be able to discover some worthwhile information by talking with customers. For example, some publishers of college textbooks recommend that people interested in becoming field salespeople in textbooks take some time to talk with professors about the role of the field sales representative.

Most industries have some trade association or professional organization. While the degree of helpfulness varies with the organization, there is little to be lost in contacting these organizations. Most libraries have a copy of the *Encyclopaedia of Organizations*, which lists these organizations by topic. As with uncovering leads on job openings, the important characteristic of an effective search on the needs of the employers is a degree of persistence and a recognition that every bit of information you can uncover will assist you in building your case. Of course as you interview you will learn more about the needs of employers. The difference between the people who are successful in getting or keeping jobs and those who aren't is that the successful people realize that their needs are met by meeting the needs of the firm.

ASSESSING THE COMPETITION

Having done your homework and uncovered job leads which you have qualified in terms of your needs and the needs of the employers, you are almost ready to begin your active campaign. The one remaining obstacle to an effective presentation is knowledge of the competition. If you were selling a product you would consider the features and drawbacks of substitute products in order to be prepared to present your case effectively. This is no different. You need some information on the availability of substitutes. How many other people might apply and what are their qualifications? You also need information on what kind of money offers are being made. Without this information it is difficult for you to have an idea of how much you are worth and how receptive employers will be to your approach.

Obtaining this information requires a variety of approaches ranging from judicious inquiry to library research. Often the information is available if you ask for it. When you call to arrange an interview you might ask the receptionist, "Have you had many inquiries on this position?" You may ask the person who arranges the interview if the other people who have called have met or exceeded the requirements as stated in the ad. It is logical that this information is of interest to you. If you ask pleasantly, you might get an answer. Of course you must recognize that the recruiter is not likely to be willing to give you the impression that the ad for the position drew little response or few qualified people. In situations where a disinterested third party schedules the interviews, such as the college placement office, the responses may be more reliable.

Although people are usually very secretive regarding earnings, compensation information is relatively easy to obtain. There are many sources of reliable information. One important source is the College Placement Council. Periodically this group surveys its member placement offices for information on the high, low, and average offers made to persons using their services. These generally represent entry level positions and are broken down by type of position and industry. While these are based on a national sample, your local office can provide an indication of whether offers in your area tend to be higher or lower than that figure.

Another important source of information is *Sales and Marketing Management's* "Sales Force Compensation" report. It provides information on actual compensation levels—but more importantly discusses many issues of concern to sales managers and salespeople in considering compensation. Other business periodicals publish occasional articles on compensation of sales people. Again the *Readers' Guide to Business Periodicals* will guide you to up-to-date sources. It is important to have a clear perception of prevailing compensation plans and levels before you receive offers. You may err by refusing an offer which is really quite attractive thereby convincing the interviewer that your expectations are unrealistic or by accepting an offer which lacks the rewards your qualifications and performance would justify.

With some realistic information on sales compensation and any information you can gather on the people with whom you might be competing, you are ready to prepare your presentation. Your objective is to present your qualifications in a manner which will convince the employer that hiring you is the best decision.

PREPARING YOUR SALES PRESENTATION

In preparing your presentation the important thing to keep in mind is that it is your objective to convince that other person that you have the necessary qualities to accomplish the job. In most situations a lot depends on how you package the product. Unfortunately many people use brown paper bags. You need to positively distinguish yourself from the other applicants. You need not be perfect: You simply have to be a little better. While the actual interviewing situation will be the focus of the next section, the pre-interview preparation critical to a successful job campaign is the topic here.

The first question to ask yourself is "Why would I want to hire me?" The answers generally fall into four categories, the four Es: Education, Experience, Enthusiasm, and Earnestness. You will be hired on the basis of expected performance. Each of these four elements is a factor in the interviewer's assessment of your promise. These factors represent strengths but are meaningful only to the extent that you interpret them to the interviewer in terms of the needs of the organization. In your preinterview preparation you must anticipate the needs, questions, and responses of the interviewer in order to plan the way in which you can most effectively present your strengths.

Begin by evaluating your educational background. Is it extensive? Is it relevant to the position? Is it recent? Clearly it is what it is. It is a documented part of your life. A B.A. in early childhood education in 1967 is not suddenly going to turn into a 1978 M.B.A. It is a given. If it is appropriate, all the better. If it isn't, you must be ready to compensate for it in each of the other areas. In addition, you should practice presenting the general benefits of education. You have had extensive practice in communication. You have demonstrated persistence. You have demonstrated a capacity for self-discipline. Perhaps you can make a case for the relevance of minor areas of study or specific courses. Did you have any math or science courses which might be significant? Perhaps your courses in psychology or social sciences are worth mentioning. You should carefully examine your educational record and attempt to develop points which will be of interest. You cannot expect the interviewer to make the effort to dig into your background, but you can expect that a logical presentation would be accepted.

Experience is another area where interpretation can actually make a great deal of difference. There are two kinds of experience: actual and vicarious. Often women lack the standard accepted forms of experience, but with a little creative thought you can relate other forms of experience to the position. Preplanning makes all the difference. In terms of actual experience there are three areas to be evaluated. First there is actual work experience. Perhaps you have had some jobs, but the titles on those jobs do not match the interviewer's expectations. Stop and consider what the interviewer is looking for in considering experience. That interviewer is looking for evidence that you are able to assume responsibility, organize your time, interact effectively with other people, follow procedures, survive adversity, and in many other ways perform to your employer's best interest. Can you interpret your job experiences in terms of your interviewer's needs? Think of instances where you demonstrated responsibility. Try to remember events that demonstrate superior performance. If your salary history indicates employer approval and self-improvement, be prepared to give some evidence of that. Were you ever responsible for your own schedule? Were you ever in a position to supervise others? This may be a difficult exercise since you have probably never tried to interpret your experiences in light of the requirements of a sales organization. However, if you lack sales experience, you can at least partially compensate in this way. If you have ever sold anything, no matter how insignificant, do not fail to mention it. One woman successfully communicated her experience selling programs at the college football games. If you have ever done telephone selling or worked in a retail store you should incorporate that experience into your presentation.

Another important area of actual experience is organizational experience. Consider every position of leadership you have ever held. Did you organize any activity for a social or professional group? Were you active in any organization in school? The planning and coordination activities that are important to success in sales can be experienced in a variety of ways. You need not shortchange yourself just because you haven't earned your living in this way. The point is exactly the same. It is your responsibility to generate every single piece of evidence that you have the necessary qualifications to be successful in sales and to present that information to the interviewer in an easily consumable form. The interviewer has no reason to put the effort into the interpretation of your experiences. It is your responsibility.

The third area of actual experiences are unique experiences. Is there anything in your background which would give you any edge in getting this job? Perhaps you have traveled extensively. One of the traditional fears about women is that they can't handle travel. Do you have a foreign language background which would be important? Do you have relatives in the industry? One woman worked her way into a job in electronic funds transfer systems such as the computerized checkouts in supermarkets because she had written a term paper on the industry as a graduate student. Remember that the interviewer will ask standard questions. If you have any nonstandard information to communicate, you are going to have to find a way to introduce it into the conversation.

Actual experiences are certainly important, but you can also effectively use vicarious experiences to demonstrate your competencies to the interviewer. Vicarious experiences are those experiences you have borrowed from others. We don't have to experience everything firsthand to learn from the experience. Reading about motorcycle accidents in the newspapers or listening to a friend or relative describe an accident is usually enough to convince us that motorcycles are dangerous. Each one of us doesn't need to have an accident. The same thing can be true of certain business-related experiences. While you may not understand all the finer points, you can gain some appreciation for the problems of the salesperson or the complexities of an industry by reading accounts of the experiences of others. There are many excellent books on selling. By reading some of these books, you can discuss the job with the interviewer in an intelligent manner.

One of the principal fears that employers have in hiring women into sales positions is that the woman will be unaware of the nature of the job and get into a situation in which she will fail. No one wants to hire someone who fails. It not only generates feelings of guilt in the person who made the hiring decision but looks bad on that person's record. If you can demonstrate to the interviewer that you have realistic perceptions of the position based on your exposure through vicarious experiences, your chances are dramatically improved. Obviously this points you back to the *Readers' Guide to Business Periodicals.* Read accounts of people and companies in the industries in which you have special interest. Try to familiarize yourself with the jargon and with names and companies significant in the industry. The principal value of experience is increased awareness. You must demonstrate that you have built upon your vicarious and actual experiences and that you have the potential to grow.

One of the important factors which contributes to your ability to grow with a position is enthusiasm for that job. Just imagine how productive the world would be if everyone enjoyed his or her work. In pursuing a sales position this idea of enthusiasm has special meaning. First of all, the person responsible for hiring recognizes that selling can be a taxing job. There will be both high and low points. In some staff positions every day is very much like the last. You experience no high highs, but suffer no low lows. In sales you will have both. Enthusiasm for your work can carry you through some of those lows and facilitate your eventual success.

Second, selling tends to be an underrated role. The interviewer facing you has probably faced many people who were reluctant to accept similar positions. It can be a little discouraging. A recent study revealed that only 1 out of 17 undergraduate marketing majors indicated a preference for an entry level sales position. If you enter the interview with a degree of enthusiasm, you can overcome a variety of shortcomings in other areas. If you can't generate enthusiasm for any position, you should find another way to earn your living. If you have it, show it.

The final strength you can demonstrate to the employer is earnestness. In most organizations the cost of training salespeople is high. There are a variety of costs to be considered. Not only are there the out-of-pocket costs for training, but there are costs in terms of your impact on customers, the opportunity lost if you fail to make sales, and separation costs if you leave. You must project the image of seriousness. The interviewer must perceive that you are intent, have purpose, and are sincerely interested in both this type of work and this company. One woman was interviewing with a publishing company. She had recently been divorced and had minimal selling experience. Her education was adequate but not distinguished. Sensing that the interview was not going in her favor, primarily because the interviewer was of the opinion that her divorce represented a disrupting factor, she blurted out, "That doesn't make one bit of difference. I know I can sell your books!" He was so impressed with her sincerity that she got the job. If you can't express confidence in your choice, who else can feel confidence in you? All of us have doubts, but the interview is a place where you should be prepared to conceal those doubts. It's not the place to expect encouragement from others.

Just as we all have doubts, we all have weaknesses. We all have limitations. While your limitations are not the points you should stress in the interview, consideration of these weaknesses is an important part of your preinterview preparation. While you are well aware of your weaknesses and would wisely conceal them, some could show through. That is no problem if you handle it correctly. Everyone has weaknesses. Some people just explain them better or build better paths around them. You must recognize your own weaknesses in order to prepare your defenses and explanations in advance.

Weaknesses come in three basic forms: imperfections, inflexibilities, and inadequacies. Imperfections are qualities you have or experiences in your background which detract from your employability. A low grade average in school, having been fired, health problems, or something such as a prison record, dishonorable discharge, or recent divorce would qualify as an imperfection. One imperfection common in women is the employment gap—time during which you were voluntarily unemployed. There is a form of collective wisdom which says that anyone who is truly interested in a career or ambitious could hardly tolerate being unemployed.

List your imperfections. Look carefully at the list. While they may never come into the conversation, you must prepare a plausible explanation or compensating point for each of your imperfections. It's not easy to contemplate your own imperfections, but you can feel considerably more confident entering the interview if you have prepared the necessary explanations. Remember that those explanations must be phrased in terms of the interests of the interviewers. Consider these examples of saying the same thing in two different ways. Imagine that you have a one-year gap in your employment record during which you traveled in Europe. You can explain, "I recognized that I would probably never have another opportunity to be free to have a good time with several of my college friends." Alternatively you can point out, "I felt that this experience would help me to develop my independence and self-reliance. I had contemplated a career in the foreign service and concentrated on absorbing the language and the culture." The first explanation lacks a career orientation while the second at least covers you in terms of ambition.

Consider another example. One of the factors which will interfere with your ability to land the job you want is job hopping. While there could be a variety of definitions, three jobs in three years will usually qualify you as a job hopper. What explanations could you offer for this imperfection? Perhaps you could claim, "I haven't been too good at choosing positions. After I actually got on the job I found that it wasn't what I had expected." Why should the current interviewer believe that your ability to assess opportunities has improved? Perhaps you would feel that an external excuse would solve the difficulty. You could comment, "I changed jobs because my husband was transferred." The interviewer is certainly to be discouraged by this type of answer. If you suggest, on the other hand, "I mastered the requirements of each job in a short period of time and moved on to a position where my talents could be more fully employed." With this answer job hopping still may not be a plus, but could be less of a minus. The interviewer would have to rate the job opening being discussed as less than challenging for such an explanation to be totally unacceptable. Of course, the nature of the jobs held during the three-year period would have to support this explanation. You would have to show that each position offered more responsibility and reward than the last.

A second weakness is inflexibility. Most firms would like a group of employees who are willing to make reasonable personal adjustments or sacrifices in order to successfully progress in their careers. While the heyday of corporate transfers appears to be waning, mobility and other issues of flexibility are still quite important. In the early 60s companies transferred people simply to transfer them. There was some idea that this added to their development and cosmopolitanism. As moving costs have increased rapidly and bottom line figures become even more important, transfers today are more often based on need. Nevertheless when you are considered for a position, your flexibility is considered. It is quite likely that you will be asked if you would be willing to relocate. The answer you give is critical, and you should consider it carefully. If you are going to answer no, your reason must be more career-oriented than the climate or your friends. In many cases, being unwilling to relocate will knock you out of consideration for the job.

The third weakness is your inadequacies. Inadequacies differ from imperfections. Imperfections are something you have which you wish you didn't have, while inadequacies are things which you don't have that you wish you did. You may lack appropriate educational credentials, experience, or skills relevant to a sales position. Inadequacies must be considered separate from imperfections because you must take a different course of action. The course with imperfections is to generate logical explanations and compensating strengths. With inadequacies the objective is to develop plans to overcome the deficiencies. Again, specific inadequacies may not arise in the interview, but your preplanning will allow you to deal with them positively if they do. Sometimes the inadequacies relate to a specific area of learning. Perhaps you should know some of the basic principles of accounting. If you've examined your inadequacies, you might be able to say, "I have been to the college bookstore and purchased the recommended basic accounting text. I've begun to work my way through the workbook and am planning to audit the course during the next session." This might be sufficient to get you the job, if only on a probationary basis. By any measure, it is a far better answer than a simple "Yes, I realize that I haven't had an accounting course."

If you can approach the interview having carefully inventoried your strengths and examined your weaknesses and are confident that you can fulfill the employer's requirements, you're in a position to help the employer make a favorable decision. It will be your responsibility to help that other person to understand. When George Burns the comedian was 70 years old he decided to stage a comeback. He went to several agents and was turned down each time on the basis of an imperfection—his age. They were reluctant to invest the time in redeveloping his career. Based upon their stereotypes, they believed that he would be unable to pay off. Finally he came across an agent who signed him as a client. It's not clear whether he became more adept at selling himself or the agent needed clients. Between the ages of 70 and 80, he earned $12 million. The agent picked up 10 percent of that. Just because you have some weaknesses doesn't mean that you are less employable.

All job applicants have weaknesses and should be prepared to deal with questions in those areas if they arise. At this point, women must be especially careful because their particular packages of weaknesses may be less familiar and hence more frightening to the potential employer. Besides that, their weaknesses are more likely to be discussed. One woman reports that she was subjected to extra tough interviewing questions. While all the questions were job-related, they reflected the doubts of the interviewers that a woman could be successful in the computer industry. Even after she had established that she felt confident in her abilities to sell, she was questioned on her choice of industry. Why didn't she consider retail selling or cosmetics—areas where women have been entrenched? She persisted and at the end of two years had managed to climb to the number one position in sales performance in her district.

MAKING YOUR SALES PRESENTATION

Your presentation begins long before you enter the interviewer's office. It begins with your first contact. Sellers of industrial products advertise those products so that the buyer has developed a favorable impression long before the sales representative walks through the door. The materials you send the employer and the calls you make are your form of advertising. They will determine if you are allowed to make your formal presentation and, if so, the employer's predisposition toward you. While this book will not discuss resumes, they are extremely important. You should consult reference materials on this subject and seek help in preparing an outstanding resume and cover letter. You should take care that your materials reflect your professional image. Can you imagine a major corporation listing the features of one of their products and then sending out mimeographed copies? Make sure your materials look professional even if it is costly.

With regard to phone calls, the biggest concern for sales managers is people who don't know what they want to say. Before you dial the number, list the points you want to make, have your calendar at hand, and be prepared to be specific. A good resume and decisive telephone practices should open the interview door.

Interviews are human interactions and are as varied as the people who participate. There are some thoughts to keep in mind to keep your perspectives in order. First, that person needs to hire someone. For most sales managers, interviewing and recruiting are time-consuming activities. There are other important issues demanding their energies. The interviewer, however, needs a reason to hire you. You must provide that reason. Second, interviewing is a two-way process. You are not being interrogated. While any interview is two-way, this factor is especially significant in an interview for a sales position. If you were seeking a position as a statistician, the interview would be a vehicle to determine your technical skills. Your effectiveness in the interview process would be relatively unimportant. With regard to a sales position, your interactive skills assume major proportions. If you have organized your presentation and can smoothly move the employer through your sales points to the logical conclusion that you are the person for the job, you will have established that you can sell. You will have sold yourself. Third, most people lack the capacity or interest to adequately evaluate your potential. They make judgments based on their perception of your perception of your worth. If you express doubts and reservations, there is really little reason for the sales manager to believe in your potential. If you express confidence in yourself, most people will believe you. Finally, remember that you are being evaluated relative to other entry level sales people. You are expected to show promise, to have some basic skills, but you are not competing for the number one position in the firm. You don't have to be perfect; you have to be a little bit better than the other entry level applicants.

With those philosophical points in mind ask the practical question "What is this sales manager looking for in this interview?" What does the interview reveal that the resume doesn't? If the interview was strictly to assess your experiences and education, it would be redundant. The purpose is to assess the package—the total you. Sales managers are looking for some indicators of self-confidence, a positive attitude, and some flexibility. They are continually asking the questions "Will this person be able to do the job?" and "Will this person work out in my organization?" Your preinterview preparation may not have made you confident in an absolute sense, but if you were conscientious, you will be as confident as possible.

Think about a presidential news conference. The President doesn't know exactly which questions will be asked or in what order, but he has prepared comprehensive answers to all of the likely questions. It is simply a matter of presenting the practiced answer at the appropriate time. You have some practiced answers too, but your situation is a bit different. The President only responds to questions. You must be more active. You must do more than respond. The sales manager isn't interested in being rejected any more than you are. One of the factors associated with being offered a job is being interested in the job. People are more likely to offer jobs to people who want those jobs. One way to indicate interest in a job is to ask questions about it. You should be prepared to ask questions about the company, the location, the other people in the office, the future, your compensation, your customers, training programs, supplemental benefits, or any other job-related issues. You might ask, "Why is this job open?" Ask specific questions and expect clear answers. If you don't get an answer, wait a few moments and ask the same question in another form. While your objective is to get the offer, remember that this isn't the only job in town. Never get down on your knees or allow yourself to be hired on a second-class basis. Try to project the image of a person who has other options but is sincerely interested in this one.

Being prepared to ask questions can have some other advantages. It can help you to protect yourself. While a great many sales managers profess that they treat men and women applicants exactly the same, that isn't always the case. If you encounter one who doesn't, your chances of maintaining your dignity are enhanced if you remember that this person is a product of a functioning male-dominated business system. This person has not had the opportunity to develop a full understanding of the potential professional contribution of women. You will have to help this person to overcome this shortcoming. Depending on the nature of the problem, your options vary. In some cases, a well-intentioned person will make an inappropriate remark out of ignorance or nervousness. In such cases, the practice of selective thickskinnery applies. You simply ignore it. To make an issue of it would belie your flexibility.

Sometimes the bias takes the form of questions which should not be asked. The rules are fairly simple; questions should be job-related and should logically be asked of all applicants regardless of sex. Your personal life is your personal life. Your marital arrangements, child care considerations, birth control practices, or other personal issues are not relevant to the job interview. You should not volunteer this information and should be prepared to fend off questions should they be asked.

If you have been asked a direct question which you feel is beyond the scope of the interview, one response is to answer that question with a question. It is important that that question is not reactionary. For example, if you were asked if you planned to marry you could respond, "Can you tell me how that would affect my job?" You will have put the interviewer on the spot and your satisfactions will be short-lived. It's better to respond with a parallel question. "What proportion of your sales people are married?" The interviewer can attempt to answer this question, which is related to the topic. In most cases, given that you have responded, the initial question will pass.

Another technique is to answer with evasion. Perhaps you are asked, "Do you plan to have children?" You could answer evasively with, "Do you realize how expensive children are? I read an article the other day which said that it costs over $80,000 to raise a child to the age of 18." You have left the impression that there is some disinclination toward children, but you've said nothing. With either parallel questions or evasive answers it is important to keep talking. This is a perfect spot to ask a substantive question on the firm, the customers, or any other job-related subject.

A final technique is more direct but still leaves you free from commitment and makes it clear that you are not to be treated differently. The interpretation technique involves uncovering the interviewer's real concern. Employers are not worried about husbands or children. They are worried that you will either move away from the job or not be able to move with the job. They are worried that you will become nonproductive. If you are asked, "Do you plan to marry?" an interpretive response would be, "I'm sure you are inter-ested in my mobility. I can assure you that my commitment to my career is strong and that I am prepared to pursue this with vigor." In each of these techniques you can preserve your dignity without destroying your chances.

It is difficult to understand how anyone involved in recruiting today could persist in this type of behavior, but it happens. You cannot change that; you can only be prepared to manage the situation if it occurs. Usually the person is well aware that these questions are off limits and will not pursue the issue. There are some indirect difficulties which may be more difficult to handle if you are not aware.

Questions about husbands and babies may be difficult, but at least they are overt. You know that you have been asked and that you are probably being treated in a different manner than male applicants. The situation is then dependent on your ability to maintain your control and shift the questioning back onto solid ground. A more insidious danger arises out of the doubt of the sales manager that you can perform the task. Some people, in attempting to protect you, actually undermine you and damage you. This usually takes the form of slanted disclosure. If a man is interviewing for a sales job, it might be assumed that he knows all of the obstacles and is aware of the problems. The sales manager may even try to sell him on the job. After all, most sales managers are drawn from the ranks of successful salesmen and can identify with men. They don't mean to damage women but really don't want the woman to make a mistake and get into something she can't handle. Therefore they are more likely to dwell on the problems and negatives of the job when interviewing a woman. Sometimes this behavior represents an attempt to see if you are really serious.

You could be unnecessarily discouraged. Even if you are concerned about some of the negatives discussed during the interview, you should never express that concern. You can check those things out later. Your mission is to get the job offer. You don't have to accept the job. If you express doubt or indicate that you may not be interested in the job, you can be certain that no offer will be made.

Every successful salesperson enters every meeting with a customer with some objective clearly in mind. The objective may be to determine if the customer is qualified to buy. It may be to secure an appointment with some other person in the organization who is the decision maker. It may be to close the deal. When you enter the interview you have an objective in mind, that is, to move to the next step in the process. Before the interview is concluded, you need to find out about that next step. You need to ask when the decision will be made, if additional information would be helpful, and how many other people are under consideration. These are legitimate questions which reinforce your interest in the position. This information provides a basis for your follow-through.

FOLLOW-THROUGH

Once the interview is over some people go home and sit on their hands waiting for the mail. This is hardly the way to sell yourself. Now that you have come this far, you can distinguish yourself with about an hour of total effort. This effort is aimed toward maintaining contact with the decision maker. First of all, thank you letters are in order. You should write to each of the people who was involved in your interview. As the decision is being made you want to make sure that your name is remembered. You can call or write providing any additional information which you feel would positively affect their decision. Some people deliberately omit some positive point from the interview in order to have it available for their follow-through. You might call to ask a reasonable question. At some point within the consideration period, it is fair to inform them if you have received another offer. This must be done carefully as it should not appear to be a pressure play. Finally, if the time for the decision has passed and you have not been contacted, it is wise to call and inquire.

This can be very difficult but is very important to your overall job search. You should call and ask if someone else was hired. If the answer is yes, you should ask, "In that I really am serious about a position such as this could you please tell me how that person was more qualified?" This becomes a part of your preparation for the next interview. Try to encourage the person to be specific by indicating an interest in self-improvement. If there are no specific reasons for the rejection, ask the sales manager if you might be referred to some other office of the same firm or to some other firm which may have a similar position. These kinds of questions will either help you to understand yourself better and thereby prepare you for the ongoing search or help that sales manager to a better self-understanding and pave the way for others.

If you are offered the job, there are two options: You can accept or refuse. Only you can establish your criteria. There are some general thoughts to keep in mind. If you have succeeded in securing one offer, you could probably get others. First, be sure the job meets your standards. Second, it is generally not wise to accept a consolation job. If you applied for a sales position and are offered a sales assistant position, keep looking. If you're hired on a second-class basis it can be very difficult to climb out of that gutter. If you refuse the job, you should do so in writing stating the terms offered in detail. This is one way of assuring that the terms offered to equally qualified people are equal. The interviewing process can be discouraging. While careful planning can pay off, there are moments when the end of the tunnel is out of sight. Remember that you are making an investment in yourself. Study the accompanying admonition.

MOTTO OF THE McDONALD CORPORATION

> # PRESS ON
> NOTHING IN THE WORLD CAN TAKE THE PLACE OF PERSISTENCE. TALENT WILL NOT; NOTHING IS MORE COMMON THAN UNSUCCESSFUL MEN WITH TALENT. GENIUS WILL NOT; UNREWARDED GENIUS IS ALMOST A PROVERB. EDUCATION ALONE WILL NOT; THE WORLD IS FULL OF EDUCATED DERELICTS. PERSISTENCE AND DETERMINATION ALONE ARE OMNIPOTENT.

4 Be assertive, not aggressive

*No one can make you feel
inferior without your consent.*
Eleanor Roosevelt, 1937

No one is going to allow you a space in this world. Indeed those who profess to allow you a space may be doing you an unintentional, but nonetheless substantial, disservice. In a recent *Harvard Business Review* article, "Two Women and Three Men on a Raft," Robert Schrank, a project specialist for the Ford Foundation, recounted his mind-boggling discovery of the concept of undermining. He had been on a test-your-survival-skills raft trip. He just happened to be assigned to a raft with another male passenger, the male guide, and two women. You may agree that people who would voluntarily subject themselves to a survival training exercise are a cut above the norm in terms of adventuresomeness, self-confidence, and a few other coping characteristics. The trip turned out to be a semi-disaster.

It started out with the responsibilities equally divided among the occupants of the raft. In the end, the women had abdicated their leadership responsibilities. While each person was supposed to take his or her turn at the helm, before the end of the trip, the men were helmsmen and the women had been reduced to permanent crew members. Shrank's analysis of the forces underlying this conversion are terribly important to any woman seeking to understand her role and responsibilities in aspiring to a traditionally male occupation, professional sales.

> A most revealing part of the raft experience, however, was not so much the power relationship between the sexes, which I think I understood, but how Bill and I unconsciously or automatically responded to protect our power from female encroachment. When the trip started, I knew I might have some difficulty accepting a woman at the helm, but I did not realize that the threat would be so great that I would actually desire to see her fail. On that trip I did something new: I actively tried to sabotage (the women's) efforts to lead. . . . (We) were unconsciously building on each woman's doubts about herself with negative reinforcement of her leadership role.[1]

The critical issue is how the men accomplished this. Had they openly challenged the women's leadership roles, the women might have resisted or fought back. But that wasn't the case. The men actually helped the women into helplessness. In a friendly and seemingly well-intentioned manner they gradually undermined each woman's confidence in herself by making it clear that she needed to be helped—that she couldn't manage independently.

Why did this happen? It happened for reasons which could be attributed to sources of influence which are not likely to change in the near future. A more relevant question is "what would have happened if the women on the raft had acted assertively rather than openly acknowledging their doubts in themselves?"

At this point you may be asking, why all this fuss about assertiveness? As a woman who would even consider a career in sales am I not far more assertive than most women already? The answer to that question could well be yes. But assertiveness, as most other human characteristics, is a matter of degree. You may be more assertive than many other women. You may even be more assertive than some men. That still leaves two questions. First, "Are you as assertive as you need to be?" and second, "Are you as assertive as you are capable of becoming?" No one is assertive or passive in the absolute sense. People are more or less assertive than other people. Nobody wrote

[1] Robert Schrank, "Two Women, Three Men on a Raft," *Harvard Business Review*, May-June 1977, p. 107. Copyright © 1977 by the President and Fellows of Harvard College. All rights reserved.

out the rules of the game, but the rules are clear. All other things being equal, confidence wins.

Some people cannot tell the difference between assertiveness and aggression, although the difference is significant. Assertiveness is a feeling of comfort in claiming a space to which you are entitled, that is, in standing up for yourself. Aggression is an attempt to claim the space of others. The reason for the confusion is that people can't always agree on who is entitled to what space. This problem is by no means limited to the question of the rightful role of women in the business environment. Most wars have or are being fought over the question of who is entitled to what space.

Space may be defined in terms of physical territory, rights, authority, privileges, or any other idea or thing of economic or psychological value. The men in the raft were unwilling to share leadership or authority. They wanted to steer the course and to be able to claim the credit for safely delivering the raft and its occupants to its destination. This being the disputed space, the women had three choices. They could have acted aggressively by insisting on particular rights and trying to back the men into a corner. By acting aggressively, they would have openly challenged the established order and the thinking of the men as evidenced by their attitudes and actions. They would have been trying to claim a space to which the men believed themselves entitled. The second choice was to react passively. This is what the women did. They accepted their assigned roles, rights, and space as defined by others. The third choice would have been to behave assertively. Assertive people attempt to logically define their spaces and then to confidently occupy those spaces. Most people are not prepared to judge the space to which someone else is entitled. They generally lack the confidence to challenge someone else for the space that person confidently occupies. It might be considered a psychological version of squatter's rights.

Why is it that some people are nonassertive? Perhaps they fear that others will not like them if they act assertively. It may be that by always bowing to another's wishes they believe they can avoid unpleasantness and conflict. Maybe they are concerned about hurting the feelings of others. Some people misinterpret assertiveness to involve ignoring the needs of others. Assertive behaviors may be avoided by people who are afraid that they won't be able to handle the pressure or the responsibility. Maybe they are willing to trade their self-determination for that freedom from the responsibility for their decisions. There is always the possibility that nonassertive people have simply never thought about it. It might be that they have never measured their actions and are not aware of the extent of their nonassertiveness.

That inaction can be just fine as long as they exist in a protective environment. As a saleswoman, you will exist in a more challenging environment. Developing assertive behaviors will help you to be more successful. Not only will you be more able to control your anxiety and withstand more pressure, but you should enjoy better interpersonal relations both with customers and other members of the sales team. Assertiveness is an important element in the process of winning respect and cooperation.

As a saleswoman, you will have some elements in common with the two women on the raft. First of all, in most business situations you will be outnumbered. There are more business*men* than business-*women* for the time being. Second, for the most part the people around you do not consciously intend to undermine your efforts. They may not be able to control themselves or may not even realize that some of their actions would be damaging to your development. Third, you are going to have a chance to demonstrate your abilities. You will have a chance to take responsibility just as each of the women on the raft was expected to take a turn at the helm. In many nonselling careers, your assertiveness or lack of assertiveness may never be put to the test. You will never be allowed the opportunity to take control. Finally, your success is to some extent dependent upon cooperation and encouragement from other people. Assertiveness can help you to inspire the cooperation and encouragement you need.

Preparation is a cornerstone to assertiveness. If one of the objectives of demonstrating assertiveness is that it can make the difference between other people encouraging you and discouraging you, it is important that the people you work with perceive you to be assertive. One of the common difficulties faced by new saleswomen is the "leprosy syndrome." Other people tend to stand back and watch you. You can begin to feel like an animal in a zoo. Some of the people are just curious. Others are waiting for you to fail. Some are sympathetic or willing to be helpful but are not sure enough of themselves to speak up. If you can get through that initial isolation period and begin to demonstrate that you will probably succeed, people will start to come out of the woodwork to offer support. It is a paradox. When you need the support the most, they are afraid to offer it. When you have gotten over the initial adjustment period and can support yourself, you will get lots of encouragement. Nobody wants to be associated with a loser. If they have no information to work with, they seem to assume the worst.

Assertive behavior can speed up that flow of support. Remember, they have no real way to judge your potential and are likely to go along with your judgment of yourself. If you go around doubting yourself, they will doubt you. If you appear confident in yourself, it will inspire the confidence of other people who can be very helpful to you. Whether your self-confidence is real or imaginary is relatively unimportant. What counts is how others perceive you. If you are comfortable with yourself, others can be more comfortable with you. One of the biggest problems you will face if you are one of the first women in anything is that other people will be concerned about what you are going to do, how to treat you, what to expect from you, and how their actions toward you will be interpreted by others. Many people are so uncomfortable that they are willing to accept the answers you provide. An assertive attitude says, "This is what I am going to do, this is how I expect to be treated, and this is what you can expect from me." It doesn't say it in a belligerent or threatening way. It projects a calm, confident, assured recognition of your space and the space of other people.

It is really amazing that most people are unable to judge the rightful space for other people. Aside from the military and other organizations where status is clearly indicated by uniforms, badges, or other external signs, most people are much more concerned about their own space than they are about yours. They will allow you almost any space you claim with confidence. As a high school student you may have discovered the key to successfully being in the wrong place at the wrong time. If you were out in the hall when you were supposed to be in class, your behavior determined if you were challenged. If you sneaked down the side of the hall hugging the wall and ducking into doorways, you probably got caught. If you stepped confidently down the center of the hall and called out a cheerful greeting to the teacher on hall duty, you were likely to receive a cheerful greeting in return and be allowed to continue on your way. The Great Imposter got away with all of his masquerades because he always exuded confidence. He was able to pose as a physician, a priest, and assume other responsible positions because no one questioned a person who acted so self-assured.

The Great Imposter was successful although he really had no formal training for the positions he assumed. Neither the men nor the women on the raft had previous experience in that particular leadership responsibility. The women cooperated with each of the men as he took his turn at the helm and thereby helped the men to be successful. Each man might have had no more confidence in his skills than each woman, but because he put up a good show, he inspired cooperation and support. Had the women on the raft acted assertively during their turns at the helm, the entire trip may have ended more pleasantly. Assertiveness is somewhat like priming the pump. If a woman expresses doubts about her skills or abilities, people are inclined to agree with her and discourage her in her attempts. She may have expressed those doubts in an attempt to stimulate encouragement, but it seldom works. If a young man expresses doubt in his abilities he is more likely to be encouraged by other men because he is more likely to be seen as a part of their team. His failure may reflect on the other men. While it may be less dangerous for a man to express self-doubt, it is still dangerous.

In the natural order of things, survival of the fittest prevails. If an animal is wounded or weakened, other animals of its own kind are likely to turn on it. If they don't, other creatures will. Think about the sharks. When something is wounded in the water, the sharks come in for the kill. The difference between people and wild animals is that people are sometimes more polite while they are killing you. Sometimes you never realize what happened to you.

Becoming assertive is like giving up tobacco. No one can do it for you. It requires careful analysis of your patterns of behavior and then changing those behaviors which are counterproductive. At times it can be very uncomfortable. It takes time to achieve the desired results. At first it is all effort with little reward. While it may never be easy, it is at least easier when the results begin to show.

Becoming assertive is something you can do for yourself. It takes a positive attitude. You must recognize your position relative to the position of others. You need to realize that the results will not be dramatic and immediate. It takes time to change behavior patterns. Fortunately there are some convenient behaviors on which you can begin practicing assertiveness. These are only a beginning, of course. Assertiveness is a complex behavioral concept and there are many good books and courses on the subject. The purpose here is to present some simple behaviors which are both easily adopted and significant to you as a saleswoman. Five appropriate practice behaviors are accepting or offering compliments, qualifying statements, initiating contacts with other people, expressing yourself in a group setting, and handling rejection.

Psychologists have argued over the question of whether behavior change brings about changes in attitudes or attitudinal change produces changed behavior. Becoming assertive requires both an attitude change and a behavioral change, although it is not clear which is the chicken and which is the egg. You have developed an assertive attitude when you can say with conviction,

> I'm somebody too! I don't expect more than my share, but I don't expect less than my share either. I don't expect anyone to allow me my share; I will step up and claim it. I am not ashamed or embarrassed to do so. I will not apologize for expressing myself. I will allow other people their rights, and I will insist upon mine. I'm somebody too!

OFFERING OR ACCEPTING COMPLIMENTS

Offering and accepting compliments gracefully is an assertive act. Apparently it is a good place to start for most people. *Psychology Today* reprinted the findings on a study on people's reactions to compliments.[2] Of the people surveyed, 65 percent reported that they felt embarrassed, uneasy, or defensive when complimented. Why does this supposedly positive form of human interaction generate a negative reaction in two out of three people? It should be a pleasant exchange. These findings reflect one or both of two possibilities. Either people are not skilled at accepting compliments or the people who offer them are not skilled in offering compliments.

Have you ever observed a compliment situation? As preparation for adopting these assertive behaviors, begin to pay attention to compliment situations. In some cases the compliment will be well-phrased and smoothly delivered, and the recipient will respond graciously. In too many cases the compliment will be poorly phrased or awkwardly delivered. The recipient will mumble, be embarrassed, turn the compliment into an insult, or behave in some other inappropriate manner. It is likely that both of the parties meant well, but

---

[2] "Newsline," *Psychology Today*, August 1974, p. 43.

they just couldn't put it all together. Why? Compliments are supposed to be nice. Aren't compliments preferred to criticism?

Have you witnessed any of these situations? In response to a compliment of her job performance a woman looks down at her feet and stammers, "I was just doing what I was told." A sales manager who meant to be positive missed the mark with, "We weren't sure you would work out, but we haven't had as many problems as we expected." Consider the intentional backhand compliment, "You aren't as dumb as you look." Most people mean it when they offer compliments and most compliments are poorly received. Why don't people accept compliments? Answering this question is the first step in developing this assertive behavior.

There are many reasons why people can't accept compliments. They may lack self-esteem and truly doubt that they are deserving. They may have been socialized to believe that it is unattractive to express any positive feelings about oneself: it is immodest. They may be practicing false modesty in an attempt to magnify the impact of the compliment. It is possible that the person has had little practice in accepting compliments. Some people hear very few of them. Maybe they doubt the sincerity of the person offering the compliment and are attempting to protect themselves from a zinger. The reasons for rejecting compliments are either the unintentional result of the recipient's lack of control over his or her social behavior or are voluntary attempts at self-protection.

When the rejection is voluntary, the person is attempting to cover himself or herself regardless of the intentions of the complimenter. If the comment was sincere, a denial is supposed to appear modest and intensify its impact. If someone comments that you have done a great job of lining up new customers and you respond, "Oh, it was nothing," it would seem to indicate that you had not yet begun to demonstrate your skills. Perhaps your response is supposed to show that you are only a humble worker and that no one could accuse you of breaking your arm while trying to pat yourself on the back. Of course that comment might also be interpreted in two less favorable ways. It might indicate that you are embarrassed and unable to handle this basic human interaction effectively. Second, it could be interpreted as an insult directed at the person who complimented you. If this person was impressed and you are not impressed, it must mean that you have higher standards. It's either that or you are accusing that person of insincerity.

If the complimenter might be insincere, a nonaccepting response is supposed to protect you. Suppose that you had just given a practice sales presentation in a sales training session and another trainee has complimented you on your performance. You could respond, "Thank you, I worked very hard on it." But then this person might catch you off guard with, "I suppose a woman would have to work harder." You let down your guard and got zapped. If you had responded, "Oh, I guess it was okay; I just threw it together last night," you would have been protected. Unfortunately, to reject compliments is not only nonassertive, but it is damaging to both parties.

If you reject compliments, people will stop offering them to you. An absence of compliments may eliminate your temporary embarrassment, but it certainly isn't going to help you maintain your self-esteem. To reject a sincerely extended compliment is to insult the person who offered it. You have clearly indicated that that person either has no taste, has made a misjudgment, or was out of line to speak to you.

Compliments offer you an opportunity to practice one small but positive assertive behavior. You know that you can train yourself to increase or decrease your use of four letter words. You can, with care, strike offensive phrases from your speech. With a little concentration, you can also begin to respond assertively to compliments. Should you give up the protection which was offered by rejecting compliments? Should you leave yourself vulnerable to zingers? You can be even more protected through acceptance. If a compliment was offered sincerely and you accept it graciously, the person who offered it will feel good inside. You will have completed a positive human interaction. You may be on your way to a positive relationship. If the compliment was offered in jest or as the prelude to a put-down, and you accept it graciously, you will have left your would-be opponent off guard. You will have hit the ball back into the other person's court. If you back away from a compliment or answer hesitantly, the stage is set for the pseudocomplimenter to drive in for the kill. If you respond in a firm and positive manner, the put-down will sound ungracious or stupid. You will have left the practical joker speechless.

Most people offer compliments sincerely, even if they are phrased awkwardly. Most compliments meet with less than comfortable acceptance due to the insecurity of the person complimented. If you accept compliments in a friendly and positive manner, you will usually be rewarded. You will also probably receive more compliments. The simplest way to accept a compliment is to say, "Thank you." A thank you and a smile are adequate in most cases:

You certainly did a fine job in wrapping up
that deal at the XYZ Company .... Thank you

We're really pleased with the progress you seem
to be making here .... Thank you

I like that suit a lot better than the one you
wore last Friday .... Thank you

If you look directly at the complimenter and say in a firm but pleasant voice, "Thank you," you can hardly go wrong. It's simple and it's appropriate. The complimenter will probably smile back and feel rewarded for having taken the time and effort to compliment you. You have respected that person's right to express an opinion and acknowledged your position of having some positive qualities.

After some success with thank you, you should be prepared to move up to a more assertive response pattern. "Thank you. I'm glad you noticed." "Thank you. Your opinion means a lot to me." You have reached the epitome of assertive compliment acceptance when you can graciously offer additional information. "Thank you. I worked awfully hard on that order. I'd be glad to tell you the whole story someday." "Thank you. I'm working on a similar project now. Would you like to hear about it?" These comments evidence confidence that the complimenter is sincere and that you are worthy.

Offering compliments is another form of easily developed assertive behavior. If you develop your skills in offering compliments, you will no doubt be able to help other people feel comfortable accepting your compliments. Remember, if two out of three people feel awkward when complimented, when you offer a compliment you have a two-to-one chance of offering it to someone who will need some encouragement to accept it.

There are some important differences between accepting and offering compliments. Accepting compliments is an other-initiated behavior. It is something which you do in response to an action by someone else. The other person has taken the initial responsibility. While you may have practiced saying thank you in front of the mirror ten times each morning, you still have to wait for someone else to give you a compliment in order to try out your new technique. Offering compliments is a self-initiated behavior. You can either decide to make an effort to compliment the next person who is worth complimenting, or you can identify something to compliment in a special person and seek out an opportune moment.

A compliment is an approaching behavior. It moves you closer to another person. An assertive woman can move closer to another person without fear because the assertive woman has defined her own personal space. A woman who is not assertive cannot compliment another person comfortably because this behavior increases her vulnerability. Since she is not really sure of her ability to occupy or protect her space, she is less able to open up to others.

In *Success with People*, Willard Zangwill offers several practical tips for offering compliments which can be more easily accepted by others.[3] First, you should direct your compliment at the action rather than the person. Second, you should be specific. Instead of saying, "You're a terrific person!" you might say, "That was terrific the way you spoke up in that meeting!" Third, you should be honest and sincere. While that might seem obvious, it is often violated. Finally, a compliment is a personal opinion and is easier to accept if you express it as one. You aren't speaking for the world, only for yourself. "I think you did a great job in landing the XYZ order." Even a person who is not particularly impressed by that feat cannot deny that you are pleased.

STATEMENT QUALIFICATION

In expressing a compliment you are expressing a personal opinion and might help another person to accept that compliment by qualifying it as such. But, in general, statement qualification is a nonassertive behavior. Statement qualification can be a very effective technique for people who are so overwhelmingly assertive that other people may be frightened by them. If the president of the firm makes an absolute statement, people who are lower on the organizational structure may be afraid to challenge that statement or to offer their opinions. If the president qualifies the statement with an introduction such as, "This is only my opinion," the way is left open for other opinions.

---

[3] Willard I. Zangwill, *Success with People: The Theory Z Approach to Mutual Achievement* (Homewood, Ill.: Dow-Jones Irwin, 1976), p. 39.

If your position is such that there is little danger that others will mistake your statements for law, statement qualification may detract from your image of assertiveness. You have heard people start a statement with a qualification such as, "This is only my opinion," or "You may not agree with me," or "You'll probably think this is crazy," or "I don't really know anything about this, but . . . ." Qualifying your statements is very much like rejecting compliments. People who do this do so to protect themselves. If after they have completed their statement the listeners do agree, value the opinion, accept the statement as sensible instead of crazy, or affirm the speaker's knowledge of the subject, the speaker has supposedly won or succeeded. If, on the other hand, having heard the rest of the statement the listeners agree that the speaker is crazy or ignorant, the speaker can take comfort in having been smart enough to have correctly predicted their reactions. "I can't really be so dumb after all."

While statement qualification may be comforting in some psychological way, it is damaging to your image of assertiveness. Assertive people say what they have to say without apology. If you are speaking and expressing an opinion which you have not attributed to anyone else, it is logical to assume that others would believe that to be your opinion. Even if you are only parroting the words of someone else without identifying that person, it is still your opinion. You have agreed with the person who expressed it originally. If people are going to think you are crazy, they are going to think you are crazy. You don't really have to give them a head start. If you don't know anything about the subject, one of two things will happen. Either the other people will know something about the subject and will recognize your ignorance, or since they don't know anything anyway, they will never know the difference.

How do you overcome statement qualification? You bite your tongue. Every time you begin to speak, you mumble, slur, or eat the first few words. Try not to be understood until you reach the meat of your statement. After having bitten your tongue enough times, you will find that you can start right off with your statement or opinion. In group situations, start to watch and listen to other people qualify their statements. Pay attention to the reactions of other listeners to the statements of the qualifying speaker. You will probably find that the opinions of statement-qualifiers generally carry less weight.

Some people qualify their statements in an effort to put the other person at ease. This is a matter of judgment. It might be useful, but only when it was a deliberate activity. Usually, statement qualification is simply a nervous habit or reaction. The use of unqualified statements signals other people that you believe that the things you have to contribute to the conversation are worth their attention. You have the right to occupy a particular space in the conversation. Of course, to practice making unqualified statements, you must be a part of the conversation.

INITIATING INTERPERSONAL CONTACTS

One way to exude confidence is to approach people. Remember, most people are not really sure about your proper space. If you assume that you have the right to approach them, they will tend to follow your lead. Observe the behavior of people at a social function. Most people wait for someone else to initiate a conversation. Most people do not choose who they will converse with but wait to be chosen. In his "Million Dollar Personal Success Plan," Paul Meyer of Success Motivation Institute asserts, "Opportunities never come to those who wait,... They are captured by those who dare to attack."

You can't afford to wait but must dare to attack. In selling it is critical to approach. You will not have the luxury of waiting for customers to come to you. There are only two types of sales positions in which the customers approach the saleswoman. In the first type, inside order-taking, the customer comes to the store or office to place an order. We call people who take these orders "clerks" and pay them in accordance with the title. In the second case, the saleswoman has control over the only source of supply or has built up a base of satisfied customers. Few people find themselves in these enviable positions. Almost all sales positions which are worth having require that you go out and find prospects. ·

Amazingly, if you step up to someone and greet that person as if you are an old friend, as if you have important business to conduct, or as if that person should be happy that the two of you will have this opportunity to talk, the other person will often take your cue and respond according to your plan. If you approach with the humble and grateful servant posture, you might be invited out the door.

A simple mechanism can help you to develop an approach pattern.

The simple mechanism is to remember and, when appropriate, repeat the phrase, "What's the worst thing that can happen?" Every time you start to falter when you should pick up the phone to follow up on a sales lead repeat, "What's the worst thing that can happen?" The answer could be that the person may be out, may not accept your call, may politely answer no, or may even be rude. If that is the worst thing that ever happens to you, you're in good shape. If the person is rude or unpleasant, it is a reflection on the person, not you. Hang up and tell your telephone what you think.

When you face a cold call, the procedure is the same, "What is the worst thing that can happen?" Again, the worst thing that can happen is probably well within your tolerance levels. It will probably be an indication of someone else's inadequacies, not yours. What if you really are worried that you will forget what you meant to say or will be embarrassed because you won't be able to answer some question? If that is the case, the worst thing that can happen is within your control. You can make sure that you are prepared.

SPEAKING OUT IN GROUP SITUATIONS

One important assertive behavior is speaking up in meetings or group situations within your office. There are two philosophies on speaking up. Abraham Lincoln was in favor of keeping your mouth shut although his words are well-remembered. He suggested that it is better to keep your mouth shut and be thought a fool than to open your mouth and prove it. That makes a lot of sense although in our business environment it makes a lot more sense for men than women. If a man is dressed appropriately for the situation, he can sit and say nothing and will probably not be thought of as a fool. He is given the benefit of the doubt. He may be reserving his judgment. Perhaps he is thinking great thoughts. He is assumed to be competent unless he proves otherwise. Remaining silent may be a clever tactic.

Women are seldom given this edge. They usually have to prove themselves. One woman recalls an uncomfortable moment at a dinner meeting of a professional organization. She had arrived a bit late with a totally platonic colleague who just happened to be a man. At first the late arrival appeared fortuitous since the only two seats left were at the table with the president of the organization. She was pleased because she felt that meeting him might be good for her professionally. Neither she nor her companion might have had the courage to select those seats if others were available. Obviously most of the others present had chosen the less courageous course. After they sat down there was some of the normal introducing of people around the table. The president, who had a nodding acquaintance with her friend, commented, "How lucky you are that your lovely wife will accompany you to these meetings." Embarrassed, her friend muttered, "She is not my wife." Of course, the president went on to offer one of those pseudocompliments of the form, "Well how did you persuade this beautiful young thing to have dinner with you?" The woman then spoke up, "You might remember my name in that it appeared in the last newsletter as a new member of this organization. I'm a sales representative for the ABC Company." She was afraid that the president would go on guessing all night and never get to the truth. It was clear that she was not able to start at the starting line but entered the race with a handicap. Without this otherwise embarrassing episode, she might have sat there through the entire meeting unrecognized. The president would have left the meeting thinking he had been sitting next to the wife of a member. She gained by speaking up.

There are probably two kinds of people—those who can't bring themselves to speak up and those who can't manage to keep quiet. If you are in the second group, you could probably skip the next few paragraphs. Learning to speak up is similar to learning to ride a bicycle. It seems awkward at first, but once you get going, you begin to wonder why you waited so long. The secret to getting started is preparation and commitment.

First, select a topic or event for which your participation would be appropriate. It might be that you could plan to make some comment at the next sales meeting. No one progresses to the top in business without the skills to speak before a group. Practice making statements as a part of a group or as a part of the audience. This activity is the first step to developing these skills. While most salespeople are obviously able to handle a one-to-one interaction, a group is a different story.

Think about a topic which is likely to come up and prepare a statement. Think it through carefully. Think about the possible responses to your statement. Then think about your responses to those responses. Practice your statement. Say it to yourself in front of the mirror a few times. When you have it organized, present it to your husband, your mother, your friend, or someone else who is both important to you and able to understand the situation. Describe the situation so that your listener may be able to make helpful comments. If there is a problem, revise your comment and try it again. Then commit yourself to your listener. "I'm really going to speak up and I hope you will remember to ask me how it turns out."

In the meeting, you may be tempted to talk yourself out of it. Try to remember your commitment. When you go home you will be asked, "How did it go?" How are you going to feel if you have to admit that you didn't follow through? The idea is to set it up so that the cost of failing to speak up exceeds the perceived cost of speaking up. Since the chances are very good that your comments will be received at least politely, the cost of speaking up will decrease each time you try it.

Why are the chances of a polite reception so good? Most people live in the proverbial glass house. They are either in the group who doesn't speak up and are therefore harmless, or they do speak up and are probably not willing to risk the chance that you will return the criticism.

HANDLING REJECTION

Assertiveness is assertiveness. It is the same for men and women, and it is the same for women in sales as it is for women in other fields. There is, however, one area in which women and men in sales are more likely to have an opportunity to demonstrate assertiveness. This is the area of rejection. For the saleswoman, or for the salesman, rejection is a fact of life. The old saying "You win some and you lose some" is nowhere more true than in sales. In most sales positions you lose a lot more than you win. You may call on accounts all day and not make a single sale. Just ask yourself when your success ratio is likely to be the highest. Do you really think that it will be in the beginning of your career? When you are getting started you will probably meet with more than your share of rejections. As you become more able to handle rejections, the number you have to handle may not decrease, but the number of successes should increase.

You can't avoid rejection and be successful in selling. The only way to avoid rejection is to call only on those accounts where you have a sure sale. This type of cautious conservative approach will lead to failure. Nothing ventured, nothing gained. You can't avoid rejection; you can only learn to deal with it constructively.

There are probably a lot of ways you can learn to live with the rejection inherent in selling. One woman in life insurance sales was really discouraged when she first started. After a particularly difficult day she dragged into the office and must have looked as unhappy as she felt. One of the more experienced agents took her aside and gave her some advice which she claims changed her entire outlook on her job. He suggested that instead of trying to minimize the rejections and only looking forward to sales, she should begin to count the refusals she got. After all, statistics in the insurance industry indicate that she would get about 25 refusals for every acceptance. She should go out each morning anxious to rack up her 25 refusals. Then she would know that she was getting somewhere.

One way to deal with rejection is to redefine the game. People who never fail haven't tried very hard. If you consider rejections to be moves forward on some imaginary gameboard, something like Monopoly, each rejection moves you closer to GO, where you'll collect $200.

You might even be able to make the rejections pay off for you along the way. There are a lot of different ways to react to a refusal. You can take it at face value. NO. This is the deadend track. A refusal could be an opportunity in disguise. To take the opportunity track, you have to read the road signs. Why did the prospect refuse? Did you interfere at an inconvenient time? Is the buyer satisfied with the current supplier? Is your product inappropriate to meet the buyer's needs? There are any number of reasons. All is not lost just because you have been refused. Some sales managers contend that the buyer really doesn't really mean NO unless you hear it at least five times.

Converting a rejection into an opportunity is a truly assertive act. One approach is to ask a question—a positive question. "When would it be more convenient for us to talk?" To ask, "Would it be more convenient to get together another time?" invites the second refusal. Imagine what you would invite with, "It probably wouldn't do me any good to try to see you at a later date, would it?" All three questions are directed at the same objective, that is, keeping the door open, but only one is assertive. An aggressive approach might sound something like "Well, I'm going to be back and I'm going to show you that you're making a mistake by passing up this offer." Aggression imposes on the rights of the other person. That person has the right to reject your offer.

Another approach is to scale down your request. If your prospect has just rejected the idea of ordering a year's supply, you could suggest, "A six-month supply would give you a good chance to test our product. Let's put that down, and we can talk about the rest later." If an order is out of the question, you could always ask, "Would you be willing to try a sample?" If a sample is unacceptable, maybe the brochure would be worthwhile reading. This is the wedge approach. You have to get started some place. If you can open the door a crack, you may be on your way to converting that rejection into an opportunity.

Not all rejections afford opportunities. Some are just plain rejections. Some rejections occur very early. You call to ask if you could set up an appointment and you are told, "Not now, not ever, never!" That's pretty clear. Other rejections occur after a great deal of time and energy have been invested in a project. You might have been working on a proposal for a year and have survived five screenings before your competitor was awarded the contract. It is not too easy to pat yourself on the back and say, "I'm glad I made it as far as I did." It is small consolation to score one for experience. It is nothing but a big disappointment, and you have a right to be depressed. You can't avoid disappointment. The question is whether or not you can bounce back from it.

You should remember that it is usually your product or your firm or your offer which is being rejected, not you. Sometimes, however, you are rejected. There is probably some solace in knowing that you are not the first or the last person who has been rejected. You may be rejected because of being a woman. No one really knows how often that happens. Saleswomen can't report that with any accuracy. They have no way of knowing how the situation would have turned out if they were men because they are not men. Each of us comes in a particular package to which others react, and we have little opportunity to judge how others would react to a different package. You can note the reaction to some changes in appearance such as hair style and color of clothing. No one has yet studied the possible differences in reactions to saleswomen and salesmen in a scientific manner.

It is very likely that any difference has been grossly overestimated. The potential reaction of buyers to women in sales strikes at the heart of management's concerns—the bottom line. While the courts have ruled that employers may not discriminate on the basis of potential reaction of customers, rumors of customer reaction have great scare value. It is comparable to the overemphasized concerns over common lavatory facilities that surround and confuse the real issues involved in the Equal Rights Amendment. If there is any substantive problem in customer reactions, it will diminish rapidly as more women enter the sales field.

Assertiveness is responsible behavior. It involves attitudes and actions which alert other people that you are willing and able to take responsibility for yourself. The mechanisms which have been suggested here are only a start. They are suggested because, while they may be a bit uncomfortable at first, if you practice them it will feel good. You will be able to demonstrate to yourself that the world is willing to allow you to claim your space assertively. The world will react negatively to aggression but will respond to assertiveness. These mechanisms are only a start. There is a great deal more to be learned. Attitude and behavior change interact and feed on each other. You just have to get started somewhere.

5 Whoever said the world is fair?

The world has approximately an equal number of men and women. In no way is there equal opportunity for women to succeed in business. There is a great deal of discussion over quotas, reverse discrimination, rights, backlash, and other emotion-charged topics. All this talk has not changed the fact that this inequality and prejudice still exists. The purpose of this chapter is not to fix the blame for the inequalities or even deal with equalities beyond those which affect the opportunities for women in the business environment. The purpose here is to answer a simple question: "How can you operate most advantageously within the existing situation?"

There are three options. The first is to ignore the realities. You could either by choice or by default remain in an unaware state. The second option is to strike back at reality. You could adopt the attitude that things should change now and become a crusader fighting back in every situation which is unfair. The third option is pragmatic positivism. This is a philosophy which combines the practical and the positive. It involves recognition of reality and careful planning to overcome barriers on a priority basis. Let's look more closely at each of these options.

TO IGNORE REALITY

Ignorance is only bliss if there is nothing which can be done to improve the situation. If you can't do anything about it, you might as well ignore it. A low level of awareness can work in two ways. On the plus side, by being unaware you may stumble into some advantageous situations which you might have otherwise avoided. If you didn't know that the men in the office *never* ate lunch with the women in the office, you might innocently invite yourself to join them. You might even get away with it simply because they wouldn't know how to refuse. They would never have expected you to ask. In some ways the increased awareness which has come about since the mid-60s has actually discouraged women from pursuing careers. The barriers which had been covert suddenly became very overt.

Being unaware of the realities of discrimination can also be very damaging. Obviously, you are less able to protect yourself and your rights. You may not be fairly rewarded or progress at the rate warranted by your performance. These are obvious dangers. The greatest danger is less obvious: you may blame yourself. If you are not promoted, you may believe that you actually are incapable of assuming the additional responsibilities. If you are paid less, you may believe that you are worth less. If you have a lesser title, you may believe that you are less important. If you are not aware of the nature of discrimination, you may believe that you are the source of your problems on the job.

TO FIGHT BACK

Being too aware of discrimination can make you the source of your own problems on the job. It all depends on how you handle it. In most business situations you will be perceived to be the intruder. Everybody got along just fine until you showed up. Even if someone else started it or you are absolutely justified in your position, you will be considered to be the cause of any disruption which results.

Not only will you be blamed if any unpleasantness occurs, but there will be a certain group of people who are ready to be an audience. Some people will be anxious to witness your difficulties. They were the ones who warned management that women on the sales force could only cause trouble. Others are just curious. You can be confident that stories about your reactions to sexually biased situations will circulate rapidly. You can allow these incidents to make you miserable, but if you handle these incidents skillfully, people will soon forget that you are "different." If you are supersensitive, hostile, or overreact, you will be plagued.

PRAGMATIC POSITIVISM

The trick is to combine the advantages of both approaches. You must try to be aware enough to protect your rights and your ego but not to let your awareness interfere with your performance. You must try to react when reaction is required but not overreact and damage your professional image. In short, you have to make an effort to carefully consider the possible outcomes beforehand and decide what you are going to do in each case. Pragmatic positivism is a possible answer. Surely you have heard the line about winning the battle but losing the war. While it may be nice to win battles, it is even nicer to win wars. Of course, you cannot expect to win any wars unless you win at least some battles. The trick is to decide who, when, and how to fight. You need a system to classify situations and people.

Classifying really accomplishes two objectives. First, it allows you to prepare standard responses to sexually biased incidents. You reduce discrimination to an *if—then* level. It isn't nearly as frightening when you are prepared for it. Second, it allows you to abstract yourself from the situation. People normally react to other people. If you view the person who is speaking to you as an individual, you will deliver a personalized response. You put a little of yourself into that response. But a person who makes a sexually biased comment is not dealing with you as an individual. You are being treated as a type of person—a woman. To deliver a personalized response leaves you with an imbalance. By classifying the situation and the person you are introducing a protective layer. You can respond with an appropriately impersonal response. You have stepped back mentally. You have removed your "self" from the situation. You are not reacting within a situation, but you are deciding how a person faced with that situation should react. You are protecting yourself psychologically. It is as though you are an observer rather than a participant. You are insulated.

It is difficult to develop a workable classification system. We all know that the same words spoken by two different people can carry two different meanings. Human interaction involves two elements, people and some object or idea for them to exchange.

PEOPLE

There are lots of ways to classify people, but for the purpose of coping in an unfair business world, the classification system should be based on the person's attitude toward equal opportunity. Be sure to notice that we're not just classifying men, we're classifying people. Women discriminate against other women.

To be usable, the system has to be fairly simple. Consider this two-dimensional system. The first consideration is degree of discrimination. Some people are equal-minded and treat people as people. Other people are prejudiced and treat one kind of people one way while reserving a different type of treatment for those they perceive to be different. The degree of disclosure is the second dimension in the system. It would be very simple if each person wore a tag indicating a preferred position of this scale (see Exhibit 5-1). Unfortunately, some people hide their orientation. Some people are even successful in hiding their true feelings from themselves.

Another quality of a usable classification system is that you can

EXHIBIT 5-1

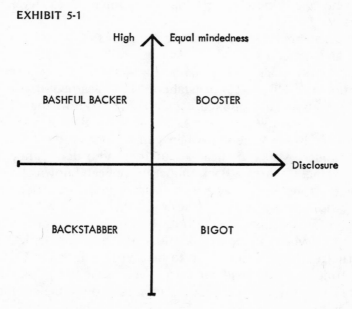

mentally carry it around with you. For that purpose, people in each of the corners have been named. As usual, the extremes are easy to understand. Bigots are people who are committed to the position that men are more capable or deserving than women and don't mind telling you about it. They know they are right despite any evidence to the contrary. While they will sometimes "humor you," they seldom miss the opportunity to evangelize. If any female who engages in traditionally male activities should meet with disappointment or failure, they are quick to call the incident to your attention. One woman in commercial insurance sales recalled the morning her resident Bigot almost gleefully presented her with a claim which had resulted from the crash of a cropduster plane piloted by a woman.

Someday there will be more Boosters—people who realize that the basic difference between boys and girls is that boys can grow up to be daddys and girls can grow up to be mommies. Boosters are committed to equality on both a philosophical and a practical level.

Between Bigots and Boosters are two other types. The Bashful Backers are philosophically in agreement with the ideas of equal opportunities but have difficulties putting that philosophy to work. If you get them alone, they are all right. Unfortunately, they can't stand up to group pressure. You can't count on a Bashful Backer to rescue you from a Bigot, but there is hope for the Bashful Backers. Given time and support, they have the potential to develop into Boosters.

The Backstabber can be the most dangerous of all unless you can identify and thereby neutralize this person. A Backstabber professes to support you. Backstabbers come in two versions, deliberate and unintentional. Deliberate Backstabbers have learned that obvious bigotry is unpopular in mixed company. They know that there are advantages to a show of fairness. They simply do not support you or may actually sabotage you when you are not around. If they are blatant enough, you may hear about it. If you don't, they can be very damaging. Deliberate Backstabbers have been known to set traps for unwitting victims. They can encourage you to confide in them and then use those confidences against you.

Unintentional Backstabbers think they are helping you but actually undermine your efforts and confidence. An example might be the sales manager who comes along to help you with the difficult calls while letting salesmen fend for themselves. While this person may be well-intentioned, the effect may be to cause you to believe that you are not as capable as the men of doing the job by yourself.

Having set up a classification system, the next step is to place people within it. Since human interaction is dynamic, that is no easy task. It requires observation over time. You may find that people don't stay in the places you place them. They may change their attitudes and behaviors over time or even from day to day. You may find that you have misjudged some people. The point is that you will begin to evaluate the actions or comments of others not on a personal basis but on the basis of the character participating in the interaction. The characters are only a part of the situations in which you may find yourself. You may also have to consider the content or the focus of the interaction.

THE FOCUS

Just as there are two dimensions along which to classify people, there are two dimensions which can be useful in classifying those topics or actions involved in your interactions with these people. It helps to consider both the frequency and the consequences of the action (see Exhibit 5-2).

A classification system is meaningful if it separates whatever is being classified into groups which deserve different treatment. Let's look at the four groups which result from this system. If a type of

EXHIBIT 5-2

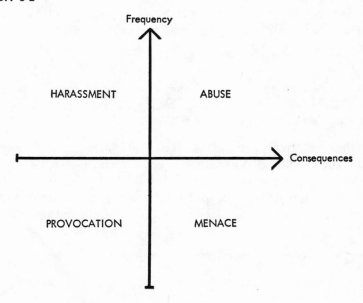

behavior is both frequent and damaging, it could be called an Abuse. An Abuse infringes on your rights and, if allowed to continue, could seriously damage your opportunities in the future. To allow yourself to be abused is to invite further difficulties of a more widespread nature. Abuse is easy to recognize, both for the victim and for the observer. A Menace differs from an Abuse in that it occurs on a less frequent basis. The consequences can be just as damaging. Instead of keeping at you or after you and wearing you down over time, a Menace is the type of episode which strikes quickly and leaves you devastated. It is the denied promotion or the unwarranted public reprimand. If you have no warning and have not prepared emergency behaviors, you can be left defenseless.

A Provocation is also an isolated event but with much less important consequences. It might take you by surprise and embarrass you, but you will no doubt recover. Harassment, on the other hand, is continuing in nature, although each incident may be minor. The effects of Harassment are cumulative. Eventually you reach the breaking point.

Let's put it all together and examine some situations which might arise.

A PROVOCATION

A simple sexually biased statement which might be considered a Provocation is "It's no wonder you get in to see the buyers. After all, you're a woman." Most saleswomen seem to run into this rationalization sooner or later. As Michael Korda points out in *Male Chauvinism*,

> The reason men behave the way they do toward women who work with them lies not in their claim to possess special qualities of strength and cunning, but in their weaknesses and fears. . . .[1]

In defining strategies to deal with discrimination, there are several points to keep in mind. First, the object is to provide for your long-run well-being. Your long-run well-being is not served by devastating those around you. If you keep Korda's thought in mind, that discrimination arises out of weaknesses and fear, you can look upon the

---

[1] Michael Korda, *Male Chauvinism: How It Works* (New York: Random House, 1973), p. 5.

person who makes these kinds of remarks with pity. It is obvious that this person is uncomfortable and is unable to deal with his or her feelings in a mature and rational manner. Your task is not to squelch this person and thereby solidify the fears and feelings of inadequacy which led to the incident but to help this person to cope within the situation. The entire world changes when you envision yourself in the superior and helping role. Your task is to determine the basis of the remark and to guide this person to more appropriate behavior. How will you respond?

To make the appropriate response, you have to uncover the reason for the Provocation. There are a lot of possibilities. If it was made by a Booster, and Boosters have been known to make such remarks, there are several possibilities. It could be that this person has had a hard day, just lost a big order, or has an upset stomach. Even Boosters have days when they slip into previous behavior patterns. The diagnosis may be that it was a lapse. Another possibility is that the remark was intended to be humorous. It could even be that the Booster intended to provide you with an opportunity to discount this rumor. The appropriate response is linked to the intention. If it was a lapse, the best move may be to ignore it. Every woman who intends to maintain her sanity in the business world should practice selective thickskinnery. There are situations in which the right action is no action. If you criticize the Booster for an ill-timed remark, you may be converting a Booster into a Bashful Backer. Perhaps you don't think the remark was very funny. Ask yourself what you have to gain for rising up in righteous indignation over an isolated incident. You may not ignore it, but you can maintain the Booster's support by bringing the point up in a supportive and private way at a later date. Of course, even if the Booster hadn't intended to provide an opportunity, you could turn the situation into one. How about responding with, "Well, I hadn't thought of that, but I bet they would throw me out a lot faster if I didn't know my stuff." You haven't insulted the person, you have made a point, and you have maintained your professional dignity.

The same approach could work on the Bashful Backer, even if the intentions were different in making the remark. Some Bashful Backers are just testing. They may be testing you or they may be testing themselves. Remember, a Bashful Backer could become an ally. Why not provide positive test results? You need to convey the message that you will offer support, that you will be comfortable to work with, and that you have confidence in your professional performance. Either an attack or a defensive response would be inappropriate. Of course, the remark could have been made out of ignorance. Maybe this person doesn't even realize that you could be offended. Maybe this was simply an unevaluative observation. Perhaps a little private consciousness-raising is in order.

While the Bashful Backer may be testing you, the Backstabbers and Bigots are probably baiting you. They would really like to see you make a fool out of yourself and are willing to provide the opportunity. Few people would recall who set the trap, but they would probably remember if you let yourself get caught in it. Provocations simply aren't worth the risk. The true Bigot won't even realize that provocative behavior is inappropriate. A Bigot believes that these are simply observations of reality. You wouldn't make much progress by arguing the point so why waste your energy? Backstabbers can't afford to persist. They would be recognized. The difference between Provocations and Harassment is frequency. When the Provocation is continued, the stakes change. You can ignore it only so long.

HARASSMENT

While you might ignore an isolated Provocation, Harassment is another matter. Harassment is deliberate. Anyone who would treat you in this way automatically qualifies as a Bigot. One of the most common forms of Harassment is sexual harassment. This is by no means limited to women in sales. It is hardly a new phenomenon. Much like rape, sexual harassment has been excused on the basis that women ask for it, encourage it, or even like it. It varies in intensity. At the low end it involves jesting behavior. "When are we going to travel together?" "At the next sales meeting we could save the company money by sharing a room." At the opposite extreme it looks more like extortion. "If you spend the night with me, I'll give you the order."

Before considering your alternatives, take a look at the evidence. If passing out sexual favors was a route to the top, why is it that so few women have made it? Ask yourself who is likely to get the axe if a relationship is discovered or turns sour? You might be the victim even if the relationship was one-sided. A sales representative for a major pharmaceutical firm was perhaps a bit too naive. She thought that her sales manager was just being nice. Slowly the conversations over lunch migrated from business to more personal issues. He volunteered to deliver some samples to her home on his way home from the office. By the time she admitted to herself that the attention she was receiving was greater than normal, he had interpreted her nonrejection as acceptance. When his wife accused him of infidelity, he accused the saleswoman of chasing him. While she had letters and cards which he had sent to her during this time, she could hardly produce the evidence. She probably would have lost her job. He undoubtedly would have damaged her further to protect himself. The world is not particularly fair. She kept her job long enough to find a new position, but it wasn't easy. He wouldn't give her a fair recommendation.

How does the saleswoman effectively deal with sexual harassment? The answers are as individual as the situations. Clearly, it is better to avoid getting into the situation in the first place. Perhaps some clarification is in order. It is not the purpose here to dictate or discuss morality. These are individual decisions. Sexual harassment is another question. People who have studied this problem carefully have concluded that most harassment is not undertaken to achieve sexual gratification. Sexual harassment is a weapon used against women in the pervasive power game. The intention, whether the harasser recognizes it or not, is to put you in your place. An individual who cannot readily accept you as a professional can put his world in order by reducing you to a sexual object or target. Even if you resist or reject his advances, in his mind you have been placed in the proper perspective. Harassment is not flattering; it is an insult. There may not be any universal solutions at this time. Let's investigate some of the possibilities.

Remember the riddle, if a tree falls in the forest and there is no creature to hear it, does it make a sound? If you refuse to perceive harassment, is it harassment? Perhaps this would be effective on Harassers. What would happen if the buyer asked you to spend the weekend and instead of being offended or accepting, or rejecting or reacting in any way, you responded with a totally unrelated question? "Would you prefer rail or truck on that shipment?" If you haven't perceived the harassment, has it occurred?

Reports from women who have experienced these difficulties clearly indicate ineffective strategies. Insults, indignation, blackmail, or other attacks not only will cause you to lose the order, but will occasionally generate retaliatory action. In order to get even, the offended Harasser may report that you are not performing adequately on the job. You can be fairly certain that if called upon to justify his decision not to give you the order, he will make no mention of your reaction to his invitation. If the Harasser happens to be a part of your organization, the problem may be even more severe.

Objections and excuses are seldom effective. Most of the people with whom you might be associated in a sales career have learned to view objections as challenges. Unfortunately, the socialization process to which most men have been subjected teaches them that women really don't mean it when they resist. They are just "playing hard to get." To postpone is to create real problems for yourself.

How can you keep people from harassing or embarrassing you? One answer is to keep yourself out of encouraging environments. Once a person has demonstrated Harassment, you should take care to avoid one-on-one encounters. It can be very frustrating to find yourself in a position of having to adjust your behaviors in order to compensate for someone else's inadequacies, but that's reality. While you should not have to take the responsibility for structuring the situation, you do. If you don't, no one will. You will be back at square one.

Several women have reported that other men in their offices have approached them to offer assistance or at least understanding in situations of public sexual harassment. While it seems that the Harasser perceives himself either to be impressing these other men with his virility or nerve or perhaps envisions himself as a crusader for the masculine cause, he is often an embarrassment to other men. Depending on the interpersonal skills and relative power positions of these concerned observers, they may be able to guide the culprit into more acceptable patterns of behavior. You may not be able to ask for this kind of help but may choose to accept it if it is offered. Obviously, the mailclerk can't be expected to make much headway with the vice president. There are some who would view this kind of help as an admission that you can't handle yourself. It may just be a practical approach. It is not your fault that this Harasser is unable to perceive you as a credible professional. Should you really expect yourself to be able to undo 30 or 40 years of conditioning? Relying on others is damaging only if it causes you to lose confidence in yourself. Think of it as using an interpreter.

The most effective technique of all is alert avoidance, that is, staying out of this person's way. Unfortunately, this is not always possible. There are three types of people. One type is insignificant to your career progress. These are the people you *can* avoid. They can be persistent but don't deserve your attention. They can be using you to draw attention to themselves. Pretend they don't exist. A second group holds absolutely no promise of helping you to advance but is capable of damaging you. They could drop a few unkind comments about you in a few important places and retard your progress. These are the people you *should* avoid. You may extend superficial courtesy such as a comment on the weather but should always hasten on your way. Finally, there are the truly significant people—the people who can either help you or hurt you. These are the people you *can't* avoid.

If you feel that you are the object of sexual harassment, one of the most important things to do is to maintain a careful record of comments, incidents, witnesses, and any supportive materials such as notes. Whether you like it or not, you may end up in court. You may want to put these materials in an envelope at particular intervals and mail them to yourself via registered mail. When the envelope arrives, do not open it but save it as officially dated material. Then if your troublemaker starts to complain about you or your performance at a later date, you can establish a history of the problem.

Harassment builds over time. If you are alert, you can see it coming. You may decide to stay and fight it, or you may just decide to seek a more supportive environment. Sexual harassment is no more common in selling than it is in any other type of job. There are reported incidents involving classroom teachers and principals. There are almost as many stories about secretaries and bosses as there are traveling salesman stories. You have surely heard about pilots and flight attendants, doctors and nurses, and on and on. While there is yet no evidence to support it, we may find that sexual harassment is less of a problem with women in sales than it is for women in these other areas. There is no way for a secretary, nurse, or flight attendant to clearly establish her level of productivity. She could be coerced or punished through denied promotions or wage increases and would have no evidence to counteract that action. As a saleswoman, you will at least be compensated on the basis of your actual performance and have some ongoing record of your productivity. If one buyer is absolutely intolerable, you could undertake some conscientious efforts to approach alternative customers. You have some control over your efforts.

96

MENACE

What do you do when someone suddenly unleashes a direct and unexpected attack? "You are the reason we lost the regional sales contest. Because of you, none of us will get that extra bonus. I knew we couldn't expect a decent performance from a woman." None of us like to be subjected to this type of treatment whether we deserve it or not. That's the first question. Did you deserve it? Of course, you didn't deserve it simply because you are a woman. While it would be nice to assume that you could muster the composure to respond, "Yes, my performance was substandard but that should not reflect on women as a group," that would be a bit unrealistic. If your performance was substandard, your only options are the same options available to any other person who has fallen short of the mark. The best course is usually to admit your shortcoming in the way which avoids long public discussion, argument, or negativism. "I understand, I'm sorry, and I hope we can get together privately and review my performance so that I may improve." If you are at fault, you should have expected that you were going to hear about it, although you might have expected more tact. You would have had enough warning to prepare your statement.

If you are a scapegoat, it can be very frustrating. If you speak up to defend yourself, you may irreparably damage yourself. If you don't speak up, you will be assumed guilty. When you are publicly accused of anything, one of the better options is the Leave-some-room-for-doubt approach. There are some stock phrases which can be plugged into any situation. "There may be some information we're overlooking here." "It could appear that way, but the picture may be more complex." "Perhaps there's another way to look at this matter." Your task is threefold. The first step is to extinguish the fire. You need to calm the person down so that the scene will be minimized. This is usually accomplished by a nonevaluative acknowledgment of the statement: "I understand what you are saying."

Second, you need to inject that element of doubt without refiring the situation. "Are you sure you have all the facts?" Third, you should suggest the next appropriate action. "Can we get together privately and discuss this?" If the other person refuses this seemingly innocent and well-meaning request, your public position is improved. You have acted in good faith and met with no success. If the attacker accepts your offer to confer, other people will believe that there is something to be discussed; you are not automatically guilty. Above all, you must appear to be in control of yourself.

You may never get together to discuss the matter. If you do, both of you will have had time to think about it. The Menace is usually an unthinking act. The Menacer has reacted in haste to some situation. There may have been some pent-up resentment toward you or you might just have been handy. Unfortunately, if you are just handy to be run over by a truck, you are just as dead as if you deserved it.

ABUSE

If someone runs over you and then backs up to run over you again, it is Abuse. Your goal is to survive. You can either survive within the situation or you can survive outside of the situation. You can seek to change the situation, or you can change jobs. There are a lot of factors to be considered. The first is the cost of changing jobs. Your Abuser may actually be doing you a favor. You may be stimulated to consider other jobs and find that there are a lot of opportunities you would have missed. Another factor is your position versus the position of the Abuser. If your performance is well above average and you have heard rumors that the Abuser is in some difficulty with other people, you may wish to hold out. A third question is whether or not your experience is unique. Perhaps you are just one of many people who are experiencing this same difficulty with this same person. If you are alone, you may just be experiencing an honest personality conflict. This may be no reflection on you or the other person. Some people are not meant to work together.

You can work your way through a series of possible solutions. Abuse is beyond the basic thickskin ignoring stage. The next step is negative kidding. It is not rare to find that an older woman in the office who, although capable, was denied opportunities in the past and is now taking out her resentment on the new saleswoman. Negative kidding might take the form, "Gosh, you sound like my mother." If the situation persists you move up to pleasant discussion. In privacy you point out to her, "I appreciate that I have a lot to learn and I'm trying, but I feel I would develop much more rapidly with praise than with criticism. Everyone deserves some constructive criticism, but I find it easier to take in private." Maybe your problem has been that you feel you have been shortchanged in terms of territories, referrals, training opportunities, or other meaningful resources. Your pleasant discussion could take the form, "I'm assuming that there is some legitimate reason for this treatment. I would like to know what it is so that I can improve."

If none of the nice approaches has worked, you have reached the crossroads. It's time to fight or switch. If you choose to fight, adherence to protocol will keep you in a more defensible position. This calls for giving the offender an opportunity to solve the problem before going beyond to the management or outside forces. Your objective is not to cause further problems but to solve the problems you already have. This step is not a formality but a potential solution. You should carefully prepare your presentation. State the matters which are bothering you as unevaluatively and unaccusingly as possible. Indicate the ways that the problem could be overcome. Leave some room for choices. State the benefits and assure the Abuser that you will be cooperative.

Imagine that you had put in a request for a change in territory. Your sales manager had said that nothing was available but you would be considered first if something came up. Then you learn that a high potential territory has just been offered to a salesman whose sales record is not as good as yours. You're really upset because this isn't the first time it has happened. What do you do? At first you should do nothing. If you march into the manager's office and make a scene, you'll really damage yourself. You shouldn't do anything until you calm down. After you've checked to make sure your information is correct, you might say, "I understand that the XYZ territory is to be assigned to a new person. I wanted to be sure that you recall that I've asked for a reassignment. If this territory is still open, I would like a chance at it. But perhaps you have some other opportunity in mind for me. I hope you know that I'd do my best."

Once you have taken this step, you certainly have committed yourself. You must now follow through. You have brought the matter to a head. If you back away without a solution, you have put yourself into the position desired by the Abuser. Because of this, it is necessary to impose some time constraints on the situation. While you certainly do not want to threaten, you should suggest some checkpoints. "Do you think we could reach some agreement by next month's general sales meeting?" Points in time seem less arbitrary if they are related to some scheduled event. You have to set up some time frame so that you will know if and when to move to the next level of the solution system.

If your previous efforts have not brought about a change in the situation, you may have to bring out your weapons. While there are isolated exceptions, most firms of any consequence have adopted official stances of equal employment opportunity and have attempted to adjust their policies to reflect that position. Unfortunately, policies are more easily adjusted than attitudes and behaviors. It is time to help the Abuser to understand that you understand the mechanism available to you. Some of those mechanisms are within the firm. It may be an affirmative action officer or committee. You may have some formal way to register your complaint with management. Some of the mechanisms are outside the company. Your state Fair Employment Practices Commission or the Federal Equal Employment Opportunities Commission are examples. Investigate the avenues and help the Abuser visualize the potential consequences.

When it comes to taking action, there are two sides to the argument. One group believes that you can hurt yourself, damage your reputation, get yourself on the list of troublemakers so that no other firm would want to risk hiring you, and that there is no guarantee that you will get anywhere. One woman who filed a complaint against a relatively small firm in Chicago in 1968 heard nothing about it until 1970. She had since moved to a different state. The EEOC called to ask if she would drop the charges so that they could clear out the case. They assured her that the firm had been made aware of the nature of her complaint and had promised that they would try to be more careful.

The other group would insist that you should take action either within or beyond the firm if you believe that you have something to gain. You may be preserving your job. You may be improving your position or circumstances within the firm. You may be satisfying your sense of fairness. Only you can judge if it is worth it. In making your decision, however, consider the idea that there is no proof that you will not win the war just because you won that battle. You could take action in a responsible manner and actually gain a reputation for determination.

There is a chance that future research will reveal that saleswomen are subject to less discrimination than women in other fields. One of the most prevalent forms of discrimination, economic discrimination, has already been demonstrated to be less important in industrial selling than in almost all other fields. As early as 1970 women sales engineers (women with technical backgrounds dealing with high technology products) had achieved income parity with men.[2] Not only were they earning the same amount of money as male sales engineers, but on the average, they were the highest paid female workers in the country. When economic discrimination is eliminated, many of the other problems can be overcome. While some forms of discrimination may persist, you can minimize the effects if you are confident in yourself and prepared to take appropriate action.

[2] Bureau of Labor Statistics, *Monthly Labor Review.*

6 The first step to successful selling: Preparation

People are not born salespeople or made into salespeople. *They make themselves into salespeople.* While many people who are not officially called salespeople engage in selling activities, selling is generally considered to be the activity of encouraging someone to exchange money for something else, but selling is a bit more complex than simply encouraging another person to part with money. Salespeople engage in a great deal of activity both before and after that exchange takes place. Actually, most people in sales spend most of their time on the job doing things other than selling. In a play or other theatrical production, the cast practices, the stage hands prepare props, the wardrobe crew develops costumes, and the musicians rehearse for hours and hours before the curtain goes up on opening night. The more preparation there has been, the more likely it is that opening night will be a success. Is the time invested in these activities worth it? Perhaps the group could have squeezed by with a little less? Of course, bad reviews could spell disaster.

No amount of preparation can fully compensate for a lack of ability. Some people just aren't cut out to be musicians or salespeople. A person contemplating a career on the stage should stop to think about all of the types of activities that are required. As you consider a career in sales you should ask the same question: What is selling all about?

The personal selling task is basically the same regardless of industry. Some products are more complex than others, some buyers are more sophisticated and some saleswomen thrive on repeat business while others must continually seek out new customers. Nevertheless, the sales task still involves three stages: the preparation before the sales call, the actual face-to-face contact with the potential customer, and the followup and followthrough after the sales call. The precall preparation and the postcall followup are sometimes referred to as the nonselling responsibility. That term is somewhat misleading. It implies that these are the duties which are taking your time away from selling. While preparation and followup do take time, they contribute to the effectiveness of the sales call. Indeed, neglect of these duties may well be the cause of nonselling. Precall preparation is likely to save more time than it consumes.

Precall preparation might be summed up as making sure that you call on the right people with the right message. As a saleswoman, you are essentially a problem solver. It is your job to seek out those who have unfulfilled needs or wants and solve their problems by fitting your product or service to those needs. Finding the right people is called prospecting. Planning the sales presentation so that you deliver the right message requires extensive knowledge of the customer, the competition, your products, and your firm. In selling and almost all other human endeavors, preparation pays off.

PROSPECTING: IS IT A GAME OF HIDE-AND-SEEK?

Remember when you played hide-and-go-seek as a child? One child was "it" and all the other children had a limited time to find a hiding place while "it's" eyes were covered. Then "it" tried to find them before they made it back to the goal. The child who didn't make it back to the goal got stuck being the next "it." The difference between prospecting and hide-and-go-seek is that you are always "it"; you are always the seeker. In the game, being "it" was something you tried to avoid. Some saleswomen view prospecting in the same way. Not only are you always the seeker, but you sometimes don't even know for whom you are looking. In the game you at least knew the other children. There are some bright spots however. The brightest one is that the prospects aren't really hiding. Indeed, they are waiting to be found.

Prospecting is one of the differences between successful saleswomen and unsuccessful saleswomen. Some saleswomen believe the old proverb "A bird in the hand is worth two in the bush." They devote most of their efforts to maintaining their old accounts and spend little time searching for new prospects. Most successful saleswomen devote at least some time to prospecting on a continuous basis. Of course, this varies with the type of product being sold. Some products, such as manufacturing materials or boxes of detergent on the retailer's shelf, are continually being used up, and you can go back to the same account on a regular basis. Other products, such as a small corporate jet or computer system, last for quite a while. If you waited to make replacement sales only, you might have some lean years.

As a successful saleswoman you must realize that there will always be some leakage from your list of customers. Some customers will retire, some will switch to another supplier, and some will find that they no longer need the product. One of the purposes of prospecting is to maintain a sufficient number of customers. Some prospecting is necessary simply for replacement purposes. A good prospect list offers insurance.

Prospecting also uncovers opportunities. If you have more customers, it is probable that you will make more sales. If you make more sales, your rewards will be greater. New customers offer opportunities. Most people could handle more customers, but even if you have all the customers you can possibly call on, there may be a benefit in prospecting. Every saleswoman has some great customers, some good customers, and some not-so-good customers. Prospecting may uncover some potentially great customers to replace some of your not-so-good customers.

Prospecting is one of those potential pitfalls. It is a potential pitfall because it is postponable. You can put it off. You can put it off until it is too late. A little bit of prospecting on a continuing basis is both more effective and more enjoyable than "crash" prospecting. Prospecting by itself is hard to swallow, but it makes a fine side dish. It is even a break from the more pressured sales call responsibilities.

Think about any kind of product, one that you are selling, one that you would like to sell, or one that you buy. People fall into three groups with regard to that product. There are people who currently need and buy that product—actual customers. There are people who could use that product but do not currently buy it. Perhaps they buy some other product, or they have not recognized that they could use a product of this type. Finally there are people who do not and will not use a product of this type. One of the cigar commercials a few years back used the tag line "Sooner or later, we're going to get ya!" While it was a great commercial, it was also wishful thinking. It is obvious that there are people who will never smoke cigars. Exhibit 6-1 divides the market into actual customers, potential customers, and noncustomers. The purpose of prospecting is to move line A to the right. Any effort devoted to people within the noncustomer area is wasted. There is nothing to be done about line B. The closer people are to line A, the more likely they are to become customers.

EXHIBIT 6-1

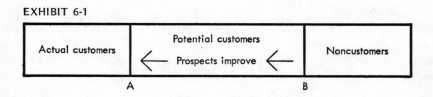

Prospecting involves three questions. First, what sources will point to people within the middle segment? Second, how can these people be contacted efficiently and effectively? Third, how much time should be devoted to prospecting? The general answers to these questions can be adapted to fit your individual situation.

There are three principal sources of new sales. First, there are current customers. It's unlikely that you will sell a single product. Most saleswomen sell some group of products. They sell one product to one customer and another product to another customer. One of the first places to look for new customers is among your current good customers. Perhaps those people or someone else within their firms would have a need for some of the other products you offer. This new business would be easy to handle. Both you and the customer would be gaining efficiency. A second source of customers is the previous customer. At one point these customers found your product and services to be acceptable but have since drifted away.

They may be ready to drift back. Maybe they just need a little nudge. Dormant accounts should be easily contacted since you have records on them. In most cases there is little doubt that a need exists. You might ask your sales manager for the names, addresses, and telephone numbers of inactive accounts. Other people within the office might be less willing to recontact these people.

The third source of new customers is that huge group of people who have never purchased anything from your firm. For most companies this would represent the largest group of prospects. It is also the most difficult to contact. Anybody could be a new customer, but the trick is to find people who are closer to the A line. Unfortunately, while they are not hiding, they do not stand up and identify themselves voluntarily. You must seek them out.

There are lots of ways to seek out new customers, but it makes sense to try the easiest ways first. One of the easiest ways is to ask old customers. A customer who is satisfied with your product and your service may be willing to direct you to other people with similar needs. Some of your customers may belong to trade organizations or other groups composed of people in similar positions. On some occasions, satisfied customers will direct other potential customers your way even if you don't ask. This gravity approach— waiting to see what falls in your lap—can be very undependable.

Satisfied customers can give you leads, and they can also provide referrals. A lead is simply the name of someone who might be interested. A referral is a letter or a phone call to a potentially interested party on your behalf. Obviously, asking a customer for this is asking a lot.

Prospects represent a source of further prospects. If you call upon someone and make a good impression, even if that person is unable or unwilling to place an order you might still obtain the name of some other prospect. It also pays to recontact previously identified prospects at regular intervals. Their situations or needs may have changed in the interim, and they may now be in a better position to buy.

Sometimes other salespeople can be a source of prospects. A salesperson within your organization may run across the name of a prospect in your territory or with needs in your specialty area. It could be that this other person does not have the time to contact this hot prospect. Senior salespeople in your office may not be willing to gamble on a long shot, but as a beginner, you may be more willing to do so. It may pay to express a controlled eagerness to others in your office. Salespeople outside of your organization can also be useful. Someone from a different firm might have a customer who has a need for which his or her firm has no suitable answer. If you have maintained a cordial relationship, that person might pass that tip on to you.

Sometimes sellers of compatible items cooperate. At the retail level, a jeweler might pass the names of a young couple who purchased an engagement ring on to a photographer or florist. This activity is sometimes called birddogging. Someone is, in effect, serving as your pointer. These relationships are often reciprocal. Although the engagement ring usually precedes arrangements with the florist, the florist and the caterer are going after the same market at the same time. Cooperation gives each one twice as many chances.

Any public information source specializing in areas related to your market represents a source of prospects. Reading trade journals may provide some clues. Every new parent knows that life insurance salespeople, photographers, and bronze baby-shoe sellers read the vital statistics in the newspaper. Equivalent sources of published information are available for every industry. Successful saleswomen see these as potential goldmines of prospects. Unsuccessful saleswomen view them as required reading or junk mail. These publications may be newspapers or bulletins, directories, application lists, or even classified ads. The trick is to figure out where names of people or firms which represent good prospects appear and then to regularly follow these publications. Published information is often the cheapest and most convenient source of prospects.

Another important source of prospects is trade fairs. These are held on a regular basis in many industries either on a national or a regional basis. You get out of them what you put into them. One vice president of marketing registered his disappointment with a new salesman over that person's behavior at a trade show. The company had sponsored a cocktail party for people attending the show. While the vice president was mixing drinks, greeting guests, and even washing glasses, this new salesperson was attending a party sponsored by another, noncompetitive organization. When the vice president indicated his dissatisfaction, the new employee countered that he had visited with several possible customers at the other party. The vice president took the position that people who were at the party sponsored by his firm were more likely to be prospects for his products. It was no surprise that this particular salesman failed to survive his first year. If he didn't even take advantage of opportunities offered at some expense by his company, it is doubtful that he really devoted himself to generating prospects on his own.

It is one thing to generate a list of prospects. There is another important step before any effort can be made to convert those prospects into customers. The prospects must be qualified or screened. Not all names hold promise. There are four characteristics which are necessary for any prospect to be considered as a potential customer. First, that prospect must have decision-making authority. Many times a tremendous sales presentation is made to someone who responds, "Wow, that's terrific! I wish I could order one but that is not my job." A second characteristic is some need or want. Does the prospect have a use for the product? Products are purchased because they fulfill some need. A want is simply a noncritical need. Haven't you appreciated the qualities and value represented by some products yet not purchased them? You can't get too far trying to sell things to people who don't need them despite all of the jokes about refrigerators at the North Pole. The potential customer, however, may not recognize the need. You can make great progress by helping buyers to understand their needs. If you can show the buyer a better way, you may indeed generate a need.

The third characteristic is purchasing power. The prospect must have something of value to exchange for your products. That something of value may be money, other products of value in a trade or barter, or a promise to pay which is normally called credit. A sale is an exchange of values. Each party must have something of value to offer the other party.

The fourth characteristic is a willingness to purchase. Some needs go unfulfilled because the prospect is unwilling to make a purchase at that particular time. Government agencies are notorious for this behavior. Because of the idiosyncracies of government budgeting, government agencies tend to spend in spurts. If you make a splendid proposal at a lean time, your proposal is wasted. All organizations have priorities. If your product is not high on the list and the budget is tight, you may be wasting your time. While you may be able to improve the position of your product on the priority list, for the prospect to represent a potential customer, there must be some hope.

In qualifying a prospect, you are really asking four questions:

1. Is this person authorized to make a purchase decision?
2. Is there a want or need which might be satisfied by purchasing one of my products?
3. Can this person pay for my products?
4. Is this prospect willing to buy my product at this time?

If the answers to all of these questions are positive, this person would be a hot prospect. If the answer to the first question is no, this prospect may still lead to someone else who is authorized. If the answers to either the third or fourth questions are unfavorable, but all of the other answers are positive, this prospect may be pigeonholed just in case conditions change. If the answer to the second question is negative, there isn't much hope.

Even if the answers to all four questions are positive and the buyer is qualified, there is an additional question to be asked: "Can I effectively approach this buyer?" In asking this question it is important to think of yourself first. The question is not "Could someone else make this sale?" Any sale you could make, someone else could probably make. Your objective is to make the best use of your selling time and efforts. The prospect doesn't have to be perfect but should be a good use of your time. If you come across a good prospect in someone else's territory, it may make a lot of sense to pass that prospect on to the appropriate sales representative.

Prospecting is a kind of revolving door process. Prospects enter from a variety of sources, but they all come in on one side. If they survive the screening process, they enter the space reserved for qualified prospects. Some are invited to sit on the hot prospect side, and some are in the standby area. Some prospects who fail the qualifying test simply continue around and are dumped back on the street. While it sounds harsh, they really don't know the difference. Other prospects keep going round and round in the revolving door. In terms of being qualified prospects, they are marginal, but there is hope (see Exhibit 6-2).

The question now is what to do with the prospects. You may wish to treat your hot prospects in one way and your standby prospects in a different way. You may not trust your ability to make the distinction and treat all of the qualified prospects the same. How do you approach prospects? Sometimes the approach is affected by the source of the prospect. You may choose to give a more personal

EXHIBIT 6-2

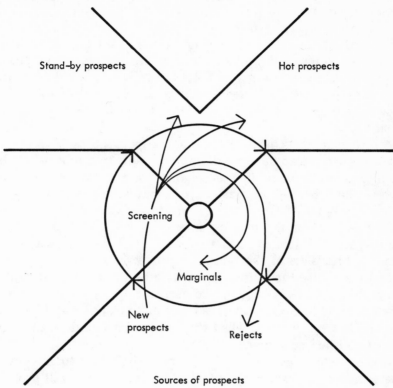

Stand–by prospects

Hot prospects

Screening

Marginals

New
prospects

Rejects

Sources of prospects

treatment to prospects which result from contacts with established customers or other more personal sources. You may use a less personal approach to contact prospects noted in publications. The type of contact you make depends on your time, your interest in the prospect, and the relationship the prospect has to any established customers.

Contacting prospects by mail requires the least time and effort but also produces the least results. You can send a standard letter to a prospect with almost no effort and follow up with a more personal approach if the prospect responds to the letter. You might combine a letter with another form of approach. While the letter may not generate a response, it may make the prospect more receptive to your phone call or visit.

Phone calls take less time than personal visits and may encourage the prospect to make an appointment. Phone calls can be an effective screening device. While direct questions from an unknown saleswoman may be rebuffed, you can determine if the prospect is qualified. While you would probably not wish to ask, "Do you have enough authority to buy my product?" you might ask the prospect a few questions about related products to determine if this person has been involved in purchase decisions at that level or for products of that type.

An unscheduled "cold call" at the prospect's office can be very effective but can also be a big disappointment. It may not be a bad idea if you are already in the neighborhood and have some time which would otherwise be wasted. You may stumble upon a person who is terribly frustrated with a current supplier and have the chance to play the role of the princess in shining armor. As you look at history you will realize that there are people who would have succeeded regardless of the times, but there are a lot of people who succeeded because they just happened to be the right person at the right place at the right time. Of course, since most of us have yet to figure out how to be in more than one place at one time, you may be on a fruitless cold call when the right place would be the office of an established customer.

Salespeople are just like other people. They tend to gravitate to those situations in which they feel comfortable. You will probably feel more comfortable in the office of an established satisfied customer than in the office of a total stranger. Prospecting is one of those activities which is easily put off until another day that never comes. If you recognize prospecting to be one of the potential pitfalls, you can establish a protective routine. The first step is to decide what proportion of your time should be devoted to prospecting. That decision is based on the nature of your industry, your product, and your customer base. The next step is to translate that time into a very concrete goal. "I will make four cold calls each week" or "I will make two telephone contacts with prospects each day." Get into the habit of measuring your performance against those goals. "Have I made my two phone calls today?" Some firms attempt to impose these types of goals upon you. You may be required to fill out prospect reports on some regular basis. If you have only contacted five people during the month and the standard is ten people, your sales manager may inquire about your prospecting activities. Unfortunately, these systems often backfire. Instead of being viewed as a system to contribute to the success of the individual salespeople, they become a sort of contest between the salespeople and the management. It is like eating spinach. Generations of children might have enjoyed it if they hadn't been forced to eat it.

PLANNING THE SALES PRESENTATION

Getting to see the right people is only half the battle. You need something to share with these people to encourage them to buy. That something is your sales presentation. The best presentation is the one that most effectively meets the objectives of you and your firm. The degree of standardization is related to the variation among buyers in terms of their needs and attitudes toward buying and the complexity of the product.

Standardized (canned) presentations are sometimes criticized for placing you in the position of a puppet "whose every word and gesture have been masterminded by a slick armchair marketer in [a] Madison Avenue ivory tower."[1] Actually, if there is great similarity among buying situations, a structured company-prepared and company-planned presentation may be appropriate. Once you have learned the presentation, there is little preparation required for each individual call. The beginning saleswoman using a well-prepared standardized presentation is assured of including important selling points and selling techniques which have been found to be successful with the "average" customer.

As the degree of difference among buyers and buying situations increases, the canned approach is less effective. There may still be some benefits of standardization. A structured approach attempts to combine the flexibility of an individualized presentation with the consistency of a standardized presentation. With this approach the basic points to be covered are preplanned, but the wording and emphasis may vary from one sales presentation to the next. You actually proceed through a memorized outline, but you attempt to adjust the presentation to the reactions of the potential buyer. The

---

[1] Marvin A. Jolson, "Should the Sales Presentation Be Fresh or Canned?" *Business Horizons*, 16 (October 1973), pp. 81-88.

importance of this adjustment increases when you are likely to meet many different types of buyers. The approach which works for one may not be successful with another.

The individualized approach requires the highest level of creativity and flexibility. In effect, you are viewing each presentation as a new experience. While you are working with the same information and selling skills, you are adapting that background to meet the needs of the buyer. Since this generally requires greater preparation for each call, it is usually used when each order is substantial.

Whether the sales presentation is preplanned by the company or developed to meet the requirements of individual customers, keep the following objectives in mind. An effective sales presentation should:

1. Conserve the prospect's time.
2. Tell the complete story.
3. Deliver an accurate, authoritative, and ethical message.
4. Persuade the prospect.
5. Anticipate objections before they occur.
6. Increase your self-confidence.[2]

Meeting these objectives will increase the likelihood of success. In order to develop a presentation which accomplishes this, you must understand your product, your company, your competition, and your buyer.

Many years ago, Charles Revson of Revlon, Inc. is supposed to have wisely observed, "In the factory we make cosmetics, in the drugstore we sell hope." There are many variations on that idea. "You are selling the sizzle, not the steak." "You're not selling drill bits, you're selling holes." Buyers are not buying physical products but the benefits to be derived from those purchases. Ford doesn't want to buy steel to have steel but to make automobiles. A small business doesn't really want a computer, it wants increased efficiency in billing, inventory control, or other routine business functions. The first step to developing a persuasive sales message is to look at the benefits which might be derived from the product. Knowing your product involves more than memorizing the specifications, options, and functions. It means all that plus an understanding of the range of benefits to be offered to customers.

---

[2] Ibid., p. 85.

When you step into a prospect's office, you are selling more than a product. You are also selling the company behind that product. Buyers may well be interested in the history of the company, the organization of the company, and the future plans of the company. All of these factors may play an important part in the sale if they help to persuade the buyer that the company is dependable, produces a quality product, deals fairly with customers, is respected in the industry, and is well-managed and can be expected to be in business in the future. It is important to know the positive points about the company, and it is also important to be aware of any unpleasant facts or rumors about your company. If you have completed your carefully prepared presentation only to find that the buyer rejects your proposal because of a rumor of a strike which might affect your promised delivery, you may have failed to anticipate objections before they occur. If you had been aware of the strike rumors you might have checked them out beforehand. Even if they turned out to be true, you might have been able to assure the buyer that the company had sufficient stock on hand to assure delivery and saved the sale.

If you don't make the sale, one of your competitors probably will. When you make your presentation, you are not making it on a clean slate. Your competitors have made some impression on that customer. The impression may be positive or negative. That customer wants to know why your product is more appropriate than the product presented by a competitor. You must not only persuade your customer that buying your product is better than doing without, you must also be prepared to show that it is better than buying any other product. Your competitors include not only sellers of products designed to provide the same benefits but also sellers of any product which is going to use up the buyer's resources. If the money is spent on new office furniture, it is not available for new office machines. Every firm has a limited budget. To answer the buyer's question "Why should I buy your product?" you must usually present some differential advantage. You must help the buyer to understand that buying your product is a better idea. You can only do this if you fully understand what the competitors are offering. You may or may not choose to make direct comparisons in your presentation, but you should be prepared to answer the customer's questions relative to the competition. Among the important points to know are the competitors' distinctive strengths and weaknesses; their histories of dependability in quality, delivery, and service; the variety of products offered; their normal prices and terms; and any plans or future developments. These factors will be measured by the buyer in arriving at a buying decision.

The buying decision is the focus of the personal selling effort, but it is perhaps the most difficult part to understand. Buyers are human. As such, their behaviors are not totally predictable. There are some factors about buyer behavior which, while general in nature, can be of some help in understanding specific situations. Most buyers are subject to multiple influences. There are other people who will be affected by and concerned with the decision made by the buyer. Buyers usually pass through a number of steps in reaching a decision. If they are familiar with the type of product being purchased, they may skip some of the steps.

In most businesses someone is assigned the responsibility of buying products and services for others within the firm. This purchasing agent is expected to become an expert at buying. People who have specific needs notify the purchasing agent of the nature and quantity of the product needed. The purchasing agent deals with potential suppliers. The purchasing agent is supposed to find a product which satisfies the need of the person who requested it while meeting the objectives of the firm (economy and dependability). Purchasing agents also have personal objectives. Most would like to maintain pleasant relations with suppliers; complete their assignments within a reasonable time; avoid complaints, delays, and aggravation; and advance within their organizations.

The organizational goals and the personal goals overlap. When the purchasing agent makes a decision which works out well, the likelihood of personal advancement is increased along with the satisfaction of the person who ordered the product. Sometimes there are goal conflicts. For example, bribes and other special favors are usually against company policies but are within the goal structure of some individual purchasing agents. Presentations which include some attention to goals in the shaded area in Exhibit 6-3, the overlap between individual and organizational goals, are usually more effective. Usually that overlap is wide. If it isn't, the person seldom lasts in the job. Appealing to goals in the individual-only area can be a very dangerous and short-run approach. Strict attention to the organizational-only area may not gain favorable attention from the purchasing agent.

EXHIBIT 6-3. GOALS OVERLAP

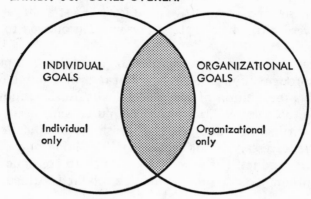

When someone within the organization sends a request to the purchasing agent, one of three situations prevails. It may be a routine request: Replenish the supply of letterhead stationery. These types of requests are usually satisfied with a straight rebuy, an automatic purchase order to the normal supplier. Some requests are for a product which is normally purchased but for some reason a new supplier may be considered. The last order from the previous supplier may have been unsatisfactory, the need may have changed slightly, or the person making the request may have heard of some interesting development in the product. The purchasing agent might treat this request as a modified-rebuy situation; while the firm has some understanding of the product, it is willing to consider new suppliers. Finally, some requests are unique. The purchasing agent is called upon to purchase some product which is not normally purchased. Then it is necessary to learn about the product and potential suppliers, that is, to treat it as a new purchase.

What difference does it make to you whether a purchase is a straight-rebuy, a modified-rebuy, or a new-purchase situation? The difference lies in whether the purchaser is already your customer or not. The best situation is to have all of your current customers view requests for your product as straight-rebuy situations and automatically reorder from you without considering alternative suppliers. Of course, it would be nice if buyers who were currently buying your competitor's product would make modified-rebuy decisions and reconsider your product each time they ordered. All new-purchase situations represent opportunities to become the preferred supplier. If the purchaser of a competitive product is in a straight-rebuy situation, it is very difficult to make a presentation or even to make an appointment.

In general a new-purchase situation requires that the purchasing agent go through buying steps. As indicated in Exhibit 6-4, it all begins with a recognition of the need. This is usually followed by a clarification of the requirements. The purchasing agent and the person submitting the request must establish the specifications of the product, the necessary quantity, and the likelihood of a continuing need for this product. If the need is expected to continue for some time, a continuing-order process may be required. Armed with this

EXHIBIT 6-4. BUYING STEPS IN THE NEW-PURCHASE SITUATION

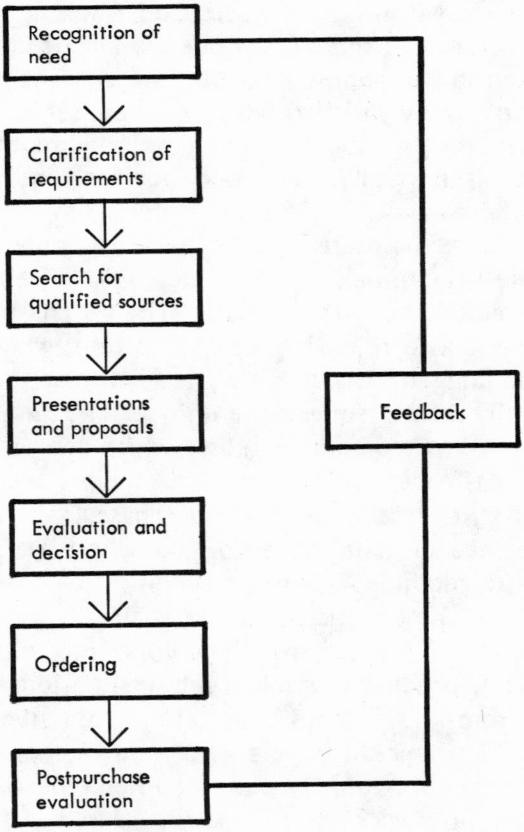

information, the purchasing agent undertakes a search for qualified sources. This step is especially important because you want to be considered as a potential source. Potential suppliers are invited to make proposals or presentations. The alternative sources are then evaluated. Once a decision is made, the order is placed. Then the postpurchase evaluation is conducted. If the product works out as planned and the users are satisfied, the product may be reordered when the need arises again. If the product or some other factor is unsatisfactory, other suppliers will be considered the next time.

There are several points in this process at which a new supplier may gain entry. You might be the one who helped the user to recognize the need in the first place. If you can show a prospect that the way a particular task is being handled is less efficient than it would be if your product was used, you may actually uncover a need. You haven't created a need; it was there but the prospect was not aware of it. One of the tasks of salespeople in the drug industry is to keep doctors current on pharmaceutical developments so that they will be able to prescribe the best drugs for their patients. The need to be cured would have been there anyway, but it might not have been filled as well.

A modified-rebuy situation follows the same pattern but involves fewer steps. Perhaps the requirements are quite clear or a list of qualified sources has been developed. The buyer would skip from recognizing the need to inviting presentations from qualified suppliers. One of the sales tasks is to maintain your position on the list of potential suppliers so that you are available for a modified-rebuy purchase. In a straight-rebuy instance the purchasing agent skips from need recognition to ordering. The opportunities for you as a new supplier may be limited.

In prospecting you are trying to locate qualified buyers. In planning your sales presentation you are trying to learn enough about those buyers so that you can interpret the benefits you have to offer in terms of the buyers' needs. All of this presale preparation pays off when you find yourself actually helping your customers to buy.

7 Help your customer buy

Preparation pays off only when you take action. Preparation without action is no better than no preparation at all. It is easy to fall into the "I'm not quite ready yet" trap. As long as you are preparing, you may feel as if you are making progress, but overpreparation can be an excuse to avoid risk. Actually putting your plans into action can be very risky. If you go out and call on the prospects you have identified and make the presentation you have carefully developed, you might meet with rejection. You might find out that your plans didn't work out as you had anticipated. You might fail. If you never try, you can't fail; of course, you can't succeed either.

All of your activities as a saleswoman are focused on successfully completing that sale. All of the steps in the process build toward the goal. Making a sales call is putting your plan into action. All of your preparation pays off if your sales call is a success. Achieving success depends on several factors in addition to adequate preparation. One is how you have defined success. Not all calls can be expected to result in orders. Some calls have less ambitious, yet important, objectives. You might be attempting to develop goodwill, to relay information, or to better understand the buying patterns and structure within the organization. Every call should have an objective. Ask yourself, "Why am I making this call?" After the call you must ask yourself, "Did I accomplish what I had intended?" At least a part of the time that objective must be to make the sale. You can only get so much mileage out of goodwill.

To a great extent the success of the sales call hinges on the way you conduct yourself as you move through your plan. When you actually go into action, there are always ways in which the situation may vary from the expected. If you can adjust to these variations you may be able to capitalize on opportunities or avoid being damaged when things go in the wrong direction. The ability to adjust differs from person to person, but it can usually be improved by first giving some thought to the possible range of situations which you might encounter. You can then develop some contingency plans, some answers to the question "What will I do if?" Having taken the time to consider "What will I do if?" can make it easier to come up with the best answer when you are asking yourself, "What am I going to do now?"

Going into a sales call is something like going into a ball game. No coach goes into a ball game without a game plan. No saleswoman should go out on a sales call without a sales plan. Coaches have some ideas about how they would like the game to go, how they think the game will go, and what might go wrong. The game plan includes some alternative formations, plays, substitute players, or other possible moves. While the objective throughout the game is to win, the strategies and tactics may vary as the game progresses. The team's performance defines the task it faces to achieve that objective.

Every sales call has three basic segments: the approach, the presentation, and the close. Each segment has a purpose and sets the stage for the part that follows. The purpose of the approach is to establish contact and set a favorable tone for the presentation. The presentation involves two-way user-oriented communication. In effect, it is an interview with the buyer. First, you must discover as much as you can about the buyer's needs and then establish that the product you are selling will satisfy those needs. The close is the real test. It is during the close that you ask the prospect to take the action you're after. You may be asking the prospect to sign an order, to set up a meeting with someone who can sign the order, or to make some other commitment in the direction of a sale. If you have done well in the approach and presentation, your chances of a successful close are substantially improved. While sales calls vary widely, what are some of the more normal situations which you might encounter during each of the three segments?

THE APPROACH

The approach segment sets the tone for the call if indeed the call is to be completed. The approach is the segment during which you attempt to make contact with the person with buying authority. Normally there are obstacles. During this segment you aren't yet selling your product; you are selling your call. The person you are approaching doesn't buy your sales call with dollars. Prospective buyers buy your sales call with time and effort. If a buyer stops to listen to your presentation, it is at the expense of some other activity. Therefore, it is common to experience some resistance, if not outright rejection. Many buyers train their secretaries or assistants to screen approaching salespeople in order to protect them from these intruders.

You can make some logical assumptions as you approach potential buyers. First of all, that buyer is probably in a somewhat satisfied state. If the buyer has needs, those needs are either being satisfied or have not yet been recognized. Few buyers will be sitting there waiting to be rescued by you. Second, the buyer attaches some value to time. Anybody in an organization who is sitting around with nothing to do probably isn't worth approaching. People who value time generally have some use for it. The buyer will probably have to interrupt some activity to see you. You will have to appear to represent a better use of that time than whatever else the buyer was doing. If that task was unpleasant, you may be a welcome relief. If the task was necessary and worthwhile from the buyer's viewpoint, you might be better off to set up another appointment. It might be impossible to set up a favorable atmosphere for your presentation if the buyer is deeply involved in some important project. Given your understanding of buyer motives, it is also logical to assume that the buyer has multiple motives. The buyer represents the company and will succeed by satisfying the needs of the users within the company in the most efficient and economical manner. The buyer also has personal motives. All other things being equal, most people would prefer to interact with people they like. Beyond that, buyers, like everybody else, like to feel good about themselves.

If you could write the script for the approach segment, it might go something like this. You called the prospect and suggested a time which was agreeable to both of you. You mailed the prospect some literature on your product. You have arrived at the prospect's office ten minutes early. The secretary informs you that the prospect is expecting you and is anxious to see you since the material you sent on the product was so interesting. Some calls do follow the script, but there are a lot of calls that don't. The script might unfold in a way which could tax your ingenuity and patience.

One of the first requirements of a successful call is to get in to see the right person. You may find that the person you are scheduled to see is not the person with the authority to buy. Hopefully you will find that out early so that you aren't both wasting your time. Sometimes you will find that a customer has shifted you off on an assistant. While this is a detour, it might eventually lead you to your intended destination if you are patient. The assistant may have more time and show more interest in your presentation. The buyer may well act on the assistant's recommendation. To refuse to see the assistant or to treat the situation as a second-best activity may cost you not only this sale but future sales to this company. Unfortunately, in some cases you will be treading water. The buyer may have been ashamed to admit a mistake in scheduling and plugged in the assistant as a stop-gap measure. If the assistant seems interested and has some knowledge of the company's needs and buying routines, you may be paving the way for your sale even though the person to whom you are talking does not have formal authority. If there is little interest or understanding, your best bet may be a graceful exit: "I really appreciate your willingness to talk with me. Let's go over the high points, and then let me leave you some materials with the details. I suppose those could then go into the file in case they would be useful to anyone else." After a five-minute once-over-lightly, you're ready to leave.

One of the most common frustrations in the approach segment is waiting. As a guest in the customer's office, you are expected to adjust your schedule to the schedule in that office. The client would probably not wait for you if you were late for the appointment, but you are expected to wait patiently. Even if you practice good time management and do some paperwork while waiting, it can be frustrating. If you wait long enough, three things could happen. You could become aggravated and less prepared to establish the necessary cordial tone for the visit. The customer may become either embarrassed or defensive. Finally, your time with the customer could be rushed because of the tendency to want to get back on schedule. The length of time you should wait depends on many factors including your alternative uses for that time, the scheduled length of time for the call, and the importance of the call. If you haven't any other appointments and can do your paperwork in that office as well as any other place, you might wait longer. If you are scheduled to spend several hours with the customer, you might wait longer than you would to make a ten-minute presentation. Of course you would be willing to wait longer to see a very important customer.

It may be better not to see the customer than to see the customer under unfavorable conditions. If you have waited too long and believe that you would be unable to achieve your sales call objective because of the time pressure, it might be better to reschedule the meeting. If you think you will find the prospect in a nonproductive mood, you might be further ahead to return another day. "Gee, it looks like your day is pretty full. Would it help if I came back next Wednesday? How about 3 p.m.?"

Sometimes you will not even be allowed to decide not to see the customer. Sometimes that will be decided for you. If you have not made an appointment your chances of being turned away increase, but even with an appointment you may be disappointed. One way to minimize these occurrences is to call ahead to confirm appointments. It is better to find out over the phone that you have been scratched from the day's schedule than to find out in the customer's outer office. Sometimes a cancelled appointment can be turned into an opportunity. If you are dealing with a purchasing agent who relays your information to the users, this may give you a chance to get to talk with those users. "Since I'm here anyway and won't be able to get in to see your boss as scheduled, how about calling the design department to see if I could chat with one of the people over there for a few minutes?" A receptionist who is embarrassed to have to tell you that you have been cancelled might set up an alternative contact.

THE PRESENTATION

If you successfully negotiate the approach segment of the sales call and make contact with the intended person, you might wish that the script continued something like this. Having greeted each other pleasantly and exchanged brief social remarks, you indicate, "I'm pleased you could see me today because I have some information which I think will be of interest to you." The customer responds, "I'm anxious to hear your story." You make your presentation, pausing several times to listen to questions from the buyer who is nodding approvingly. You are both aware that your product meets the need and are prepared to move comfortably into the close segment of the sales call.

The presentation is your chance to learn more about the customer's needs and to interpret your product for the customer in light of those needs. This is much easier if the customer is open and aware of these needs and is interested in learning more about how you can help in satisfying those needs. The assumptions you made in the approach segment still hold true. If the customer has needs, there is a good chance that these needs are currently being satisfied with some alternative product or that the customer is not aware of the needs.

The responsibility to stimulate the customer's interest rests on you. A good presentation does several things. First it arouses and maintains the customer's interest. It provides the customer with specific solutions to needs and wants as they are perceived by that customer. A good presentation inspires the buyer's confidence because it is both believable and understandable. The objective is not to impress or confuse but to communicate benefits. By communicating benefits you are able to move the customer toward a purchase decision.

Psychologists who study learning have long understood that people are more able to maintain interest and learn from some experience if they participate actively in that experience. A good presentation is a two-way communication experience. The customer has an opportunity to ask you questions or is encouraged to respond to your questions. You must maintain the buyer's interest. You can maintain interest more effectively if you appeal to more than one of the buyer's five senses. It is much more difficult to pay attention to a tape-recorded message than to a real live person delivering that same message. If you can see, hear, feel, smell, and taste something, it makes a greater impression on you. Not all products are subject to demonstrations, but the conscientious use of selling aids to make points, demonstrate concepts, or appeal to multiple senses increases the effectiveness of your sales presentation.

While a good presentation covers the points important to the customer in an interesting, informative, and thorough manner, your objective is not to barrage the customer or to stage a dog and pony show. You need to present enough information, but you can also overkill the sales presentation. Some salespeople keep on talking until they have talked themselves out of a sale. The prospect might have been excited and ready to buy, but as the presentation went on and on, the prospect got bored or irritated and decided against the purchase.

You may have planned a good presentation and hoped that things would go according to your script, yet you encountered one of the many potential disruptions. Disruptions come in several forms. Some divert the customer's attention. Others interfere with your ability to deliver your message as planned. Most disruptions are technically outside of the control of the saleswoman although it is possible to take some actions which might minimize them. One of the more common disruptions is the interruption. Many buyers are interrupted mid-presentation by telephone calls or people stepping in to "ask a quick question" or deliver a message. While each of these interruptions takes only a few minutes, it diverts the customer's attention and breaks the train of thought. You have to reestablish the customer's interest and get back on track. If you become annoyed by the interruptions it can interfere with your ability to concentrate on the buyer.

There are at least two ways to deal with these interruptions. Your options are limited because you are usually a guest in the customer's office. You can hardly dictate what that person will or will not do. Sometimes you can attempt to minimize the interruptions by asking the buyer, "If you could ask your secretary to hold any phone calls, we can probably cover a lot of ground in a short time." This may meet with resistance unless the buyer is particularly anxious to hear what you have to say. But note that the request offered the buyer the benefit of saving time. You could minimize interruptions by taking the customer to a neutral setting where you can exercise more control: "How about going out for a cup of coffee?" While you will still experience some interruptions, they are not of a business nature.

The second approach to interruptions is to attempt to turn them into an advantage. An interruption may provide a few minutes to review your notes against points you have made or to come up with an answer to a question for which you were not prepared. You might partially prepare the order form or make some other use of the time. It is better than sitting there and listening to a conversation. In fact, if the buyer is interrupted by a phone call, the polite thing to do is to ask, "Would you like me to wait outside?" When the interruption passes, you can take the opportunity to briefly review the positive points you had made prior to the interruption. You now have an excuse to repeat your selling points for the buyer.

Disruptions can force you to make your presentation under conditions which you had not anticipated. Perhaps you had anticipated making your presentation to one person and you find that you will be presenting your message to a committee. You might have anticipated a professional atmosphere and arrived to discover that your buyer has just returned from a very long lunch, or is feeling ill, or is unduly affected by some event. While these are not directly related to your call, they are likely to affect its outcome. You must balance a lost opportunity against the danger of a lasting negative impression. While it is usually difficult to abruptly refuse to make a presentation, it may be wise to make a very short introductory presentation and seek a later appointment: "Today I'd like to give you some basic information and then leave these brochures for you to study at your convenience. You may want to discuss some of the specifications with your associates. I'll come back and we can discuss the details. How about next Wednesday? Would you be free around 10:30?"

Your presentation may be disrupted because the customer introduces unanticipated information. On a routine call you may learn that the buyer's company is making some major change which affects your sales. They may be expanding production dramatically, acquiring one of your competitors, changing their ordering procedures or their evaluation criteria, or making any of hundreds of possible changes. Perhaps your buyer is the first one who has told you about a significant change being made by your competition. You might have prepared your presentation based on one expected selling price only to learn that your competitor has drastically cut prices. Depending on the potential impact of the information, you may want to reconsider your presentation. You may be called upon to make a graceful exit. "I wish I had more time to explain that now, but let's get together next week and talk about it. How about Friday at 2?" If you should have been aware of this new information, your credibility may be damaged.

What looks like a disruption may actually be an opportunity in disguise. Professional salespeople have long recognized the value of customer objections. While objections may seem to be a problem, if properly handled, they can be important selling tools. Objections are at least evidence that the buyer is interested. A person has to pay attention to raise an objection. Objections are important clues to the buyer's real buying motives and needs. Most objections are not new and may even be predictable. One trick is to establish an objections file. You should keep track of objections you hear and prepare responses to those objections. You can easily trade responses with other people in your office. People are flattered if you ask for their advice in handling a particular type of objection. While the specific objections vary with the type of product or the type of buyer, objections generally arise in some standard areas. Price is a common objection. "I think that's a wonderful product, but it's too expensive." Buyers may object to specific features or lack of features. They may not like its color, its size, or its limitations.

In any sales situation you are not only selling the product but you are also selling your company and yourself as a representative of that company. These areas are also the focus of objections. The buyer may not be familiar with the company or may have had a bad experience with the company. The objection may be based on some third-hand report of some impropriety or misunderstanding. The buyer may have a question about the company's capacity to adequately service the product after the sale. The buyer may like the product and like the company but object to you.

Some objections have nothing to do with you or your product or your company. The buyer may simply not be in a position to buy. Perhaps the funds are not available or an order has just been placed with your competitor. Some people are just reluctant to make decisions. "Oh, I don't know if I should." These people don't last long as purchasing agents.

Converting objections into selling opportunities takes both thought and practice. While there are many recognized techniques, you must be sensitive to the buyer and be able to judge the importance of the issue to that buyer and interpret the objection accurately in terms of the buyer's needs and motives. Some objections are simply tests of you and your knowledge of the product. Some objections are formalities. The buyer-seller relationship has been characterized as an adversary situation for so long that some buyers feel a responsibility to protest. Some objections are pleas for help. The buyer is actually asking you to be more persuasive or informative. Some objections are actually legitimate first-class objections. The person understands fully, has contemplated the possible outcomes of purchasing your product, and objects to some substantive factor involved in the sale. Not all objections can be overcome. Some objections represent substantive reasons why the buyer does not choose to buy your product.

While the actual points will differ, there are several basic techniques which you can use in overcoming objections. The trick is to apply an appropriate technique. You must consider several questions. One question is how important the point is to the buyer. If it is a serious objection it may be necessary for you to deal with it immediately before it interferes with the buyer's ability to develop a positive attitude toward the purchase. But spending time dealing with a casual objection may unnecessarily interrupt the flow of the presentation. Another question is whether or not you can provide a soothing response to the customer's objection. Perhaps the customer has identified some reason why your product is not suitable, but you have additional information which would show that it is. Your technique would be different if you had nothing to say. What about the nature of the objection? Some objections are based in fact. It may be a fact about the product, the company, the buyer's situation, or any other element in the sales environment: "Our workers have always used left-handed machines." Other objections are based in opinion. Personal preferences, impressions, and predictions of the future are a few examples: "But I don't think the legislature will ever pass that bill so we won't need to redesign our product."

These three questions will give you some clues as to the most appropriate technique. If the customer raises a serious objection, serious in the eyes of the customer, that is, some type of direct and immediate response is probably required. Even though it will temporarily disrupt your presentation, to allow the customer to go unanswered may interfere with your ability to make other points anyway: "I'm glad you raised that issue. Let me explain before we go on." If

128

the point does not appear to be very important to the buyer, you might take a more passive approach. Passive techniques are attempts to smooth over the issue: "I'm going to get to that in a few minutes, but let me talk about a few other points first." A passive technique might also be the best approach if you are unable to provide a satisfactory response to the buyer's objection. Of course, if the buyer has a serious objection and you are passive because you have no answer to offer, the buyer is likely to notice. If the objection is based in fact, you may choose to agree with it or deny it depending on the available information. Provided that you have some relevant information, objections to factual information are more easily denied than objections based in emotions or opinions. If a buyer objects to excessive energy usage with your product and you can produce test results which demonstrate fuel economy, both of you are focusing on an issue: "I can understand why you asked that question. Our test results show that energy usage is minimized." You haven't denied the person: you have denied some fact or information. If, however, the buyer states an opinion and you deny it, you have denied the person. To say that the person's opinion is invalid is an insult: "I understand that you think that but you're wrong." You may be tempted to deny other people's opinions if they conflict with yours or stand in the way of making the sale. After all, it's your opinion against theirs, isn't it? In some situations that might be the case, but when you are trying to sell something, it is the buyer's opinion that counts. If the buyer is objecting on an emotional basis, one of the techniques which builds on an agreement with the objection might be indicated: "Yes, that's an important point. I have some test results which point to an answer."

Having evaluated the situation and decided whether your techniques should be active or passive and whether you should agree with the objection or deny it, you could apply several standard techniques to handle the objection.

Passive techniques are those which are intended to divert the customer's attention away from the objection. Passive techniques can involve either agreement or denial. You may, for example, use postponement: "I have to agree that you have raised an important point and I'm sure that I will have answered that question before my presentation is over." The important point is that the customer feels that you have recognized the issue and will provide some reasonable answer. Often just being recognized is sufficiently soothing. Simple listening can be an effective technique for overcoming some objections. The opportunity for self-expression may relieve some of the buyer's tension and smooth the way for further communication. Listening may work because it makes the buyer feel important. Sometimes the buyer simply runs down like a wind-up toy. If you had attempted to discuss the points being raised, you might have, in effect, wound the buyer up tighter.

Of course, listening works only when you recognize that there is a big difference between listening and waiting for another person to stop talking. In the context of overcoming objections, listening means that the buyer believes that you are getting the message. *Remember, you can't learn anything while you're talking.*

Objections are important because they provide clues to the buyer's needs and motives. A successful sales call is based on understanding the customer's needs. Active techniques to overcoming objections are really additional selling efforts in the areas in which the customer is not yet convinced of the wisdom of making this purchase. Active responses may provide solutions which the customer had not considered, provide the customer with a different frame of reference, give additional information to fill in a gap, or correct a misinterpretation or misunderstanding.

Often the problems which come up as objections have been faced and solved in past situations. If you can identify the problems you may be in a position to suggest a solution which worked for one of your other customers. Sometimes, as an outsider, you are able to suggest solutions which might not have occurred to someone who is closer to the situation. If most of your buyers face a particular problem you might even go a step further and anticipate the objection. Anticipating an objection is a technique in which you bring up both the potential difficulty and a proposed solution before the customer points out the problem to you: "You may be worried about service. Let me explain our service policy."

Sometimes a problem melts away when you take a different view of it. Imagine that you had a customer who was objecting to the price of your product. There are several established techniques for changing the frame of reference. One is called reduction to the ridiculous. Suppose that your product cost $100 and had an expected useful life of five years. A little quick division and you can say, "This is less than 6 cents a day." The price hasn't changed, but it looks a lot different. Perhaps you can reverse the focus. Instead of concentrating on the $100 it will cost to buy the product, you might help the buyer to think about the time, energy, or money which will be saved by using the product. Sometimes it helps to put the issue in perspective: "$100 may sound like a lot, but it's only 1/70 of the price of an average new automobile."

One of the worst situations occurs when you are thinking one thing and the customer is thinking something else, but neither of you realizes that you aren't sharing the same thought. You can try to test your customer's understanding of the points which you have made during the presentation as well as trying to uncover any misperceptions, biases, or misinformation which the customer picked up from other sources. Objections can often provide the necessary opening to introduce information which rounds out the buyer's understanding or at least introduces some doubt as to the reliability of conflicting information sources. If the buyer had not objected, these misperceptions might have persisted unchallenged.

Viewing objections as an opportunity to focus the selling effort where it will do the most good points to the need to probe for objections. Sometimes the objections you hear first are the socially acceptable objections. It may be less threatening to say, "I just don't like the color," than to admit, "I'm really not willing to pay the price." Separating real objections from smokescreens may not be easy. One of the clues is the buyer's interest in your response.

The responses of the buyer should be your guide throughout your selling effort. Hopefully the buyer will at some point begin to give off what might be interpreted as signals of a readiness to buy. These signals are your cue to close. Closing is one of the most frequently cited difficulties of people who are not successful in sales. Closing is simply asking for the order. At some point you must take the responsibility of asking if the customer is going to buy your product. Of course, there are important timing and technique questions in closing.

THE CLOSE

Every sales call comes to an end, but not all sales calls end with a closing. Regardless of the way the call ends, the person you called upon has given you some time and attention and deserves to be thanked for that at least. Either you or some other person will be calling on this person in the future, and there is great value in departing on a pleasant note. That is much easier, of course, if you are departing with an order. The obstacle which stands between most people and the things they want is that they don't ask for those things. Although it may seem difficult to believe, saleswomen have been known to go through all of the steps of the selling process from conscientious prospecting to a well-prepared customer-oriented presentation and then never ask for the thing they wanted, never ask for the order. Closing is not easy. Aside from the mechanics of timing and technique, there are significant emotional questions.

If you could go on with your sales call script you might open the third act with the buyer looking up from the product specification sheet and exclaiming, "That looks like it is exactly what we need! Where do I sign the order?" You then gracefully hand over a completed order form and a pen, comfortable that your academy award presentation moved the buyer to action without any unpleasant pushiness on your part. It might be nice to be able to wait for other people to extend themselves and to take the risk out of the situation, but the gravity approach isn't very dependable. If you wait for someone else to take the responsibility, you may wait a long time.

Closing can be both tense and risky. It is tense because you are finally asking for action. To this point you have asked your customer for some time and some attention, but you haven't asked for any commitment. Now you are going to ask your customer to part with some resources, to give up something in order to buy your product. Now you are getting down to business. You may worry that you will offend your customer. You may feel that you are imposing on the customer. You may be concerned that you will place your customer in an embarrassing position. What if your customer wants to refuse you? No one likes to have to speak up and refuse someone.

All these concerns for your customer are one thing, but what about concerns for yourself? You may be rejected. You are actually putting your presentation to the test. To this point you may have been playing the game according to the rules, but now you are about to find out the final score. You will either win or lose. There is no in-between. Doubts may begin to creep into your mind. Maybe you should try to make more points before you close. Maybe your customer should be allowed to think about it for a while. Maybe it would be better to come back again. After all, nothing ventured, nothing lost.

While all of the emotional concerns are common, the truth is that your buyer is expecting you to close. It is your responsibility to close. That is the way the rules are set up. You are the seller and the buyer is the buyer because you are supposedly taking the responsibility for bringing about the sale. That means that you are supposed to ask for the order. If you weren't going to ask for the order, why did you set up the appointment? If the buyer wasn't expecting to be asked, you wouldn't have been given an appointment. If you don't feel that what you have to offer is worth the buyer's consideration, you have been wasting everybody's time in making the call.

Your buyer not only expects you to close but may actually welcome it. The close signals the end of the sales call. This buyer has allocated a certain amount of time to your call and may be pleased with this signal that your visit is about over. If your buyer has decided whether or not to make the purchase, it provides the opportunity to express that decision and then to move on to other business. If your buyer hasn't decided, a well-phrased close provides the opportunity to ask for a clarification on some troublesome points. The attempted close is a signal to your buyer that you are serious about your mission: you are attempting to keep the discussion focused on the appropriate issues rather than allowing it to wander aimlessly. It shows that you, at least, are convinced that your product is suitable.

While closing has emotional overtones, it is the necessary and natural conclusion to the sales presentation. There are some general guidelines to closing and some accepted practices which can help you to be more successful. The two considerations in closing are timing and technique. You are striving to cinch the deal by saying the best thing at the best time. The two most general guidelines are that your close should be made in response to some signal of readiness by your buyer and that your close should be of a positive nature.

The personal sales call is an interactive process. Good presentations stimulate that interaction and develop two-way communication. This two-way communication has the benefit of keeping your customer alert and involved, but it is more than a presentation technique. It is your guide to your customer's buying readiness. You may make some judgments based on the questions asked by the buyer. A buyer who asks, "Can you tell me more about the maintenance requirements?" is still interested but is not ready to buy. But when that customer switches to, "What are your credit terms and delivery policies?" it is your signal to close.

Your buyer may not be asking questions but might begin to acknowledge positive points about the product or make positive points about the benefits of owning or using the product: "It certainly seems to be well built." If you respond, "It certainly is, and I'm sure it will meet your needs very well. When would you like to have it delivered?" you might have a sale. Neutral or negative statements indicate that more selling effort is needed. You can't measure buying readiness unless you listen to the buyer. Listening is critical to effective closing.

Your measuring of buying readiness depends in part on comments and questions volunteered by your buyer and in part on your buyer's responses to your direct questions. Your objective is to move your buyer to the positive purchase decision. A few well-placed questions might be helpful in measuring your progress. These questions are sometimes called trial closes. Throughout the sales presentation you can be testing buying readiness. You can seldom use the very direct approach: "Are you ready to buy yet?" but you can ask in other ways. Any question which requires your buyer to take a position on the benefits offered or the suitability of the product gives you indications of buying readiness. "Which color do you like best?" "Do you think you would be interested in our trade-in option?" Of course, you don't want to provide too many invitations to express unfavorable opinions.

In general, whether trial or actual, closes should take a positive tone. If you ask, "You don't want to buy my product do you?" you will probably hear, "No." By the time you close you should have some indication that your customer is ready to buy. You should have already answered that question for yourself. You can hardly ask a person to buy your product with confidence if you lack that confidence yourself. Closings should be phrased so that it is easier for your buyer to come up with the answer you want to hear than it is to come up with an unfavorable answer.

One technique, the assumption, practically answers the buying question for your buyer. "Well then, you just sign right here and I'll make sure that this order gets the special attention it deserves." The easiest path for your buyer is to go along with your assumption. It takes a lot less effort to comply and sign on the line than to protest.

"While you sign this order, I'll check on those delivery dates for you." Of course, this technique is most appropriate where the buying readiness signals are strong and your customer appears to be in a cooperative and relaxed mood.

A second technique allows your buyer more participation in the buying decision but still guards against the wrong answer. In the positive choice technique you offer your buyer the opportunity to choose between two or more alternatives, each of which is equally desirable from your standpoint. "Would you like that in brown or green?" While this is a variation on the assumption technique in that you have clearly assumed that your buyer wants it in the first place, it offers the more nervous buyer a chance to express some opinion. Instead of imposing the decision on your buyer, you have given your buyer some options: "We can have that delivered Thursday or Friday. Which would be better?" Of course, any one of the choices would accomplish your objective: "Do you want to take advantage of our predelivery payment discount or shall we bill you?"

Some closings start small and move ahead as the path clears. The one-step-at-a-time technique begins by gaining customer acceptance on smaller issues or more general questions and then moving toward the big question or the specific decision as the level of agreement builds. Your questions should lead to easy and obvious positive responses. "It's likely that costs are going to continue to rise isn't it?" and "Are you going to be more interested in conserving your financial resources?" are both general questions with reasonably predictable responses. You might start by gaining approval of relatively unimportant product features. "How do you like the finish on that machine?" While the main question at hand is the function that machine will perform for the buyer, the risk involved for either of you in agreeing that the finish is attractive is small.

In other closing situations you might start big and back off. "According to my study of your production schedules, an initial order of 10,000 units would be advisable." If your customer gives signs of resistance you then quickly follow up with, "Of course, it would work out well if you ordered 5,000 now and place a second order for 5,000 in January when you see how things are working out." If there are no strong signs of action, you could continue to scale down your action plan for your buyer. You may end up with, "To get you started, I'll send over some samples." This statement would only be made after you had convinced yourself that your more ambitious plan was out of the question (see Exhibit 7-1). You could comfort yourself with the knowledge that you had tried.

EXHIBIT 7-1. START BIG AND BACK OFF

"Now remember, ask for a snake first, then the puppy!"

Family Circle, October 13, 1977.

Some buyers are moved to action by a closing which involves a note of urgency: "I hope you can place your order now since we anticipate an industrywide price increase as the costs of materials rise." Sometimes time is an important consideration: "If you order now, I can assure you that you will have delivery before Christmas." Of course, if you use this technique on your buyer without justification, you may not be welcomed back. If there is no price increase or the buyer finds out later that the delivery date wouldn't have been a problem, you have lost your credibility.

A professional selling situation involves two or more rational people discussing a potentially mutually beneficial transaction. If you have done your job well, you have identified a person who has a need for your product and sought to define that product's benefits in terms of that buyer's needs. If your buyer is operating effectively, listening attentively to your presentation is a part of the buying process which advances both the interests of the firm and the interests of your buyer. Your buyer has a problem or a need and you are offering a potential solution. Sometimes the best close is the direct approach. "Today I have discussed with you the benefits which our product can offer you. It is inexpensive, easy to operate, and dependable. Let's write up the order." In this closing you would probably briefly summarize the points which seemed to be of greatest interest to your buyer. If your buyer agrees that you have made your case, you may be rewarded with the sale.

Closing is one of the biggest pitfalls in selling. People are reluctant to close either because they lack confidence in their performance or their product or because they fear that an attempted close will be upsetting to the buyer. A close can be upsetting to the buyer if it is poorly timed or poorly phrased. If the buyer is in a state of buying readiness, a failure to close may be even more upsetting. It is your responsibility to initiate the closing segment of the sales call. If you have moved through the approach and presentation segments of the sales call with the benefits of prior preparation and flexibility based on your sensitivity to your buyer's needs, you have no reason to fear the closing segment. Rather than an obstacle, the close represents opportunity. It is your opportunity to turn all of your efforts into rewards.

8 Follow-up and follow-through

Professional selling involves a continuing relationship with customers. Satisfied customers are not only a source of future sales themselves, but also serve as an important base of references for new prospects. Your selling job is far from over when the order is signed. Building a successful sales career requires both follow-up and follow-through. Follow-up is the process of evaluating your own performance. It is only from self-evaluation that you can hope to improve your selling skills. Follow-through involves continued attention to your customer's satisfaction. When the order was signed, what you actually promised your customer was the benefits to be derived from the use of that product. You are an agent of your company. Therefore it is your personal, legal responsibility to make sure that those promises are fulfilled.

Indeed, both follow-up and follow-through are important steps even if your sales call did not result in a sale. You would benefit from analyzing the unsuccessful interaction to try to uncover the reasons why there was no sale. If you or your sales presentation are the cause, you need to admit it and be better prepared before the next sales call. If the buyer was unable or unwilling to purchase although you had presented your story well, you may need to reevaluate your prospecting standards. Perhaps it was only a matter of timing. Following through with a nonbuyer may produce that sale at a later date. Whether or not a sale occurred, both follow-up and follow-through should be undertaken after each sales call.

FOLLOW-UP

Follow-up is essentially a self-analysis. Your objective is to try to understand your performance better so that you can improve it. Most companies make some attempt to assist their sales people with follow-up. Unfortunately these attempts generally involve the most dreaded of all sales-related activities—paperwork. It is understandable that people who like sales tend to dislike paperwork. Sales is a people-oriented career. It involves human interaction. To be successful you need to develop your abilities to be creative, flexible, and adaptive. Paperwork is an individual noninteractive activity. It is generally somewhat rigid and usually requires conformity. While it might seem that the contrast would be a welcome relief, paperwork tends to hang heavily over the heads of people in sales.

The real problem with paperwork, however, is less obvious. While paperwork is often the company's attempt to make you evaluate your performance on a per call or per day or per week basis, it is often inadequate in itself. Nevertheless you may think that you are actually undertaking adequate follow-up. If the company required no reports whatsoever, you might more clearly realize the need and devise your own system. Because you had devised the system, it would be more meaningful. It may cover the very same areas or even ask you to answer the same questions, but because you had created it rather than having it imposed upon you, it would be more meaningful.

A good follow-up system has three characteristics. First, it forces you to ask yourself questions about *your* performance. It doesn't allow you to externalize or always find some excuse outside yourself. Second, it allows you to easily compare your performances over time. Each individual evaluation is meaningful only as it indicates patterns in your behavior. Are you improving or not? Third, it is fast and simple to complete. Your system is supposed to help you do a better job, not become your job. Self-evaluation is usually only comfortable when we really don't need it. When there is room for improvement it can be very painful.

While your company system for self-evaluation may be your starting point in developing your own system, there are several reasons why you should look it over with care and possibly adapt it to your needs. While some systems are very good and have resulted from studies of many salespeople and their sources of difficulties, the company's system still isn't your system. It is a system designed for the company's average salesperson. It may cover in great depth some areas where you have no difficulties and skip over your weakest areas. It is a standardized system, and you're not standard.

The best systems are designed for your personal use. If your company requires that you turn in self-evaluation paperwork, it can be much less useful to you. When people fill out that type of form for someone else to read, they naturally tend to write the things which they believe the other person will want to read. There is a strong tendency to accentuate the positive. You not only fool your sales manager, but you may well be fooling yourself. If you are going to effectively follow up on your sales activities it must be through a system which encourages you to be honest with yourself. If you have carefully analyzed your company's reporting requirements and feel that they are suited to your needs, you might consider filling out two sets of paperwork—one set for public consumption to be turned over to management and one set for your personal records. On your own set you should feel free to write between the lines.

A follow-up system usually involves two kinds of reporting. First, you need some system to record your performance on individual calls. Beyond that you will need some way to summarize your performance over a particular time period. That may be a day, a week, or a month. The frequency depends on the relative frequency of your sales calls. In some industries you may make only two or three calls a week. In other industries you may be in contact with more than a dozen prospects every day. The purpose of the per call analysis is to make you consider your behavior on that call. The purpose of the summary sheet is to help you evaluate changes in your performance.

No system works unless you use it regularly. You will only analyze your sales performance on a regular basis if you can do it quickly and easily. The evaluation will be more valuable if you do it immediately following the call. If you are tempted to put it off until the end of the week or until the forms are due at the office, the results will be much less helpful to you.

Sometimes it is tempting to try to sneak by with a quick mental analysis. While that would be better than no analysis at all, there are substantial benefits to writing down your thoughts on your sales performance. When you analyze the call in your mind alone, there is a tendency to slide over the tough questions. As time passes, your memory fades. It is much more difficult to assess your individual progress over time. Paper and pencils are powerful tools.

While your follow-up system should fit your situation, some of the topics which generally are included in a self-evaluation of a sales call might be covered with questions such as:

1. Did I achieve my precall objective?
2. If yes, how? and if no, why not?
3. How did I handle objections?
4. Was my closing effective?
5. If I could do it over, what would I do differently?

Each of these questions deals with your effort, not directly with the buyer or the situation. While you were interacting with the buyer within a particular environment, the question is how well you con- ducted yourself. There is really little you can do to change the buyer or the situation. You can work much more easily on yourself.

A precall objective is critical to success in sales. If you can't state an objective, you shouldn't be making the call. Your precall objec- tive is a statement about what you intend to change. After you make the call, something should be different from the way it was before you made the call. You didn't have an order, and now you do. Your prospect was unaware of you or your product and now understands what you have to offer. A regular customer was dissatisfied, and now either you or the customer better understands the problem and will be able to correct it. Without some precall objective, any postcall evaluation will be quite meaningless. How can you say how well you did if you have no idea of what you were supposed to be doing? The more specific you were in stating your objective for the sales call, the more value you will derive from your postcall evaluation. If you have a vague objective, such as generating goodwill, you can always give yourself a self-satisfying if not helpful good score. Unless you got into an argument with the customer, you should be able to claim that you increased goodwill. You would be playing a game with yourself, and you would lose in the end.

If you have stated a specific sales call objective, you can answer with a distinct yes or no. "Yes, I did get that order for 10,000 units" or "No, I was not successful in getting the purchasing agent to set up an appointment for me to meet with the design staff." If the answer was yes, you should ask yourself to review how you accomplished it. Examples might be, "I was prepared to compare my product to the three most popular competitive products" or "I had prepared an analysis of the money that could be saved by using my product." While the entire sales presentation affected the likelihood that you would achieve your objective, you will probably be able to identify one or two points which seemed especially significant to the buyer.

If you didn't achieve your objective you need to seriously ask yourself, "Why did I misassess the situation? Was my precall objective unrealistic?" Be careful not to use this last one too often. On the other hand, if you are achieving your objectives all the time, you may be setting your objectives too low.

Maybe your answer to the question of why you failed to achieve your objective is, "My customer asked a question which I wasn't prepared to answer." That would point to the need for better preparation. If you found your customer to be resistant, you might conclude that you weren't reading the cues quite right. Maybe you need to try to be a bit more sensitive to your customer's signals. Perhaps you found that you were talking to the wrong person. Is your prospecting effective? In some cases you will conclude that there was nothing you could have done, but it can't always be the other person's fault. The most important thing about this evaluation is to be honest with yourself. If you're not honest with yourself in this process, someone else will be painfully honest with you at a later date.

Since objections are such an important part of any sales interaction, you may want to consider your handling of any which arose during the call. If there were no objections you may wonder whether you failed to stimulate any interest at all or failed to leave your customer some time to express them. Did you handle your customer's objections well or did those objections linger and damage your performance? How did you handle the objections? Did you use an active approach or did you postpone or simply listen to the objections? What was your customer's reaction to your technique? Did your customer accept your alternative way of looking at an aspect which had been bothersome?

Every sales call should have a closing. Even if your purpose was not to make a sale, you had some other action in mind. How effective were you in asking your customer to take that action? You may have been seeking agreement to an adjustment on the purchase price of a previous order which had been damaged in shipment. Did the customer respond favorably to your request for that agreement? In most cases you are asking your customer to place an order. Did your technique work well? How could you improve?

The last question is what would you do differently. There is a big difference between the question "What would I change?" and "What would I do differently?" The second question addresses your action. A suitable answer to the first question might be, "I would increase my customer's budget for products of my type." That answer is essentially useless in terms of improving your sales performance. You might answer the second question with suggestions relative to any segment of the sales call. You might change your procedures for making appointments, confirming appointments, dealing with receptionists, or any aspect of the approach segment. You might change your presentation so that it more directly addresses the concerns of your customer. You might have learned something about the buyer's motives which could be useful in planning future calls. You may change your closing. This would be especially true if the technique you used was not effective. As you continue in your selling career you will probably find yourself in a similar situation. If this started as an unfavorable selling situation and turned into a disaster, your next try in a similar unfavorable situation may be less of a disaster. If this was a highly successful call, reviewing your behavior may help you to stage a repeat performance.

Follow-up is one way to help yourself to improve your selling performance. Unfortunately, it is not easy. There are several difficulties which keep people from taking advantage of the benefits which are offered by follow-up. Follow-up is an investment. You put the time and energy into it now and it will pay off in terms of improved performance later. You are required to pay the price now for some expected benefit in the future. Sometimes people would rather spend their time on something which promises more immediate returns, even if those returns are less.

Follow-up is postponeable. If you have an appointment scheduled, you should honor the appointment. If you missed lunch, your stomach will let you know. If you put off filling in your follow-up form, it just sits there waiting patiently. Unless you are required to turn it in to your manager, you could postpone it indefinitely. It is something you can put off in favor of something which may be less important in the long run but is more pressing at the moment.

It is especially easy to postpone follow-up when you need it the most, that is, when things aren't going too well. Some sales calls are unpleasant enough the first time and the thought of an instant replay is not too appealing. Although that call was a miserable failure, there is still some benefit to be gained by reviewing it. While that idea may sound good on paper, it is difficult to put into action.

The best solution to all of these problems of follow-up is habit. Brushing your teeth is not a particularly satisfying activity either, but once you established a habit so you didn't have to think about it anymore, it got easier. Once you have established a habit, you are more uncomfortable if you don't do it than if you do. If you can get in the habit of filling out your postcall follow-up form as soon as you have left the customer's office, you will have provided yourself with an important self-development opportunity.

While the call forms provide you an opportunity to immediately review your performance, the second benefit is that they allow you to measure your progress over time. Some factors are easier to measure than others because you can attach numbers to them. If each week you reviewed your precall forms and recorded the number of times you achieved your precall objectives and the number of times you failed to achieve your precall objectives on a summary sheet, you could measure your performance from week to week. That part would be easy, but the rest is far more difficult to measure. Are you improving in your ability to handle objections? Are you making beneficial changes or are you repeatedly encountering the same weaknesses? You can only answer those critical questions about your progress by using your precall forms to go on a kind of mental treasure hunt. The second stage of follow-up is a critical review of your performance over time. This review should answer the question "Am I improving at an acceptable rate?" Look at the changes in your precall reports. You should sit down with your reports and ask yourself:

1. Is my percentage of achievement of precall objectives increasing?
2. Have I been able to repeat those actions which seem to help me to achieve my objectives?
3. Am I able to avoid repeating my errors?
4. Have I improved my techniques for handling objections?
5. Have I improved my closing techniques?
6. Am I making the changes I have recommended for myself?

If you can comfortably answer yes to all those questions, you should be noticing an improvement in your performance. If your answer to any of the questions is less than an unqualified yes, you have identified an area that needs work. Good sales managers try to help their people go through reviews of their performance in order to improve. But stop and think for a moment. There is no one who can or should be as concerned about your improvement as you. If you are the most concerned, shouldn't you take the initiative? Conscientious postcall follow-up is your responsibility.

FOLLOW-THROUGH

Follow-through is another responsibility after the call, whether or not the call resulted in an order. Obviously the type of follow-through is different when you make a sale, but some follow-through is always required. When you make a sales call, you have established a contact with someone and that person was considerate enough to listen to your story. To follow-through with a simple thank you note, even on a postcard, shows the buyer that you are thoughtful of that relationship. Selling is just another form of human interaction. Courtesy has been developed over the years to make human interactions more orderly and enjoyable. Beyond the thank you note, the treatment of buyers and nonbuyers diverges. If a call did not result in a purchase order, you must now decide on the appropriate course of action relative to that prospect. If an order was the result, you must follow through to be sure that you provide that buyer with all of the benefits you promised.

Nonbuyers fall into three groups. There are some people on which any further effort would be a waste of your time. Eliminate them from your prospect files. Other people are possible future buyers. You can put these people in your tickler file. A tickler file is usually set up on a date basis. For example, you might have a folder for each month. If you judge that this prospect might be in a better position to buy in two months, slip that name into the file for that month. At the beginning of each period you can take out that file and remind yourself of activities you have postponed.

In the third group are those prospects who did not place an order because they have not reached the decision stage in the buying process. They are still considering alternative suppliers. Follow-through in these cases involves taking the appropriate next step in convincing the buyer that you are the supplier who should get the order. You may be required to prepare or revise your proposal. Perhaps you were asked to supply some additional information. There are numerous possible actions, but there is one truth which persists from situation to situation. The follow-through is your responsibility.

During your call you may have gotten a clear indication of your next move. The buyer may have asked for some additional information on the product. You may have been asked to draw up a sample contract. You may have been asked to take some other action which would give the buyer something more to consider. If you have been asked to do so and it appears possible that you are able to meet the buyer's need, your course is clear. Take the steps to advance within the buyer's evaluation system. If you know what to do, the only problem is to get it done well and on time. Remember to do it. Every salesperson needs an effective reminder system. A notebook or calendar on which you can keep track of things is essential. Some people scribble notes to themselves on bar napkins, memo pads, gas receipts, or anything else which is handy. Since there is no order, it is easy to allow one of your notes to get lost or slip your mind. By the time you remember, it may be too late. You need an organized way to keep track of your responsibilities.

A second problem arises if you must rely on someone else. If you have to work with someone else to put together the proposal or wait for someone on the staff to supply you with some figures or materials, you may run into a bottleneck. If your ability to follow through on your customer's request is dependent on someone else, it is your responsibility that that other person fulfills the requests. To go back to the customer after the deadline and blame someone else is really inexcusable. You need to establish checkpoints for the people who will be contributing to your project and to make sure that you are aware of any delays or difficulties in time to take some action. While you see yourself as a representative of the company, to your buyer you *are* the company. If you fail to deliver on promised actions during the negotiation period, it will surely affect the buyer's opinion of your potential reliability as a supplier.

Sometimes before you can deal with the mechanics of follow-through, you have to ask, "What should I do?" In some cases your next step is not clear. You may have supplied all of the information which you believe would be useful to your customer. On your last call you asked if there was anything which might be more helpful and got no response. Now you are stuck waiting. How do you follow through? Sometimes you just have to wait. If you feel that your buyer is in a stage of the decision process where additional contact would be considered an intrusion or would make absolutely no difference in the outcome, you might as well devote your time and thoughts to other prospects.

If you feel that additional contact might make the difference, develop some reason for that contact. You certainly cannot waste the buyer's time by calling simply because your curiosity is getting the best of you. If you had some warning that the decision period would be drawn out, you might have withheld some tidbit of information. While you would certainly have wanted to provide the customer with all of the substantive information before this, you might have "overlooked" some minor option and now call to correct that oversight. New information is always a good reason to call, especially if it is good news. While you can't expect to be lucky enough to be able to announce a price decrease or technological breakthrough, you might justifiably pass on information on improvements in production or delivery schedules or any other development which might be interpreted as improving your buyer's chances of being satisfied in dealing with you.

A stronger form of information is the sweetener. You might have some extra benefit to throw in at the crucial point in your buyer's consideration process. You can call with some special incentive to buy. Of course, your buyer may resent this because you waited so long to offer it. Another possibility is that your buyer will keep you dangling even longer hoping that you will come through with more incentives. Regardless of the technique you use, it is usually to your advantage to keep your name and your product in the mind of your potential buyer. If everything else is equal, simple familiarity may make all the difference.

Follow-through is often the difference between making the sale and not making the sale. Follow-through after the sale is also worthwhile. Placing an order involves decision making. Any decision involves risk. Risk makes people feel uncomfortable. The bigger the decision, the more risk there is associated with it. After making the purchase decision, your buyer is subject to several sources of psychological discomfort. While your buyer's discomfort may not be so great as to justify cancelling the order, it may make your selling task a bit more difficult on your next call. By following through after the sale, you may serve as an important source of reinforcement and reassurance.

If the buyer placed the order for a product which is to be used by someone else, that other person may be a source of discomfort. If you call the purchasing agent you may find that you can answer some question raised by the intended user or counter some additional postpurchase resistance which will put your buyer at ease with the purchase decision. While you may have explained these very same points to your buyer in the past, some of the message may have been lost when your buyer transferred it to the user. You may even be called upon to communicate directly with the user.

Your buyer may bring on some of the problem. It is not uncommon that after a person makes a big decision little doubts begin. It is easy to dwell on the benefits of all the choices which were not chosen. When you decide to buy one product you are in effect deciding to do without all of the benefits offered by all of the products which you did not choose. Of course, you have also foregone a lot of the disadvantages of those products. At the time you made the decision, the advantages were overshadowed by the disadvantages, but that may be forgotten. Whether your buyer is subject to internal or external doubts, you may be able to offer the necessary reassurance. Even if your buyer has experienced no doubts, you can't do any harm by reaffirming your intentions to provide that buyer with all the benefits which you promised.

When you left your buyer's office you held an order which was your buyer's promise to pay, given that you fulfilled your promises on product quality, product quantity, delivery date, and other details. You will either be able to deliver on those promises as they were stated at that time, or you will discover that there is some need for adjustment. Your buyer is counting on those promises. A good follow-through program would include either confirming those terms as soon as possible or contacting the buyer immediately if any adjustment became necessary. If you anticipate any delay, it may be tempting to avoid notifying the buyer for a little while, just in case things turn out better than expected. You may be placing the buyer in an extremely difficult position. If you cannot deliver, it is your obligation to notify your buyer in time to allow for some alternative action.

As the sales representative, it is your responsibility to follow through both externally and internally. You are the company's representative to the customer, but you are also your customer's representative to the company. While your customer placed the order with you, nothing is going to happen unless you place the order with your company. Much of the paperwork required of you is part of the order-processing operation of your firm. Production, delivery, billing, and sales compensation functions must be coordinated if your buyer is going to receive the product as promised and you are going to be rewarded for your work. While it seems unlikely that you are going to work to get an order only to let it lie around in your briefcase or the corner of your desk, it has happened. Sometimes when you put a great deal of effort into the sale, the paperwork is a big letdown. Then, of course, accuracy counts. A simple clerical error could ruin the entire deal. A saleswoman in business forms recalls with great embarrassment the time that she sent in a good-sized order well in advance of the required delivery date. She checked back two days before the promised delivery and the shipping department had no record of the order. Checking back through the system she was horrified to learn that she had dated the order 11/7 instead of 10/7. It was on the schedule for the following month. With considerable extra effort, the parties involved managed to get the order out on time, but she had used up all of her goodwill in the process.

She was fortunate that she had at least shown the good sense to check back on the progress of her order. Setting up a procedure and a schedule for checking on the progress of your orders at certain points could save both you and your buyer a lot of problems. All of the people who are involved in processing your order are also responsible for the orders of all of the other salespeople. While they no doubt fully intend to pay careful attention to all of the orders, accidents do happen. If there is going to be some problem, it is better to discover it earlier than later.

Even after the delivery you have remaining follow-through responsibilities. In some industries the postdelivery responsibilities are substantial. If the product requires installation, servicing, or the training of employees, you may be involved in substantial interaction with the customer. If your product is relatively simple and has been in use by the firm for a long time, your responsibilities may be limited to a brief follow-through to be sure that the customer hasn't experienced any unusual problems. Everybody likes to feel that they are important and that their satisfaction matters to someone else. This callback may serve as an opportunity to generate the names of other prospects or to make additional sales to this customer. By this point you have come full circle in the selling process. The end of one sale represents the starting point of other sales. The process goes on and on. By following a few simple guidelines and analyzing your behaviors as you pass through the process you can improve your performance.

Once the process is underway, many of the sales you make will be to people with whom you have developed continuing sales relationships. Most successful saleswomen are constantly building on a base of satisfied customers. In order to protect that base, you must maintain records which will allow you to become aware of any changes in your customer base which represent either opportunities or potential difficulties. While you will surely want to be careful to pay attention to any industrywide developments, your personal records of your clients can provide you with some vital information if you are systematic and look for the signs.

Some of the factors which might alert you to possible difficulties are related to the sales activity between you and the buyer. If, for example, one of your customers changes normal buying patterns without explanation, you may want to check to see if a problem is developing. The buyer may be ordering smaller quantities or ordering less often. Some problem with which you are not familiar may have caused this buyer to order from another supplier. The problem may be easily corrected. Perhaps the buyer has heard a rumor that your firm might go on strike and is seeking the protection of an established relationship with one of your competitors. Maybe one of your shipments didn't arrive on time or in the proper condition. A slight difficulty might have been interpreted as a sign of deteriorating service or quality on your part. The buyer may have been reluctant to call the matter to your attention. Unless you bring it up, you may lose a valued customer.

Sometimes the buyer is not at all reluctant to bring up some unpleasant matter. In fact, constant complaining would seem to be a certain sign of customer dissatisfaction. Sometimes the difficulty lies in the area of the complaints and sometimes the complaints are only symptoms. In fact, some people complain all the time. The complaints themselves may not be as much a sign of a problem as a change in the number or the nature of the complaints. A single complaint over a substantive issue coming from a person who never complains should be more of an indicator of possible underlying problems than a barrage of minor complaints from a born complainer.

Sometimes otherwise pleasant comments are signals of difficulty. If one of your customers begins to make repeated positive references to your competitors and their product, you might well sense that what had been a straight-rebuy situation in your favor may be coming up for reconsideration. When your steady customers begin to pay special attention to your competitors and report back that they like what they see, you may be in for some trouble with those accounts.

Whenever there is a change in the atmosphere or the circumstance of the sales situation, your relationship with your buyer may be affected. Some of the changes are predictable, and you can begin early to lay the groundwork for a smooth transition. If, for example, one of your valued customers is retiring, you would probably be aware of the change well in advance and be able to start a relationship with whomever will succeed to the position. Your customer would probably even be willing to put in a good word for you. It may not go as smoothly as you would like if the new person believes he or she has to make changes simply to establish that the department need not be bound by the decision of the previous management, but at least you are forewarned.

Some changes come about without warning. You may arrive for an appointment one day to discover that your contact has been fired or worse. If your contact departed under any cloud, you may well need to seek out some new customers. Even if you are conscientious about your follow-through activities, you may not be able to anticipate all the changes.

The responsibilities of selling do not end with the order. After the order is placed, there is some minimum level of follow-through required of all salespeople. While it is possible for you to survive or even to be lucky without going beyond that minimum, conscientious self-evaluation and attentive customer service can be well worth your effort. Some people claim that they don't have time to follow up and follow through. We all have the same amount of time. The difference is in how well we use it.

9 Use your time: Don't kill it

The benefits of effective time management are obvious. Either you can get your job done in less time and have more time left over for other activities, or you can get more done on the job and earn more. It is equally obvious that some people have learned to manage their time more effectively than others. Time is a common denominator. We all have exactly 168 hours each week. If it is used wisely, it will pay dividends. If it is wasted, it can never be recovered. We're all moving in the same direction and at the same speed through time.

A time management system only works if you follow it. You will only follow it if it fits your situation. There are three bases on which any system fits into your life. First, it must be simple to initiate and maintain. It doesn't make sense to try to use a system which uses up more time and energy than it saves. Second the system must offer differential advantage. At the very beginning, it must be obvious to you that you will be better off to adopt the system. Finally, it must be compatible with your lifestyle. For example, since your deepest sleep occurs during the first two hours, it might be suggested that you sleep for 2 hours and work for 4 hours in four cycles over every 24-hour period. You would supposedly benefit more from your total of eight hours of sleep and avoid those less productive evening hours. The thought of four mornings each day may be bad enough in itself, but just imagine the problems this would cause in your relationships with family, friends, and business associates. For most people, a system of this type would lack compatibility.

While time management should be important to everyone, it is of particular importance to you as saleswomen. First of all, it may be easier to allow yourself a diversion or a delay since you don't have to punch a time clock. Most people have deadlines and time constraints imposed upon them. If you are not at your desk at most jobs, someone will notice and encourage you to correct your behavior. As a saleswoman, if you are not at your desk it will be assumed that you are out calling on potential buyers. The truth will come out when you have no orders, but by then it may be too late.

Ben Franklin cautioned, "Remember, time is money." This may be more personally significant in selling than in many other fields. If you are on a salary your time is money—someone else's money. If you are in sales, your time is your money. *If you can manage your time so that you can squeeze in one more call each day, you can add 250 calls each year.* While we may not understand all of the factors which account for success in selling, we do know that the more calls you make, the more chances you have to make sales.

Adopting an effective time management system is a three-stage process. The first stage is the philosophical acceptance, recognizing the value of such a system. The second stage is the psychological acceptance, modifying attitudes toward *yourself* and the value of *your* time. The third stage is the practice stage during which you develop mechanisms which work for you. Obviously no one can prescribe a system for you. The purpose here is to expose you to some thoughts and suggestions relative to the use of your time. You can accept some, reject others, and probably add some ideas of your own.

THE PHILOSOPHICAL STAGE

Ben Franklin went on to say, "Early to bed and early to rise makes a man healthy, wealthy, and wise." Perhaps in recognition of the quickening pace of life and the trend toward equality Tony Barretta, the maverick TV detective, observed simply, "If you snooze, you lose."

Do you remember having wished a part of your life away? When you were young you may have wished that you could pass through some period of time more rapidly. Perhaps you were anxious to celebrate your birthday or could hardly wait to open the presents under the tree. Maybe some particular unpleasant event was upcoming, and you wished it was over. Every January a lot of people in the colder climates start to wish it was spring. One of the beer companies ran a truly philosophical commercial not too long ago. While they were obviously touting their beer, the message had widespread implications: "You only go round once in life, and you have to reach for all the gusto you can get." In 1750 the Marquess of Halifax observed, "Misspending . . . time is a kind of self-homicide."

What are some of the philosophical concepts underlying effective time management? Two critical ideas are the Law of Diminishing Returns and the Theory of Comparative Advantage. The Law of Diminishing Returns contradicts the idea that more is always better.

Imagine that you went to your local ice cream shop and ordered a chocolate malt. It would probably taste pretty good. Imagine that you enjoyed the first malt so much that you ordered another. Do you think it would taste as good? What about the seventh chocolate malt at one sitting? It might even be disgusting. When applied to time, the Law of Diminishing Returns implies that additional amounts of time devoted to a particular task will at some point return fewer and fewer rewards. You might have derived more satisfaction from spending your money on a book instead of the third, fourth, fifth, sixth, and seventh malt. There is a point at which additional units of time spent in trying to get the order from a resistant potential buyer might be better spent in prospecting for new potential buyers. On a philosophical level it is not too difficult to accept the idea that each unit of your time should be spent where it would do the most good.

The Theory of Comparative Advantage is also related to the way in which you spend your time. Virgil, a Roman poet, observed, "We are not all capable of everything." This idea is the root of the Theory of Comparative Advantage. We are not all capable for a variety of reasons: natural talent, learning, access to information, and so on. Doesn't it make sense for each of us to do those things which we like to do and do well? We should leave the other tasks to people who do those tasks better than they can do our tasks. Consider the story of the attorney and the typist. The attorney was prepared to practice law. It also happened that having practiced on term papers and projects, this particular attorney was also very capable of typing. In fact, the attorney was a better typist than the typist who was hired to type in the attorney's office. Does it make sense that the attorney should devote a certain number of hours each week to typing? Of course not. Even though the attorney is an accomplished typist, that task should be left to the typist who was hired for that purpose. The typist is hardly prepared to practice law. Eventually neither of the people would have anything to type. They would both be out of work. The system is better off if the attorney turns the typing over to the typist. Law is the attorney's best act, and typing is the typist's best act even though the attorney is capable of typing. Just because you are capable of it does not mean that you should do it. Many people waste their time on projects for which they are only marginally qualified and then do not have the time to complete the projects which would bring in the greatest personal returns and the greatest productivity in the economy.

Accepting the philosophical justifications for efficient time management is perhaps the easiest step. It is not too difficult to accept the idea that time is important, that time moves in one direction, and that time past is time past. It is a bit more difficult to develop attitudes consistent with the effective use of time.

THE PSYCHOLOGICAL STAGE

The philosophical stage may require some thought, but it does not require commitment. In the psychological stage, the task is to relate those ideas to your situation. There are two elements, priorities and perspectives. Alan Lakein, in *How to Get Control of Your Time and Your Life*, recommends that you constantly ask yourself, "What is the best use of my time right now?"[1] The best use of your time is to spend enough, but not too much, on projects of higher priority before projects of lower priority. It may sound simple, but it isn't. The process requires evaluation and decision making. Two factors interfere.

---

[1] Alan Lakein, *How to Get Control of Your Time and Your Life* (New York: Signet Books, 1974), p. 96.

First, there tends to be an inverse relationship between true priority and immediacy. Consider two time-consuming activities, a phone call to line up an appointment to see a prospective buyer and taking out the garbage. Each would take about the same amount of time. In the abstract, most people would agree that the phone call should have the higher priority. After all, this contact could have substantive effects on your sales record, your income, your promotion, and other professional measures of accomplishment. What are the benefits to be derived from taking out the garbage? The best you are going to do is to obtain some relief from the possibility of smelly garbage. In practice, most people take out the garbage. Why? If you don't take out the garbage, the garbage lets you know about it. If you don't call the potential buyer, nothing happens. Nothing good happens and nothing bad happens. Nothing happens at all. Not right away anyhow. Most of the high priority projects in life are postponeable. There was once a popular song titled "Mañana." The message was that tomorrow is good enough; tomorrow never comes. Put those calls off in favor of the garbage long enough, and you can get fired.

The second difficulty in setting personal priorities is that the answers are seldom clearcut. Some projects of low priority may appear to be more important. It is easy to say that time is important, but it is much more difficult to decide that spending time on one project is more important than spending it in the hundreds of other possible ways. It gets into an apples compared to oranges situation. Is one hour spent completing necessary paperwork more important than one hour listening to your child describe the school play or a birthday party? We are not machines.

These are the basic realities which underlie the common human tendency toward fire fighting as opposed to fire prevention. In some cases important tasks are postponed until they must be completed in haste or simply neglected. Some seemingly unimportant tasks fester until serious consequences arise. Ben Franklin also warned us, "For want of a nail, the shoe was lost; for want of a shoe, the horse was lost; for want of a horse, the rider was lost." Sometimes hours are wasted on tasks which could be performed better by others or which could have been ignored without serious repercussions. These wasted hours are sometimes the outcome of distorted perspectives.

Supposedly a young man wrote home during World War II and

described his experiences in the Army: "We hurry up and wait." Lots of people are able to accomplish this without the benefit of military training. They hurry through some tasks only to spend too much time on another. It is difficult enough to establish priorities, but to actually decide that one task deserves two or three or eight times as many hours as another task is brutal. Imagine that you had time tags on every project. The time tag was equivalent to a price tag, but instead of paying in dollars you had to pay in hours. Instead of being symbolized by $, it was symbolized by $\mathcal{H}$. You can probably envision that it takes half of your yearly earnings to buy a new car, but have you thought of your weekly allotment of time? Does it make sense to spend almost 10 percent of your nonsleeping $\mathcal{H}$ (hours) driving back and forth to work? Lots of people pay $\mathcal{H}$10 each week in that activity. The difference between $ and $\mathcal{H}$ is that you can expand your $. Your supply of $\mathcal{H}$ is predetermined and fixed. You can decide whether you want to spend or save your $. You don't have that choice with $\mathcal{H}$. You are spending your $\mathcal{H}$ at a constant rate and will continue to do so as long as you live. You can't deposit $\mathcal{H}$ in the bank. Napoleon once said to an aide, "You can ask me for anything you like except time."

You can probably clearly envision the $ leaks in your financial system. You know that you pay taxes, a big leak. You see the grocery bill each week and have watched inflation eat away at your buying power in the department store. Are you as aware of the $\mathcal{H}$ leaks in your time system? Think about slow starts in the morning, disorganization, diversions, and disruptions. All of these are leaks in your time reservoir. While $ aren't exactly $\mathcal{H}$, $\mathcal{H}$ may be more important. Which one counts in the end? Lots of people have $ left when they die. No one has $\mathcal{H}$ left. Ironically there are high school and college courses in personal finance. Since you probably never had a course in time management, let's look at some of the mechanisms which might prove useful to a woman in sales.

TIME MANAGEMENT MECHANISMS

Time management mechanisms are the little subsystems or routines you can adopt in order to minimize time waste. Many of the mechanisms which are suggested in general purpose books and seminars on time management must be adapted to meet your special situations as a saleswoman. They are based on some assumptions which are inappropriate in sales. First, they assume that there is going to be a secretary to help you manage your time. The normal salesperson is lucky to share the services of a secretary with a dozen other people. Second, they assume a fixed work location and schedule. While salespeople usually have some desk space, their work is conducted in the work locations of other people. It requires a great deal more creativity and determination to control your time in someone else's territory.

Time management mechanisms fall into six broad categories: elimination, simplification, substitution, standardization, delegation, and organization. Your objective is to answer three questions: "Is this worth my time?" "Is this the best use of my time right now?" and "What is the most time-efficient way to do this?" No one can come to you and impose a system on you (see Exhibit 9-1). You can't even impose a system on yourself. The best system is developed through experience. It is a sequential and evolutionary process.

Demands on your time enter at a continuing, although irregular, rate. Some demands are anticipated. You know that you will spend a certain number of hours over the next 24-hour period sleeping, eating, and attending to various physical needs. Some demands are unanticipated. Someone may call with a problem, the house might catch fire, or a friend may call to ask you to lunch. Other demands are fixed. There is a sales meeting scheduled Thursday afternoon. You are required to attend.

Demands on your time come from a variety of sources. The simplest way to think of this is in terms of external and internal sources as shown in Exhibit 9-1. External demands are made upon you by others, and internal demands are those which you generate

EXHIBIT 9-1. BUILDING YOUR OWN
MANAGEMENT SYSTEM

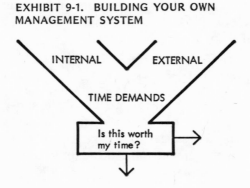

INTERNAL   EXTERNAL

TIME DEMANDS

Is this worth
my time?

yourself. The two may overlap. When you sit down to think of the things you have to do, many things will be done to satisfy either previous or anticipated demands made by others. If you are going to make the best choice with regard to the use of your time you must be aware of the demands. You don't have to worry too much about the external sources. They will usually make themselves heard. You do have to worry about the internal sources. You need to review and recall the internal demands. The list is the most common and useful crutch.

IS THIS WORTH MY TIME?

Whether you are reviewing your list of things to be done or responding to a request for your time, the first question is "Is this worth my time?" This is a screening process and is truly personal. Only you can decide what is and what is not worth your time. Think of it in terms of the V (value) of the output versus the cost in $\mathcal{H}$, $V/\mathcal{H}$. Imagine that you had set a standard for yourself. You had decided only to do those things which returned you two units of V for each $\mathcal{H}$. If you assessed the project as requiring $\mathcal{H}4$, you would decide that it was worth your time only if it was likely to produce eight units of V. Maybe you had no standard but had two choices and only $\mathcal{H}1$. If the first choice promised $3V$ and the second choice could only offer $1V$, which would you choose? Wouldn't it be nice if the choices were that simple? Is the immediate satisfaction of staying in bed an hour longer on a rainy morning of greater value than the possible benefits of making an early call? You may have expected that Ben Franklin would have had a few wise words on that subject: "He [She] that rises late must trot all day." Even if

EXHIBIT 9-2. BUILDING YOUR OWN MANAGEMENT SYSTEM

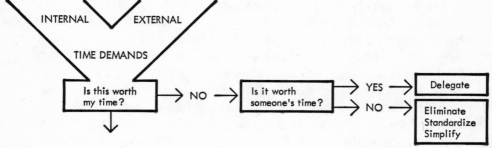

the evaluation is subjective, you should still ask yourself, "Is this worth my time?" Whether the answer is yes or no, the next step is another question (Exhibit 9-2).

IS IT WORTH SOMEONE ELSE'S TIME?

Even if the answer to your first question is no, someone else's $V/\mathcal{H}$ may be different. Suppose you had been given some tickets to a tennis match. It may not be worth your time because the V of watching a tennis match for you is very low. Someone else may thrive on spectator tennis. What if you are right in the middle of a big proposal and you receive a referral? Wouldn't it be better to pass it on to someone else? Someday that person may return the favor.

If it is worth someone else's time, you may choose to delegate (see Exhibit 9-2). Delegation is the answer when someone else's $V/\mathcal{H}$ is more suited to the task. This might be the case because they value the output more highly, because they have fewer alternatives and by comparison this looks good, or because they will, for some reason, be required to spend fewer $\mathcal{H}$ to complete the task. Delegation must be one of the best kept secrets in the world. People continually toil over projects of a lower $V/\mathcal{H}$ than alternatives available to them because they lack the skills or attitudes necessary to delegate. They may be able to accept the idea of the Theory of Comparative Advantage, that is, the attorney ought to practice law and the typist ought to type even if the lawyer knows how to type, but they just can't put it into practice.

It might be worthwhile to hire an assistant. Some salespeople have recognized the value of an assistant and then complained because their firms do not supply this kind of help. Complaining about an established reality is certainly a waste of time. Your objective is to cope with reality. One woman who is a manufacturer's representative in paper products and works out of her home has hired a high school girl to handle her paperwork. She is free to make more sales calls and hence more money. The 16-year-old is being exposed to a type of work she might otherwise have ignored, is earning money, is able to fit her hours to her schoolwork and teenage social life, and is a devoted worker. The situation is mutually beneficial. The saleswoman earns more than enough extra money through the more efficient use of her time to pay the young worker. Besides that, she confesses that she never liked the paperwork anyway. Another woman contracts out assignments to her own teenage children. She also has an office in her home. Her children file, fill out order forms, and process routine paperwork. They have accepted her working better since they have shared in some of the responsibilities.

Both of these women acknowledge that it was initially more difficult to get the work done through someone else than to do it personally. Generally the stumbling blocks to delegation are a lack of confidence in one's supervisory skills or a lack of willingness to invest in the short run in order to gain in the long run. While the second woman turned to her children first, the other woman had to interview several people before she found someone who could and would do the job. There is always the fear that the situation won't work out and you will have to fire someone. You would not deliberately expose yourself to that risk, would you?

Both of these examples are situations in which the V someone else attached to the work exceeded the V attached by the delegator. The delegator had more important uses for her time. What about the other situation? What about specialists? The manufacturer's representative is an independent businesswoman. She is not on the payroll of the companies whose products she represents but, in effect, rents her sales services to them. As an independent businesswoman, she has to file tax forms which are even more complex than the individual forms. While our first woman had struggled through those forms for several years wasting precious sales time or equally precious leisure time, the experiment with the paperwork and the high school worker turned out so well that she sought out an accountant to do her taxes. She had always operated under the "I can do it so I should" or the "I have to be good at everything" approaches to her business. The accountant's $V/\mathcal{H}$ is much more suitable to the task. The $\mathcal{H}$ is much lower.

Delegation is not easy. There are several steps which you can take to increase the usefulness of this mechanism. First, take the time to carefully analyze the task to be done. Write down exactly what you expect to be done, how, and when. Then establish a feedback or reporting system. A clear job description eases supervision.

BUT IT'S NOT WORTH ANYONE'S TIME

If you decided that the task was not even worth someone else's time, you have three choices. You can eliminate it. Scratch it off the list and go on. You can attempt to simplify it. Simplification should decrease the number of $\mathcal{H}$ required to complete the task and could bring the $V/\mathcal{H}$ into balance. Finally, you could standardize the task. Standard treatments may not be the most appropriate but might be a suitable alternative to elimination. Let's look at an example. Perhaps it occurred to you one day that it might be a good idea to send a letter explaining an addition to your product line to all of your customers who had not placed an order within the past six months. It would serve as a reminder and might stimulate some business. You go through your records and compile a list of 35 customers who fit that description. Your first question would be "Is this worth my time?" The potential V seems high, but the $\mathcal{H}$ required to write 35 letters would be high too. Assuming for a moment that you had not yet invested $\mathcal{H}$ and $ in delegating some of these tasks, your next question should be "How can I simplify this task?" An obvious answer is to send the same letter to each person instead of trying to compose 35 separate letters. You could further simplify it by saying very little in the letter and enclosing a copy of the appropriate catalog page. Once you had composed the letter you might take a step toward delegation by contacting a word-processing service. With their automatic equipment they can run off a letter to each person on your mailing list for much less than the value of your time.

One of the areas in which salespeople have recognized the value of standardization is in travel accommodations and business gifts. One of the major nationwide hotel chains stresses the value of standardization in their promotions. While it may be interesting to stay in a different place and eat in different restaurants every time you go to a particular town, it is far more time efficient to find an acceptable pattern and stick to it. You can cut down the time necessary to buy ten gifts by 90 percent if you buy ten of the same thing. No one but you would know the difference.

There are hundreds of opportunities for standardization in your normal routine as a saleswoman. Consider the area of correspondence. When you were a child, did you have one of those booklets in which each page showed a different person or animal but was cut in three sections? You could flip the pages and combine the head of a duck with the torso of a monkey and the feet of a chicken. Letters aren't much different. If you compose a series of standard paragraphs, writing letters becomes a simple matter of combining these paragraphs. You are well on your way to delegation. You can assign your helper to send a 3 + 6 + 11 + 18 letter to one person and a 3 + 7 + 9 to another person. It takes about a minute per letter to pick the right paragraphs.

If you travel a great deal, a packing list is a great help. Instead of wasting time trying to think of what you should pack, you simply work your way through the list. The purpose of standardization is to help you avoid reinventing the wheel. It may take you a little time to set up the standard treatment, and the results may not be as perfect as they would be with a fully customized treatment, but perfection is seldom worth the price, especially when the price is paid in time.

IS THIS WORTH MY TIME RIGHT NOW?

The stream of demands on your time keeps coming. You might be in the middle of a project when the phone rings. You may have to ask again "Is this worth my time?" If the answer is yes, you move to the second question, "Is this the best use of my time right now?" (See Exhibit 9-3.) It may be worth your time but not at this minute. It could be that something else is more critical at the moment. It could be that you are not psychologically or physically able to undertake a particular task at a particular time. It could be that this task would fit in nicely with some other task which you intend to

EXHIBIT 9-3. BUILDING YOUR OWN MANAGEMENT SYSTEM

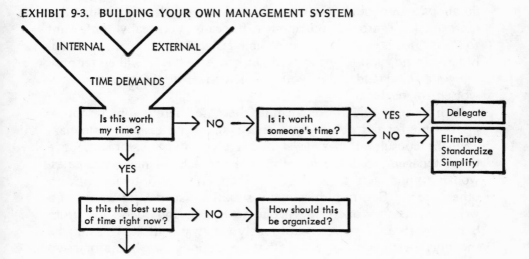

undertake later. If a task is not the right task for the moment, the appropriate time management mechanism falls under the heading, organization.

One of the standard recommendations of time management experts is the list. You should have a list of things to do. You may choose to have several lists. You may have a list of upcoming responsibilities, a list of continuing responsibilities, and a list of daily responsibilities. When a task comes up which cannot be effectively handled at the moment, it should go on a list. Maybe you save up your orders and process them once a week. On your continuing list it says "Process orders." Each time this task arises you put the necessary papers or reminders in the "Order pile." The same technique works for expense records. If you got out the forms and filled them in each time you made a phone call, you'd spend your life filling out forms. Those are the kinds of tasks which are well-suited to clustering. You do them either when a sufficient volume builds up to warrant your attention or on some regular schedule.

Especially as a beginner it is tempting to do this kind of necessary, but nevertheless busy, work ahead of some other less-defined tasks. It can be comforting because when you are done, you have something to show for it. You have filled in a form. If you make ten telephone calls to prospective buyers, you may end up with nothing but scratches on a list. You may end up with ten "No, I'm not interested's." The expense form can be far more comforting.

There are several questions to ask yourself when deciding what to do about a task which is important but is not worth your time at this moment. First, are you putting it off because you really don't want to do it? If it is one of those miserable tasks which you will eventually have to do, you might as well get it over with. It will either prey on your mind and make you less effective, or the situation may worsen for neglect.

Perhaps it should be rescheduled because there is a more appropriate time for it to be done. Alan Lakein, a professional time management consultant, has developed a concept critical to effective time management and especially suited to saleswomen. As a saleswoman, your success is dependent on effective interaction with other people. Contrast this to the situation faced by a writer. If a writer wants to work from 4 a.m. to 8 a.m. and then sleep from 8 a.m. to 10 a.m., she could probably get away with it. This may be the only occupation in which that continuous two hours of sleep and four hours of work schedule might work. It may cause serious problems in terms of family life, but it could work. As a saleswoman you are to a great extent dependent on the schedules of your potential buyers. You usually see those people at their convenience. Imagine the reaction if you suggested that you are most alert at 6 a.m. Lakein talks about external and internal prime time.

> Internal prime time is the time when you work best—morning, afternoon, or evening. External prime time is the best time to attend to other people—those you have to deal with in your job, your social life, and at home. Internal prime time is the time when you concentrate best. . . . Try to save all your internal prime time for prime projects. . . . External prime time is when external resources (usually people) are most available for decisions, inquiries, and information.[2]

When you become aware of a new demand on your time, it may go on your list because there is some other time which is more "prime." You may have a great idea on Friday afternoon. This is usually not the best time to approach your sales manager. It might better wait until Monday afternoon. You may collect routine tasks to do in the evening when your mind is run down. There are some simple tasks which are best completed while watching TV. One woman who travels a lot by plane collects projects to work on while in the air or waiting for her plane. These are not projects which require a great deal of creative thought. As a matter of fact, she always writes a letter to her grandparents. It is a necessary task as she has structured her priorities but is not appropriate to her internal prime time. Many saleswomen who travel by car try to get started early in the morning. If you get up at 6 a.m. you can be dressed and on the road by 6:30. You can make a 100-mile trip and have breakfast before calling on a client at 9 a.m. This usually allows you to travel during the day, to check into hotels during daylight hours, and to avoid being on the road during the hours when traffic accidents are most common. People who are driving down the highway at 6 a.m. tend to be serious about their destinations.

External prime time may be phrased in terms of hours of the day, days of the week, or weeks of the year. It is largely dependent on industry. If you are selling a product to private firms which operate on a year-round basis, you will normally be concerned with hours of

---

[2] Lakein, *How to Get Control*, pp. 48-50.

the day, although you may expect better results on Wednesday morning than Friday afternoon or on any given December 10 as compared to December 23 or 26.

Insurance saleswomen who are selling to individuals may find the evening hours to be external prime time. If the target market is small businesses, the morning hours may be more fruitful. If you are selling to any government agency you need to pay attention to fiscal years. Government units follow a strange but justifiable spending pattern. They usually receive a certain amount of funds which is supposed to last for a year. Early in that year they tend to be very frugal so as to save funds to protect themselves against unforeseen expenses. Near the end of the budget period they are in a hurry to spend the remaining funds because unspent funds work against them. If they don't spend the money, it is assumed that they don't need as much during the next budget period.

The women who sell college textbooks face an equally spasmodic, although predictable, prime time pattern. Twice a year the college bookstore badgers the professor for a textbook selection for the upcoming semester. Between the time that the first notice goes out and the date on which the order is due, the professor has an interest in selecting a text. It is an all-or-nothing situation. Either you sell lots of copies of your book or you sell nothing. If you show up on campus before the first bookstore notice, you may meet with a disinterested reception. Professors may be willing to go to lunch, to accept free examination copies of texts, or to discuss personal writing projects, but they are not ready to make a textbook selection. If you show up after the order has been sent to the bookstore, you would almost have to walk on water to get an order.

It is too bad if your internal prime time conflicts with external prime time. One of them is going to have to give, and chances are very good that you are not going to be able to change the world. Most of the people who have tried that have failed. You need to define your best time for paperwork other than normal working hours. You may be an early riser. Most saleswomen with husbands and/or children find that it is better to get up early to do whatever paperwork and planning they want to do, to make sales calls during school hours, and to relax and spend time with their families in the late afternoon and evening. There is no "best time" for everyone. Your objective should be to discover the best time for you. If a particular task is worth your time but is not the task which deserves your time right now, you should be able to set a time for that task.

Setting up a time for a task brings up the subject of time budgeting. We are all familiar with money budgets. We usually begin with expected revenues and start to assign uses. First we take out the necessities. Indeed, some of those are taken out before we even see our checks. The various governmental levels which take a tax bite are afraid that we won't put them first in our budgets, so they withhold their expected share. Our gross income is reduced to a net income. As a reasonably fiscal-conscious individual, the next step is to allow for necessities. From that net or disposable income, you must subtract all of the nondiscretionary expenses, those expenditures to which you are committed. You subtract your insurance premiums, house payment, car payment, minimum grocery bills, necessary health care, and other unavoidable expenses. If you have anything left it is considered to be discretionary income, that is, income which you can spend as you choose. A time budget is quite similar.

You could seriously consider your priorities and attempt to set up a budget which places the various elements of your life in perspective. A budget differs from a schedule. It can be extremely difficult to maintain a rigid time schedule in unstructured occupations such as sales. It is that flexibility which can make sales more attractive than some of the other career options. A time budget may be a suitable alternative.

A time budget is a paper and pencil exercise. Off the top of that gross of 168 hours each week you have to subtract time for the necessities of life—the minimum number of hours required for sleep, eating, basic personal care, and other absolutely unavoidable time expenditures. From your disposable time you can allocate a number of $\mathcal{H}$ to your job. The time that is left is discretionary and will hopefully be spent advantageously. That is a matter of personal choice.

What should you do with the hours you have budgeted for your job? Can you list all of the tasks involved in your job and attempt to balance the time spent against the benefits? Most sales jobs include calls on customers, calls on prospects, sales meetings or training sessions, self-study of products and applications, keeping up on the industry including the competition, paperwork, travel, and prepara-

168

tion for calls among other responsibilities. One technique to improve your effectiveness is to make a list of the tasks you face and then to assign a certain proportion of your time to each area. Then over the next few weeks, record the actual amount of time spent at each task. It will probably vary from week to week. The objective is to uncover areas in which your actual time spent is out of line with the prescribed time allowance. You may be surprised.

You may further interpret the time allowances in terms of units. If you have allocated two hours each week to prospecting for new business, you might set up a personal quota of ten phone calls or two cold calls each week. Perhaps you could even make your paperwork more enjoyable by timing yourself and trying to improve your time. Getting the same amount of work done in less time implies efficiency.

WHAT IS THE MOST EFFICIENT WAY TO DO THIS?

Efficiency and effectiveness are closely related (see Exhibit 9-4). You can hardly be using your time effectively if you are inefficient,

EXHIBIT 9-4. BUILDING YOUR OWN MANAGEMENT SYSTEM

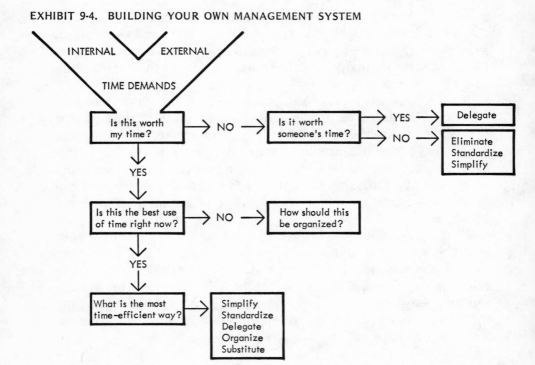

but you could be very efficient and still be ineffective. Effective means accomplishing those tasks of the greatest value to you. Of course, this is interpreting the term task in a broad sense. A "task" may be enjoying a vacation trip. You could efficiently complete a worthless activity. Time effectiveness is efficiently completing worthwhile activities. If you have decided that a particular activity is worth your time, that is, it is the appropriate activity at this time, the next question is "What is the most efficient way to go about this?" Efficient means more than fast. Efficient means getting the greatest output for the input. It means avoiding waste.

While by this point in your analysis elimination should be out of the question, any of the other time management mechanisms may be appropriate to increase efficiency. As you begin to develop your own system for effective time management, you should run through a series of questions each time you are about to begin a task. After your system is well underway, you need only review the questions when you face a new task.

Is there an easier way to do this?

Have I done this before?

Will I have to do this again?

Could someone else do this?

Could someone else do this more efficiently?

Could this be combined with some other activity?

Is there a different way to get the same result?

Perhaps you have heard the phrase "Work smarter, not harder." A few minutes spent in planning your attack may save hours later on. Answers to these questions may indicate the opportunities for simplification, standardization, delegation, organization, or substitution. "Is there an easier way to do this?" You may have noticed more people responding to your correspondence by writing their reply on the bottom of your letter. This is certainly a simplification. It even has the added benefit of immediately reminding the recipient of the nature of the original communication.

If you have done this task before and will probably do it again, it may be a good candidate for standardization. One of the benefits of standardizing is that it is the first step toward delegation. Of course, if it is a task for which you lack the skills or someone else has more skills, delegation is the answer. Time invested in seeking out appropriate help is an investment.

One of the areas which generally provides the greatest opportunities for combining activities is in scheduling sales calls. In studies of salespeople and their time usage, two activities which consistently show up as big drains on time are traveling and waiting to see customers. Travel time is, to a great extent, a function of the size of your territory. For the most part, that is a given. If your territory is the downtown business district of a major city, travel may be much less significant than if your territory covers four states. Beyond the territory size, the amount of time you spend on travel is largely a function of your ability to organize. There are three wrinkles which make this a real challenge. First, sales calls are indivisible. You can't make half a call. If you only have enough time to make half a call, you have to find some other use for that time. Second, you are usually at the mercy of someone else's schedule. Many of the courses on time management stress techniques to keep salespeople from interfering with your schedule. Third, the time consumed by a sales call is somewhat unpredictable. You have to allow some flexibility. What if you had just solved all of the buyer's problems but didn't have time to write up the order because you had to hurry to another appointment? Some of these problems are more controllable than others. It's logical to start with the controllables.

The first controllable is making appointments and confirming those appointments. It's far better to be a part of the buyer's daily schedule than to attempt to interrupt that schedule. It's also better to call ahead and discover you have been bounced from the schedule.

The second controllable is the route. If you make one appointment on the east side of town, it would make sense to make the rest of that day's appointments in the same area. It may help to keep a geographic card file. Customer files are kept according to different systems. Perhaps the most common and least functional is the alphabetical system. For the purposes of selling, it would be more useful to organize files by sales volume, by product or industry, or by geography. Regardless of the system in your firm, you can set up your own geographic card file. Instead of searching for another customer in the area or calling on accounts you remember, you can methodically organize your day. As you run through the stack of cards for the east side you will be reminded of a prospect or customer. Without the cards, you might be tempted to call it a day.

A third controllable is the pace of the day. Most experienced salespeople use what might be called the sandwich approach. They set up several key calls in a day and fill in with less critical appointments. Scheduling two critical calls back to back is asking for trouble. If the first one runs late, the second gets off to a bad start. The critical calls are scheduled during prime times.

A fourth controllable is alternatives. While you cannot control the customer, you can control your response to disappointments. If a customer cancels at the last minute, is in a bad mood, leaves you waiting, or in some other way disrupts your carefully planned schedule, you can't control that customer, but you can control yourself. Rather than looking upon this as a disappointment, you should consider it to be an opportunity. It is an opportunity to call upon that prospect whose name and number you brought with you from your geographically arranged card file. It is an opportunity to make those phone calls, do some paperwork, work on your list of things to do, or try to think up ways to simplify or standardize your other tasks. There must be some use for your time.

Your time is one of your most valuable resources. You can decide that you want to use it effectively and make a serious attempt to develop time management mechanisms which work for you. There are some things you can control and some things you can allow for, although they are beyond your control. You have no control over the amount of time you have to spend, but you can control how you spend it.

10 Vive la différence: Special concerns of women in sales

Women are women and men are men. Women aren't men. While the basic differences should not matter in terms of opportunities, intellectual abilities, talents, or attitudes, our social system has not yet reached that sublime state. Selling takes place within the general social structure. That structure has been struggling with the adjustment to the changing roles of women. It's not perfect, and the adjustment, while encouraging, is far from complete. Women in sales encounter all of the enjoyment, satisfaction, challenge, disappointment, fatigue, and turmoil experienced by salesmen. Sometimes the saleswoman's experiences are a bit more intense. Some of the differences among the experiences of saleswomen and salesmen represent opportunities or advantages for you. Some of the differences come in the form of additional obstacles or problems. Whether or not those differences, good or bad, are justified or will persist could be argued for hours. The question is how you can handle these special concerns.

Saleswomen are generally reluctant to discuss how their experiences differ from the experiences of salesmen. Perhaps they have been quite successful in dealing with any problems and therefore those problems no longer concern them. Obviously none of them has had the opportunity to see what it would be like to be a salesman, and so they may be unable to perceive the differences. Maybe they have been careful not to discuss the differences for fear of fueling the rumors that they enjoy special advantages because of their sex. It could be that they are concerned that by openly discussing the differences, they may discourage other women or in effect condone differential treatment. Perhaps they believe that any difficulties they have encountered are theirs alone, that is, that these difficulties spring from some personal deficiency not from the environment.

In discussing differences the intent is neither to discourage you nor to condone any differential treatment either to the advantage or the disadvantage of saleswomen. Fair is fair. It is simply that women are in the process of developing some answers to questions which haven't even been asked in the past. It makes little sense for individual women to reinvent the wheel. If you can learn from the experiences of others, you can make more progress yourself. You may be able to avoid some unpleasant surprises. On the other side, some of the more widely assumed differences may not be differences at all. Sometimes supposedly difficult problems disappear when they are exposed to enough light. It may just be a matter of learning the rules.

The rules of the business game have been clearly defined for men although it has taken a long time. Men have been playing the business game since before the first Phoenician traders rowed away from their homeland in search of foreign treasures, but women are relatively new to the game. As women play the game in increasing numbers, there will be some adjustments in the rules of the game. By and large, however, women will first have to learn to play by the established rules. Where the objectives, resources, and obstacles are the same, it makes sense that the rules should go unchanged. The only problem is that no one has ever written the rules in a rulebook. They are handed down much like folklore. They have been handed down from father to son, not from father to daughter. It can take a long time for you to figure them out for yourself. Wouldn't it be nice if the business world would take the time to pass on this knowledge?

The business of business, however, is to conduct business. While it might be argued that the business world would benefit by taking the time to encourage the more active participation of women and hence take advantage of this human resource, the business of business is not to foster the inclusion of diverse groups of people. Only when the main business is threatened does this task achieve priority. Unfortunately that same threat which brought about action generates some inhibitions and fears which make the inclusion of women more difficult.

As women begin to move into selling in larger numbers they will be treated in much the same way as a group of immigrants to a new country. As any new group of people came to the United States, they encountered a certain degree of resistance on the part of the established residents. That resistance varied, although few groups were accepted without some reservations. The more rapidly the people in these groups of newcomers were able to adopt some of the accepted behavior patterns, the more rapidly they were accepted. Of course, the more they looked and acted like the established residents in the first place, the easier that adjustment was for them. The arrival of a new group of people caused two kinds of changes. First, the new arrivals changed some of their behaviors to conform to some of the expected patterns of behavior in the United States. Second, they made some slight changes in the existing environment. They brought with them some languages, foods, or customs which they contributed to the culture. As women learn the rules, they themselves will experience some changes. Similarly, as more women choose careers in selling, they will bring about some changes in those rules. To ignore the established rules or to expect to bring about any immediate or widespread change is to fight against overwhelming odds on the opponents' field.

There are several areas which may be of special concern to you as a saleswoman. Some concerns arise because the rules are rigid and do not fit or allow for women. Other concerns stem from a lack of defined rules. In some cases you could get along just fine with existing rules if others would only allow it. Some of the special concerns are directly related to your job and others develop outside of the job because of the requirements of the position. Some concerns are self-induced and other concerns are imposed by other people as a reflection of their attitudes toward saleswomen or women in general. In some cases, these concerns are over restrictions on your opportunities. In other cases, the greater extent of your opportunities may actually create problems.

What are some of the specific situations faced by saleswomen?

Some are actually opportunities. Your objective should be to capitalize on those opportunities. Other situations turn out to be disadvantages. Your skill in handling these disadvantages may be equally important to your success. While the rules may be exactly the same for men and women, there may be some slight differences in interpretation. There are at least three areas in which these differences seem to stand out clearly. The first area is travel. Travel has long been assumed to hold special concern for women. Some of these concerns may be justified and others may be imaginary or temporary. The second area is customer relationships. You may have to work a little harder or be a bit more creative in establishing productive long-term working relationships. The third area is the establishment of workable relationships with other people within or outside of the organization who are not potential customers but whose actions and attitudes are important to your success.

TRAVEL: CAN YOU, SHOULD YOU, WILL YOU?

Most selling positions require some travel, although the amount varies widely. The record may go to a man in the musical instrument business who reported that he had been on the road 316 days in a single year. Some sales jobs in major metropolitan areas involve little if any overnight travel as a part of the regular routine but may require occasional trips for training or sales meetings. Travel can present problems for both salesmen and saleswomen, but some of these problems may differ. Men and women share the problems which accompany being absent from home. You may encounter additional problems in terms of the actual mechanics of travel or the attitudes of other people toward your traveling.

Travel is not the insurmountable obstacle that it is sometimes imagined to be for women. There is some truth to the generalization that women are unwilling to travel. Some women don't like to travel. Of course, some men don't like to travel either. Men who don't like to travel are simply expected to get over it. Men have traveled more than women because men have had to travel more than women. That is no indication that women can't or won't travel. Nevertheless, the issue of travel seems to be a special concern of male managers when they contemplate integrating their sales forces.

The managers of a midwestern firm recently hired their first saleswomen. In the discussions which preceded the decision to hire women, travel was questioned in several ways. While none of the points raised would rate as submissible evidence in an EEOC action, they were all very real to the executives involved. Some of the concerns were for the psychological and physical well-being of the individual women. Other fears were for the stability of the organization.

"Are women willing to travel? All of our territories involve some overnight travel." You could suffer because of this unjustified assumption that as a woman you are less willing to travel. Women in fields other than selling travel extensively. Women in news reporting, entertainment, law, government, and other fields travel without apparent difficulties. If the job requires travel and women are assumed to dislike travel, it would seem to be logical not to hire women. As an individual your biggest problem with the travel issue might be that it interferes with your chances of being hired. Even if you are hired, the travel stigma may restrict your advancement opportunities. This problem may be compounded if you do not even realize why you are being restricted. You can't expect your sales manager to come to you and say, "We've decided that it is in your best interest not to offer you this challenging territory. We are afraid that it would upset you because you wouldn't want to admit to us that you really don't want to have to do all of the traveling which would be required." The manager may not even realize the impact of inbred stereotypes in eliminating you from serious consideration for the assignment. You may be dealing with one of those ghost issues which would disappear with sufficient exposure to the sunlight.

The key to the solution of this difficulty is your own awareness. It is only by being aware that you can protect yourself. One woman was being interviewed for a job and sensed that the male interviewer had some reservations which he was not expressing. Guessing that travel might be his concern, she opened the issue up for discussion, "I expect that this position will require quite a bit of traveling. I've had to travel on some of my other jobs and managed to get along quite well." She was fortunate in that she was in a position to take this direct approach. Her previous work experience had included business travel. Her carefully worded statement implied a recognition of both the good and bad aspects of travel.

Even a woman with business experience appears naive if she overemphasizes the positive aspects of travel. If you have business travel experience, it may be equally damaging either to overemphasize the positive or to express doubts in your abilities to handle traveling.

Travel can be both exciting and exhausting. It pays for you to gain some experience in business traveling early. Most management positions of any consequence will require that you travel, even if the entry-level position did not. After ten years of working her way up the management ladder of a major midwestern manufacturer, one woman reports that she has reached her upper limit in the management structure. She will be unable to accept the next promotion because of her fear of air travel. Her company has facilities nationwide, and she would be unable to travel to conduct important business. While her travel fears have little to do with her gender, travel may involve some special fears for women.

Your travel objectives, however, are the same as salesmen's objectives. You have a particular job to do at a particular time and place. To do that job most efficiently you want to minimize the time, energy, cost, aggravation, and danger which can be involved in travel. At the same time you want to maximize your reliability, comfort, and enjoyment. If your job is a big part of your life and travel is a big part of your job, it shouldn't be something to be endured. You should strive to make it worthwhile. Recognizing potential difficulties is the first step in overcoming them.

Traveling increases your vulnerability to both physical and psychological damage. The physical dangers to the woman alone are covered in the news every day. Most can be minimized by using a little common sense. One saleswoman carries a mental safe zone/danger zone map wherever she travels. For example, in most hotels the safe zones are your own room, the front desk, and the coffee shop. The danger zones are the bar, the elevator, the stairways, parking lots, garages, and hallways. While she can't stay out of all the danger zones, she tries to be more alert to any signs of danger while in those areas. There are also safe times and danger times. She takes those into consideration in scheduling her travel. She always tries to arrive at her destination before dark. If she must travel long distances by car she tries to make the trip in the morning before working hours rather than in the late afternoon or evening. While women can travel safely, the margin of safety tends to be narrower than it is for men. Consequently, prior planning is more important.

The psychological dangers are more complex. Almost everyone has heard a traveling salesman joke. There are no really reliable statistics on the sexual behaviors of traveling males, but rumors fly. There are probably three types of males: those who talk more than they act, those who are reasonably honest about their activities, and the quiet ones. Whether the activities of women will match the activities of men is not known, although the rumors will circulate since all of the publicity on aggressive women makes good press. Individual moral standards or personal sexual behavior is not the issue.

Our social structure has generally defined men as pursuers and women as the objects of that pursuit. The world has been a little retarded in adjusting to the unescorted woman. If you are in a public place after working hours by yourself, you may be seen as inviting pursuit. You may simply be hungry and want to enjoy a peaceful dinner. Maybe, just like a lot of other people, you have had a hectic day and would enjoy a quiet and private drink. You may be able to eat your meal or drink your drink alone, but many saleswomen feel uncomfortable with the knowledge that their actions may be mis-interpreted. Our social structure has granted men both the pleasures and responsibilities of initiation options. A man is supposed to choose whether or not to attempt to establish an interaction with a woman. Women have not been expected to have that option. They have been expected to wait until they are chosen. Of course this option brings benefits at a price. Being allowed to initiate interaction provides flexibility and choice. It embodies a sense of self-determination. If you have the initiation option, you can choose whether or not to attempt to interact and, subject to availability, with whom to interact. You are also protected from intrusion. If you don't initiate the interaction, the other person is supposed to leave you alone. Of course, by initiating you increase your vulnerability to rejection. You must assume the active role and take responsibility for bringing about the interaction.

Women have not generally exercised the initiation option, but they are still vulnerable to intrusion. While you may wish to be left alone, as an unescorted woman you may be subject to uninvited interaction. Men who have always been responsible for the initiation of interaction may simply be behaving according to a set of rules which do not fit you and your situation. The question is how to protect yourself from undesired interactions. How do women who travel and consequently find themselves alone in public places at social hours handle these intrusions? Some bring their briefcases or work on papers to try to appear occupied or to establish their identity as a legitimate business person. Others have practiced their rejection skills realizing that they don't owe anybody else in the establishment anything beyond basic courtesy. You do not need an excuse to end a conversation. It seems more likely that most women simply avoid that situation. They simply try never to allow themselves to be unescorted in public places during the normal pursuit hours.

Imagine a large hotel. If you had a giant X-ray machine aimed at that hotel at the dinner hour, how many women would you find hunched over a room service tray in front of the TV? Avoidance is the solution favored by many women. A major hotel chain which has been concentrating on the woman business traveler has been emphasizing its extensive room service menu as an attractive feature. The avoidance solution probably has two advantages other than decreasing your visibility and vulnerability. It may increase your productivity on the job. Eating in your room takes less time and there are fewer distractions. You are in a better position to settle down to your paperwork for the day. Second, it can be more relaxing. But it does lead to a feeling of being trapped, confined, or even being something less than a first-class self-determined individual. You are compensating for a system which should be changing more rapidly.

Avoidance contributes to two related problems. First, by absenting themselves from these public places, these women retard the adjustment process. The world is not going to learn to respect the rights of the unescorted woman business traveler if we spend hours cooped up in our rooms. Further, you might resent being forced to change your patterns and habits just because of the nearsightedness of others. Why should you have to sit isolated in your room because it is dark out and going out after dark might cause problems. If you want a drink, you should be able to go into the lounge and order a drink. In some limited areas of the country the transition is fairly complete. These behaviors are very normal. In most areas the difficulty persists.

Few people, man or woman, seem to enjoy eating alone in a public place. One of the partial solutions is to go to the best restaurant you can find. The only logical advantage is that you have a more pleasant atmosphere in which to suffer the depressed feeling generated by eating alone. A reservation and attentive service may help the lonely diner to feel more accepted. Perhaps the atmosphere at an expensive restaurant would discourage unpleasantly aggressive behavior.

There are some very real concerns shared by women who travel on business. The solutions vary with the type of travel, such as automobile travel versus air travel, and the amount of travel. Most problems can be overcome with a little forethought and planning.

The concerns of the male managers of that midwestern firm with the history of a totally male sales force did not stop with the physical and psychological dangers of travel to the potential saleswomen. Their comments reflected some concern for themselves and the stability of their organization. Any organization's personnel objective is to develop a group of employees who can accomplish their assignments effectively and efficiently. Management's concern is that the sex issue will interfere with the ability of the organization to achieve that objective: "Will our sales meetings turn into orgies with company personnel involved?" Clearly such a development would be unsettling to the organization. Executives in male-dominated organizations might be concerned that the presence of women in the sales force might interfere with the ability of the men in the sales force to concentrate on their responsibilities for the company, but this is more of a comment on the men. Beyond that, they are concerned that the woman wouldn't be able to withstand the pressure, either from individuals within the company or on the outside. As another executive expressed the thought, "How will the husbands of these women react if they spend ten days in a hotel with 75 men at a sales meeting?" Of course, in the purist sense, that should not be a concern to the management. You are responsible for you. If you can't keep your own house in order, that should be your concern not theirs. Unfortunately, it is true that difficulties outside the job sometimes affect a person's performance on the job. People take their work home and their home to work. Of course, that behavior is not limited to entry-level saleswomen. The management of this firm was also concerned about itself. "How will the wives of existing executives react when these men are called upon to travel with women?"

While you may be tempted to dismiss these issues as ridiculous, the question is not whether these concerns should be concerns. They are concerns for you to the extent that they are important to people in positions to constrain your opportunities. Many of these concerns appear to be susceptible to reason. The problem is one of interjecting that reason without creating other problems. There are some things which you are just not supposed to talk about. For example, most of these concerns about intracompany sex are based on the assumption that you will be a cooperative partner. That's a monumental assumption. Regardless of personal moral convictions, it has long been established that mixing personal relations and business relations can bring about explosive results. While your behavior is your responsibility, you should know the dangers. It has been clearly established that the woman is most often the loser in the end. There is no firm basis for the assumption that saleswomen would encourage or even cooperate in the activities which concern management. The problem is how to convey that message up front. It's easy to say that if you act professionally in every way you will convey to management a promise of appropriate behavior. While over a period of time your behavior could establish your credibility, you may never be given that chance to prove yourself. Beyond that, you may find that you have to compensate for the real or imagined misbehaviors of other women. The actions of any member of a highly visible group reflect on the other members of that group, and women in sales are currently visible.

CUSTOMER RELATIONS

Any visible group of people tends to become the subject of rumors. Some of the rumors about saleswomen relate to the second area of special concerns—customer relations. To be effective both saleswomen and salesmen have to build their relationships with their customers on the same basis, trust. You may have to work a little harder at developing that trust. The rumors don't help. One of the rumors is that saleswomen are more likely to be able to get in to see the customer. This, of course, is often extended to the idea that you will be able to use your "feminine charms" to get male customers to do something. This implies that an otherwise rational male business executive is unable to make rational decisions in your presence.

Often the problem is not the reality but the expectation. You may not be seeking any special consideration because of your sex. The customer may not be intending to give you any consideration because of your sex, but the customer may fear that you are expecting special consideration or you may be afraid that the customer thinks you are expecting special consideration. Either way, a cloud hangs over your interaction. The system has spelled out little scripts for each of you which may not be comfortable for either of you. The question is how to let the customer off a hook which he may not deserve to be on at all. He may be acting out one of the prescribed roles because he believes that you expect him to act that way. He may not know any other way to act. Few men have had the opportunity to become accustomed to interacting with saleswomen. If you are going to establish a workable business relationship, you may have to guide him into a different role. If he has chosen one of the standard scripts, such as Romeo, and you respond with the lines written for Juliet, the drama will continue.

Since you are the source of his confusion you must also be the source of the solution. Unfortunately you wouldn't get very far with a comment such as "Why don't you cut out that act so that we can get down to business here." If he has performed his best act, whether it is Romeo, Macho, Mama's Boy, or Father, he'll probably expect some applause in order to determine that his act is over. The trick is to give enough applause to signal the final curtain but not enough to encourage an encore. While the entire scene may not be comfortable for you, your objective is broader than immediate comfort. Your objective is the establishment of a longer term business relationship. Remember the philosophy of pragmatic positivism. Your objective is to make progress within reality.

Sometimes rather than playing Juliet, Mama, or Daughter, it is better to play the role of a sponge. Perhaps you have heard about courses in modern dance where all of the participants act the part of a water sprinkler or some other inanimate object. A sponge may seem to be less exciting but it is an equally challenging role. Visualize the inappropriate comment of the customer as a ball being thrown at you. As a sponge your task is to absorb the energy from those comments so there is no rebound. If there is no rebound the customer will soon run down and have to settle into another pattern. If you object to his performance or play a supporting role, you are providing fuel for a continued drama.

There are several sponge techniques. All of them require some action. To simply ignore the ball is to act more as a wall than as a sponge. The balls will keep bouncing back because the other person won't know when to quit. The simplest sponge act is the unevaluative acknowledgment. If the other person plays a Macho line which is supposed to press one of your sensitive buttons such as "What you women really need is a man to keep you in line," you'll only start an unproductive argument by protesting your independence. An unevaluative acknowledgment would be "Some people say that." Your objective is to leave him with nothing to say but without offending or embarrassing him. You haven't agreed or disagreed. You have not opened up further avenues of discussion on the matter. You have provided a nice comfortable dead end for that phase of the conversation. Of course, you must then be prepared to immediately open up another line of discussion.

A second sponge technique is the deliberate misinterpretation. What if you were to receive strong hints that your cooperation beyond the line of duty would assure favorable action on your sales proposal? "You're an awfully cooperative young lady, and I'm sure you and I could find some way to work this deal out together." A deliberate misinterpretation would be, "I'm sure we can. Just last week I was talking to my sales manager about our service to our customers. He said that he'd be glad to go over any of our special customer needs with me and help work out a plan to make the best uses of the resources available within the company." Delivered with a sincere look designed to convey a confidence in your mutual professionalism, a deliberate misinterpretation can almost convert a threatener into a believer.

The most sophisticated sponge technique is the bridge. You try to provide an easy transition from a nonproductive or damaging conversation to a situation which you believe will be better for both of you. The idea is to change the subject without letting the other person know what has happened. There are several bridging phrases which seem so natural to most people that you can slip them onto another track smoothly. All you need is a key word or two. Imagine that you are being asked to answer for the entire female population: "I don't understand what you women want these days. Why do women make such a fuss about everything?" While the question is obviously unanswerable, by using a bridge you could start this person off in a more productive direction. "It doesn't make much sense to make a fuss over things which can't be changed. Speaking of change, have you seen the improvements we've made on next year's models?" By using bridging phrases you can cause the other person to feel as if the topic change was natural. "Speaking of..." and "That reminds me ..." are common bridges. Sponge techniques may be helpful in redefining the roles to be played by your customer and yourself. If contact with a woman in a sales role is a new experience for this customer, your skill in defining the appropriate roles may be an important factor in establishing a mutually beneficial working relationship.

As a part of building that working relationship, it is not at all uncommon for a salesperson to take a customer to lunch, dinner, or some other appropriate event. If a customer isn't quite sure how to handle a social exchange in his office, how well could he handle an invitation to meet outside of that protective office? There are two problems. First, there is the problem of dealing with a nontraditional salesperson. Second, there is the stigma of male dominance which implies that men are supposed to initiate, men are supposed to drive, men are supposed to decide when and where, men are supposed to pay the check, and men are supposed to control these kinds of events. Customers readily recognize that there is no such thing as a free lunch. They know you are taking them out in order to talk business or to establish a workable sales relationship, and they usually accept these invitations.

One woman in a male-dominated industry was perplexed when her luncheon invitations were repeatedly declined. Confident that she didn't have the plague, she sought to identify the source of her rejection. She finally concluded that the men with whom she was dealing weren't psychologically prepared to be entertained by a woman. So she tried a new approach. She stopped asking customers to go to lunch with her and tried suggesting that the two of them, she and the customer, should let her company treat them to lunch. Her acceptance rate picked up dramatically. The situation was the same. She was still initiating the invitation, arranging the details, and paying the check, but the customers were more comfortable. She had been successful in redefining herself as an agent of her company. Seeing her as an agent of the company rather than simply a woman, the customers were able to comfortably assume the customer role in the customer-salesperson interaction.

A sales manager at a business machines firm identified another potential difficulty which resulted from the customers' inclination to view the saleswoman as a woman rather than as a salesperson. He had recently hired several women whom he felt were capable of developing effective sales skills. Their first contacts with customers seemed to go well. He had had a number of postcall discussions with them as he normally did with all his new salespeople. They reported that the customers seemed quite pleasant and quite satisfied, but after some time he started to get some complaints from the customers. He was concerned because he normally received very few complaints directly from customers. When he talked to the saleswomen, they were surprised by the complaints. They had not been aware of the difficulties. Fortunately, there was more than one woman involved. If it had been a single person, he might have attributed the difficulty to her. With more than one incident to think about, he was inclined to search for another explanation. He concluded that the customers had been playing a protective role. They were apparently reluctant to complain to a saleswoman or to be gruff or unpleasant with her. Instead they swallowed their aggravation and took it out on her sales manager over the phone. While they protected her for a few moments, they actually put her in a more difficult position. If she had done something wrong, had failed to do something, or could have done better, she was unaware of it until it came back to her through the management of her firm. A new salesman might have the opportunity to correct his errors on his own and learn from the experience. This difficulty in confronting or arguing with a woman might have had other implications. It might be that customers were less able to express objections to a saleswoman during a sales call. Since customer objections are important guideposts during the sales presentation, you might have to be especially attentive to stimulating objections if confronted with a protective personality.

Not all of the special concerns of saleswomen are directly related to the selling aspects of the job. Some of the concerns involve relationships with other people who are not managers or customers but who are nevertheless important to your success and peace of mind.

WORKING RELATIONSHIPS

Believe it or not, some of the more difficult situations faced by saleswomen have been in connection with other women. These situations develop out of the visibility factor. You look more like other women in traditional roles than like salespeople. This creates a peer-group definition dilemma. Are you a salesperson or are you a woman? One new saleswoman realized what was happening just in time. While the adjustment was difficult, she was able to extricate herself with just a few scratches.

The problem developed innocently enough. She still believes that all of the people involved meant well. During her first few days on the job, her male manager was trying to be considerate. He made sure that she was welcomed and shown around the office. Since this tour logically included the women's room, he turned the duty over to the woman secretary. At noon he made sure that the other women in the office, all secretaries, included the new saleswoman in their plans. He assumed that they would probably have more to talk about together. After all, she looked more like them. The women were pleased to include the newcomer and tried to be helpful by filling her in on the office history, personalities, and other useful information about the organization.

As things progressed the women in the office sought to include her in other activities. They invited her to a baby shower, to join their bowling league, and to go to lunch whenever she wasn't out on a call. The peer-group dilemma began to emerge. Was she a woman or a salesperson? Couldn't she be both? Could she balance both roles or would one dominate? The answer came back loud and clear. No! She could not balance the roles. She had to make a choice. It wasn't that she couldn't be associated with women. It was that within the organization, any organization, there are defined levels. While it is certainly to the benefit of the organization and the individuals that the people from the various levels of the organization interact pleasantly and considerately, few people can maintain their identity at their rightful level if they associate more comfortably and continuously with a group at a lower level in the system. This problem sometimes arises with newly promoted men. If a man was a salesman and associated comfortably with the other salesmen, but was then promoted to sales manager, he might make the mistake of trying to continue to be one of the guys. Since this is against the established rules of the business game, some older and wiser male might take him aside and point out the difficulties caused by this behavior. The newly promoted man would be encouraged to affiliate with a new peer group at the appropriate level within the organization. It isn't that women suffer the problem of peer-group definition alone. It is just that women have more opportunities since other women tend to be concentrated at lower levels in most organizations. Besides that, there are fewer older and wiser people willing to pass on the necessary advice.

Even if this saleswoman had realized or been warned of this dilemma in the beginning, it would have been difficult to avoid it.

The women had been willing to include her and the men had been willing to allow it. A salesman can converse pleasantly with women secretaries, and it will cause no problems in his role. A man can even talk about his children for a few minutes and still maintain his professional distance. If you cover exactly the same ground, the outcome is likely to be far more personal. You are risking becoming "one of the women in the office." This is a natural role for you to assume in the eyes of the salesmen, the sales manager, and the other women. Everyone is more comfortable if they can squeeze you into the more traditional and visually consistent role of a woman.

When this saleswoman realized that she was headed for trouble, she quit the bowling league, declined invitations which she judged would not have been extended to the men in her position, and tried to exit gracefully. It was not easy. Despite her attempt to make the change gradually, it was noticed. It is much more difficult for you to reestablish a professional distance than to maintain it in the first place.

Sometimes you will experience the opposite difficulty. Instead of being overly accepted by women who occupy traditional roles in the business structure, you may be resisted and rejected. Have you ever heard about the Queen Bee Syndrome? Perhaps because of previous experiences with the peer-group dilemma, the Queen Bee sets herself apart from other women. While she may be in a position to offer advice or assistance, she declines. She has been described as a successful woman who believes that she has reached her particular position because of some unique effort or ability. She is hesitant to make any effort to assist less experienced women climb up the ladder to success. At this point there are few women in positions to become Queen Bees, but there are lots of women who can be Spider Mites.

Several saleswomen have encountered the Spider Mite, a distant cousin to the Queen Bee. The Spider Mite, unlike the Queen Bee, has little formal authority within the organization. She occupies a traditional position, such as secretary, receptionist, or "assistant to." To the unaware saleswoman, she may be almost as inconspicuous as the tiny plant parasite from which she takes her name. While she lacks formal authority, she spins webs of informal power. From her position she is able to grant or withhold certain necessary favors or privileges. She can choose whether or not to schedule an appointment for you with her boss. She can relay your message with a positive or negative inflection. She can remember or not remember to remind you of some upcoming responsibility. If she favors you, she can pass on some valuable tips. She knows who has seen her boss, who is scheduled after you, what kind of mood her boss is in, and many other things which have a direct influence on your success. She can divert interruptions and make your life easier, or she can surreptitiously make you miserable. She is a modern keeper of the keys.

Some saleswomen have identified Spider Mites within their own organizations, and others have encountered them in the offices of clients. Why do Spider Mites behave as they do? This resentment on the part of some women in traditional roles can represent a real problem for a woman who is moving in a nontraditional direction. The principal causes are confusion and resignation. The widespread publicity on changing roles of women has left many women whose roles have not changed in a state of confusion. Does the move toward new opportunities and responsibilities mean that they are wrong? Maybe they were pleased with their positions before their consciousnesses were raised and would still be pleased with their positions but are confused because all of the messages say that they shouldn't be happy in traditional roles. Your presence as a woman in a nontraditional role may bring these feelings of confusion to the surface.

Some women are not at all happy in their traditional roles but feel that they have little choice in the matter. They have resigned themselves to their positions because of family pressures or other restrictions. Some very capable women feel trapped in traditional roles. Perhaps they passed up the opportunity for an education at a time when education for a woman was considered less important than an education for her husband. They may have tried to make the best decisions for themselves at the time, but now the times have changed. They may feel too old to start over at something else, yet they still face decades of work in jobs which are not only less than rewarding, but are less than stimulating as well. The future seemed acceptable when it was all that could be expected. You may be forcing one of these women to acknowledge that there are now alternatives. When the lines were drawn on the basis of sex, she had few alternatives. Men sold and women typed. She may not have liked her job any better, but she could at least identify a reason why she had that job. Now she is resigned to a job although the reason has disappeared. When you show up and remind her that there are greater opportunities for women today, she may consciously or unconsciously stand in your way.

This may not be all her fault. Your feelings and actions may aggravate the situation. Men in the traditional role of salesman and women in the traditional role of secretary are comfortable with each other. Neither is a threat to the other. Neither has reason to question the other's position, privileges, rewards, ambitions, goals, or interests. When a woman is dealing with another competent woman who is "only a secretary" she may unconsciously treat that secretary in a demeaning manner. If you are thinking, "Gee, I'm glad I'm not a secretary" while you are trying to interact productively with a secretary, it will probably show. Society has set the stage for this other woman to react defensively to the slightest indication that her role is inappropriate.

How can you minimize the potential for Spider Mite damage? You can't do anything to change the social messages or to soothe their resentments or frustrations. You can only try to avoid arousing those feelings. First of all, you must remember that it's not your responsibility to recruit or convert these people. It may be tempting to say, "You seem bright. Have you ever thought of getting into sales?" If she has, she's rejected the idea. You may just be reminding her of her frustration. You may be asked about your job. If you are, it's still not a good idea to evangelize, but it's worse to be falsely negative: "It's really a hassle. I almost wish I was back at a desk job." Comments like that lead to a patronizing "I bet you enjoy being a typist. You must get to read lots of interesting memos." You can only magnify the traditional/nontraditional issue. In short, the best bet is to avoid any discussion of occupations and roles. Don't bring it up, and if asked, give a neutral response, "There are good points and bad points to any job."

Another group of women who can complicate the life of a saleswoman are some of the wives of coworkers. Some wives of policemen objected when women were assigned to patrol cars with their husbands. Some wives of firemen objected to women moving into the firehouse. It seems logical that some wives of men in business might show some concern. The wives of the firemen and the policemen claimed that the new women officers would be less capable and hence endanger the lives of their husbands because they were unable to perform the duties of the office. There could well have been some underlying concerns about potential intimacy. While that may be possible, there are certainly endless examples of men and women working together on a purely professional basis for extended periods of time. While intimacy does require proximity, proximity does not require intimacy. Proximity will provide the greater possibility of intimacy, but whether or not it occurs is up to the individuals.

In addition to the issue of physical intimacy, there is still the issue of mental intimacy—shared understandings and experiences. Consider the problems presented by any company social function whether it is a Christmas cocktail party or a sales meeting in a pleasant location to which the spouses have been invited. One saleswoman recalled her awkward feelings at the first cocktail party she attended at the home of one of the salesmen. When several people with the same responsibilities for the same company get together in the evening, there is a tendency to let some business creep into the conversation. Three men were standing in the kitchen talking about an important account. She was joining in on the conversation. Most of the wives were in another room. The hostess came into the kitchen and pleasantly, but specifically, invited this saleswoman to join the group of wives. Most conversation groups at parties form on the basis of interests or gender, but the breakdown is usually the same. She realized that she wasn't supposed to be the only woman talking with the men in the kitchen, but they were discussing something which was of interest to her. Later when she discussed the incident with her husband, she found out that he had felt just as awkward. He really didn't fit in with the spouses, but he didn't work for the company either. While he had toyed with the idea of going out and sitting in the car, he'd stuck it out in the corner. This type of difficulty may diminish as women become more common in sales. In professions where the numbers of men and women have been balanced, this problem is less severe. At social functions there may be four groups: husbands, wives, male employees, and female employees.

You will have some concerns regardless of the career path you choose. As a saleswoman you will have the concerns inherent in the job for any person. Beyond that you may experience some special concerns. These concerns are not overwhelming but require forethought and consideration. A woman in business can be more productive, more businesslike, and more promising in every respect but still be confronted by challenges simply because of her gender. You had better develop appropriate techniques and attitudes early in your career because mistakes in these areas can be costly and time consuming. Women are successfully coping with the demands of business travel, with the expectations of customers, and with the need to establish workable relationships with all of the other people who are a part of the business environment. You can too. There is a lot of help available if you learn to use it.

11 Helping your sales manager help you

Management has been the focus of seemingly endless courses, conferences, seminars, and publications. Apparently the hope is that by studying the concepts and practices of management, managers can become better managers. Over the history of business, these concepts and practices have undergone continuing change as more and more is learned about human behavior and motivation. Management is defined in a number of ways. One popular definition is "accomplishing through other people." Much of the material which is available on sales management is intended for sales managers. It reads as though management is something which one person does to another person.

But management is a two-way street. Although some people are called managers and other people are managed, the process is highly interactive. If by studying sales management sales managers can become better managers, doesn't it make sense that a better understanding of sales management would help the salespeople to be better managed? But being managed seems to have some power or status implications. Why would anyone want to be better managed? Maybe people don't want to be better managed. Most of the material on sales management seems to place the burden of improved management on the sales manager. Those who are being managed seem to be freed from the responsibility for the outcome.

It is true that in a formal organizational sense you may not bear the burden for the effectiveness of your sales manager, but clearly you stand to lose in a personal sense if you are poorly managed. There are several ways in which you personally benefit from effective management. Each of these is a reason why it is to your advantage to help your sales manager in managing you. Another way to think of this same idea is to think not of being managed but of managing your management.

There are probably two interrelated keys to successfully managing your manager. One is a positive attitude and the second is constructive communication. Your positive attitude requires both an understanding of why you benefit from effective management and a confidence that your manager intends to do what is best for you in terms of your professional development and success. Your constructive communication helps your manager to understand just what you need to develop and succeed.

You can gain all kinds of benefits by working with an effective manager. First of all, a well-managed office is a more pleasant and productive work environment. There are fewer emergencies, conflicts, and misunderstandings. You are free to spend a greater proportion of your time and energy on productive activities. Things happen when they are supposed to happen. Good management provides you with the kind of support you need to do your job as well as you can.

Second, well-managed people know what is and is not expected from them. These expectations are clear and consistent. It is much easier for you to maintain the level of motivation necessary to be a success in sales if there is consistency. If you know what is expected of you, you can channel your energies toward those objectives. Consistency and fairness go hand in hand. Fairness enhances sales force morale.

Third, good management rests on the development of people. A good manager challenges people to develop up to their potential. A good manager encourages you to grow. While there are many measures of management, these three emphasize the value to you personally of being well-managed. While a good manager may be able to inspire a satisfactory performance out of an otherwise marginal individual, truly superior performances require the active cooperation of the persons being managed. Some capable people withhold this cooperation. Apparently they would prefer to feel that they alone were responsIble for both their successes and their failures.

Several years ago there was a commercial for a headache remedy which showed women in a variety of stressful circumstances. Each woman resisted the help offered by another with the comment, "Please Mother, I'd rather do it myself!" One of the characteristics of many women who find themselves in the first wave of the new career women is a fierce independence. In some cases this actually represents an inability to depend, even when some dependence would be wise. When Frank Sinatra sings "I did it my way," listeners can feel comfortable because Sinatra's way obviously brought him a substantial measure of personal success. There are probably a lot of failures who could be singing that song.

There are a lot of reasons why you might as well take advantage of the benefits your sales manager has to offer by actively cooperating in the sales management process. There is a great deal of evidence that you have more to gain than to lose from being a manageable person. Regardless of other issues, your manager has obviously been able to understand some of the requirements for success in this organization and to perform up to those requirements. The promotion to sales manager is an indication that this person has been successful in selling. If you want to be successful in selling and to advance within the organization, you could probably learn a lot from your sales manager.

Your sales manager has seen a lot of new sales people and at one time or another has probably shared in experiencing almost all of the frustrations or elations you will be experiencing. While you are having your ups and downs, it can be comforting to lean on someone who has been there often enough to keep it all in proper perspective.

Third, the relationship you build with your manager now may be important to you as you progress in your career. Your sales manager is already at least one rung ahead of you on the management ladder. If you and the other people in your office continue to produce for the firm, your sales manager's track record will continue to improve. You are contributing to your manager's success. As your manager moves up the management ladder, your positive relationship may improve your chances of moving up that same ladder. It doesn't hurt to dream a little. One of these days you may well find yourself in your sales manager's shoes. If you do your job well, that opportunity may materialize sooner than you might expect.

One of the fears which seems to crop up when the issue of women as managers is discussed is the fear that subordinants would not react favorably to a woman in a managerial role.

> What . . . will happen to sales force morale, the bottom line, and the company's ability to recruit promising sales representatives if the field manager is a woman? If the company makes the investment in developing her, will she be tough enough to stick with the job? . . . The experiences of such companies as Continental Air Transport, Del Monte, General Time, Hoffman-LaRoche, Jewel Companies, 3M, NBC, National Merchandising, New York Telephone, Philip Morris USA, RCA, R. J. Reynolds Tobacco, Viking Press, Wang Laboratories, and Xerox clearly show that women can and do make successful field sales managers.[1]

As these and other barriers continue to fall, your opportunities to step into a sales manager position will become even better. One of the best ways to prepare yourself for that responsibility is to carefully observe those who are currently assuming those responsibilities. One of the traditional responsibilities of good managers is to train their own replacements. You could be that replacement.

Recognizing all of the benefits to you in being properly managed is only half the battle in developing a positive attitude toward management. The other half is generating confidence that your manager has your best interests in mind. The sales management system has endured and is widespread throughout the business community because it tends to achieve the objectives of the organizations and of the people within those organizations. The people who are currently in managerial positions have developed their skills within this system. As a product of this system your sales manager has enjoyed a positive relationship with sales managers and is probably anxious to help you have the same experience.

It makes a lot of sense for your sales manager to make every effort to help you to be a success. If nothing else, your failure would be a reflection on your manager's judgment. In most firms, the sales manager has a great deal of influence or actually makes the final

---

[1] Sally Scanlon, "Manage Sales? Yes, She Can," *Sales and Marketing Management,* Monday, June 13, 1977, p. 33.

decisions on who is to be hired. Your success is evidence that hiring you was a good decision. In those firms which are only beginning to hire saleswomen, your manager may have had to make a special case to hire you. If the firm has been conscientiously stressing affirmative action, your sales manager may be concerned about paying a special price if you fail.

Another reason why your manager wants you to succeed is that employee turnover is costly. Your manager is responsible for the cost efficiency of your office. If you quit or are fired, not only has all the time and energy spent on finding you and hiring you been wasted, but training expenses are usually the highest early in your career. Some technologically advanced industries, such as electronics, spend up to $10,000 on training during the first six months you are on the job. Your manager would have a lot to lose if you were to fail. Even if training expenses aren't that high, there are other turnover costs to be considered. It may have an unpleasant effect on established customers or the image of the firm within the industry. If these people see a parade of new salespeople, they may begin to wonder about the stability of the organization or the quality of its management. It is also disruptive within the office. Excessive turnover can be demoralizing. Those who remain may begin to wonder if those who left know something that they don't know either about the company or about the opportunities elsewhere. On top of all that, sales managers are human and may feel guilty for having encouraged you to take a job for which you were not suited.

All of this is just evidence that your sales manager wants you to stay with the job. Your sales manager not only wants you to stay with the job, but would probably love to see you be supersuccessful. Your success has a direct effect on your manager's material and psychological welfare. Sales managers are usually compensated in some direct relationship to the productivity of their salespeople. The direct tie between productivity and compensation is extended to management. Your sales manager produces through you. If you perform well, your manager is rewarded.

Sales managers also like to brag about their salespeople. This may be especially true of their more visible salespeople, and women tend to be more visible. There is great satisfaction from a feeling of contributing to the development of another worthy person.

There is every reason to believe that sales managers are sincere and conscientious in their attempts to improve the performance of every person in the office. It is through the success of their people that they themselves succeed. They share in the rewards and recognition earned by the people under their supervision. The question is not whether they would want to help you to constantly improve but rather how you can make the most out of the help they are capable of offering you.

It is unfortunate that the manager-subordinate relationship is so often represented as an adversary situation. In many TV serials or even on commercials the boss is characterized either as an incompetent bungler from whom the conscientious employee is well-advised to conceal information or a vindictive and selfish person who takes every opportunity to squeeze an unreasonable level of performance out of the employee. While there must be some people in supervisory roles who fit these models, for the vast majority of managers these stereotypes are a disservice. This distorted picture tends to interfere with the development of a mutually beneficial working relationship. If you consider all of the reasons why your manager is interested in your progress, it may be easier to develop a positive attitude which is the first requirement in helping your sales manager help you.

Your sales manager has a number of tools to use in helping you to develop your sales career. Most of these tools depend on constructive communication. Constructive communication is the art of keeping your manager up-to-date on all the matters which may affect your working relationship. Your manager needs at least three kinds of information from you on an ongoing basis. The first kind is evidence of your accomplishments. While it would seem that everyone would be anxious to communicate positive information, sometimes there is interference. Because your manager probably receives regular reports on your sales volume, you may be tempted to think that this is sufficient evidence of your accomplishment. Throw in a little modesty, real or otherwise, and you may refrain from communicating the positive. Your immediate sales performance, however, is only a part of the positive information needed by your manager. Your attitude is also important. If you are going to continue to perform well, it will only be because you derive satisfaction out of your work. Your attitude is reflected in your actions and conversation, not on paper.

The second kind of information is the bad news, confessions, or reports on matters which haven't turned out as you would have hoped or expected. One of the basic principles of being a manageable person, and one which is often violated even by the well-intentioned, is not to cause your manager to suffer any unpleasant surprises. Everybody has inadequacies, suffers from temporary lapses, has errors in judgment, or has unfortunate but unavoidable difficulties at some time or another. Sometimes in attempting to cover up these events, you actually set the stage for a bigger problem. If you have run into some difficulty, your manager may be able to help you. Even if your manager can't help you, you will probably be able to recover more quickly or at least avoid lasting damage if you are the first one to discuss it with your manager. If the story reaches your manager through some other channel, that counts as an unpleasant surprise. You have probably left your manager in an embarrassing situation. If you have concealed some event and someone else could innocently mention the matter, your manager will be very unhappy. You will be in double trouble.

The third kind of communication is informing your manager of your needs. While you are important to your sales manager, all sales managers have a variety of job-related responsibilities. Your sales manager can be most helpful to you if you communicate your needs. This is sometimes perplexing. Many people are authority-oriented. A manager is an authority figure. People in authority generally possess the power to both grant rewards and inflict punishment. Therefore people have a tendency to filter the information they provide to authority figures. There is the tendency to restrict the flow of negative information and to emphasize the positive information.

A person who needs help may be considered to be inadequate. If you are inadequate, the authority figure may withhold rewards or punish you. When your authority figure is the same person who is supposed to be helping you to overcome those inadequacies, you face a perplexing situation. Do you expose your inadequacies, thereby possibly displeasing this authority figure? Your other choice is to attempt to conceal your inadequacies and do without help. Your best course of action depends on three factors. The first is the availability of alternative assistance. If there is something which you can do to improve yourself independent of your authority figure, you might pursue that solution first. That is only a wise move if that alternative is efficient. For example, if your sales manager can readily answer your question, it wouldn't be wise for you to spend three days ferreting out the answer in the library.

The second question is whether your inadequacy is normal. If you are a new person on the job, you are not expected to be an expert. No one expects perfection. They expect you to have questions and to make mistakes. They expect you to seek out guidance and advice. Indeed if you are new to the job and seek out the advice of more experienced people, they usually find it flattering. It is evidence of their status and expertise. But if you have inadequacies which are not to be expected of a person at your experience level, such as not being able to read, you should be seeking outside help.

The third question is whether the situation will only get worse without help. If you judge that the inadequacy is minor and will probably not interfere with your progress, you may choose to wait to see if it resolves itself. Maybe, like all new salespeople, you find that you're nervous making cold calls, that is, approaching a new prospect uninvited. That should improve by itself with time. If your problem is likely to divert your attention from more important matters or stand in the way of your development in some more important area, you might as well get it over with as soon as possible. For example, if you seem to be having problems organizing your time, you could be seriously affecting your productivity. Perhaps your sales manager could help.

While most organizations provide for some formal evaluation at regular intervals, your needs may not occur on schedule. If you think that your sales manager might be able to help you, it is really your responsibility to ask for that help. Unless you ask, your manager may assume that you are progressing on schedule until the sales figures reveal your difficulty. At that point, it will be far more difficult for both of you.

Constructive communication is an important responsibility of all new salespeople, male or female, but can be especially critical to a saleswoman. Not all sales managers are equally comfortable managing salesmen and saleswomen. While the managers who have had experience with both seem to find that any differences soon disappear, statistics would indicate that most sales managers have not yet had the opportunity to share these experiences. Some sales managers find themselves in a position something like that of the emperor in the children's story.

Remember the story about the emperor's new clothes? While in today's market the emperor would have had recourse under consumer protection laws, as the story goes he was literally left out in the cold. It seems that two fraudulent operators approached the emperor and made a sales presentation which he couldn't resist. Assessing the emperor to be a vain individual, they offered to make him a set of new robes which were distinguished by a unique competitive advantage. These robes, which incidentally sold for a price substantially above competitive products, could be seen only by those persons who were truly loyal to the emperor. To all others the robes would be invisible. The emperor placed his order.

As the con-men tailors cut, stitched, and sewed, the royal press corps kept a constant vigil interviewing each person who was privileged to enter the royal fitting room. The reports were uniformly flattering. Anticipation filled the air. Finally the magical garments were finished and a royal procession was staged. The emperor strode regally through the streets to the ohhhs and ahhhs of the loyal subjects until a small child cried out, "But the emperor is naked!"

Many otherwise competent sales managers may feel that they have been left in a position only slightly better than that of the emperor. While they may have every intention of being fair and supportive to saleswomen, they may have some uncertainties regarding the best way to translate those intentions into action. Yet it can be difficult for them to admit those uncertainties. After all, at this point in their careers they are supposed to be able to handle these situations. They may be reluctant to ask for help in handling this unfamiliar situation. At the same time, other people may be reluctant to suggest that help might be in order for fear of belittling the manager's capabilities.

While hopefully you would display more tact than the child who exposed the emperor's condition, you may find yourself having to guide your manager through constructive communication. With a positive attitude and constructive communication you can contribute to the management process to the benefit of both your manager and yourself.

One of the keys to effective management is an understanding of the nature of the tasks to be performed by the people being managed. Your manager has already been successful in sales and probably understands the nature of your tasks very well. If you are going to effectively manage your manager, you will need to make an extra effort to understand the manager's tasks in managing you. While your sales manager has a variety of responsibilities in managing you and the other people on the sales force, let's look at three specific areas in which your positive attitude and constructive communication can help your sales manager to help you. Your training is one of your manager's important concerns as soon as you have joined the organization. It is to everyone's advantage that you are provided the opportunity to develop the skills which will help you to be more productive in your work. A second very important responsibility facing your sales manager is the care and feeding of your motivation. Measuring your current productivity and estimating your potential is the purpose of the third managerial activity—performance evaluations.

To better understand your sales manager's responsibilities in any of these areas, you need to ask yourself three simple questions: "What is my manager trying to accomplish?" "What tools or resources are available?" "Is anything likely to interfere?"

The answers to these questions could be very useful to you in defining your plans to work with your manager toward your own success. If you make the effort to look at the situation from your manager's vantage point, many potential conflicts or difficulties could be avoided. You may even be able to save yourself from some of those unpleasant surprises.

If you asked these three questions about training, what might the answers be? What is your manager trying to accomplish through training you? Your manager is investing in your future. That investment is supposed to be returned in the form of increased productivity as you develop your potential. There are several very specific objectives in most training programs. One of these is to familiarize you with the products or services offered by the firm. Perhaps the most widely accepted dictum on success in selling is "Know your product!" Your manager wants you to know what your products will do, what they won't do, how they work, how they are made, and all of the other details which will help you to present your story more effectively to potential customers. Another objective is to familiarize you with the characteristics of the company's customers. To sell successfully you will need to know who buys the product, how they buy, and why they buy. While the company may not have a perfect picture of the behavior of the buyers, the information which has been accumulated gives you a head start. Third, in most training programs you learn a lot about the competition. Fourth, to represent the company well it is important for you to understand not only its current practices and policies but also some of the events in its history which account for its current position and future plans. Of course, one of your manager's objectives in providing training is to equip you with the basic selling skills you will need to do your job well.

What are the tools and resources available to your sales manager to accomplish these objectives? These obviously vary widely, but among the more common resources are the individual manager's time and attention, the assistance of experienced salespeople, booklets and sales manuals, and specialized sales training programs. If there is no specialized training program, the training is usually called on-the-job training. This approach can have both advantages and disadvantages for you. It is usually individualized rather than a standard course. You are expected to progress at your own speed. It is certainly realistic. You are immediately exposed to all of the thrills of the real thing. It is usually quite short and soon you are testing your skills. If your manager or the person to whom you are assigned for a sales apprenticeship is a highly competent teacher, on-the-job training can be both exciting and worthwhile. While on-the-job training is sometimes associated with firms which experience high employee turnover, it should not be taken as an indication that the company is not interested in your future. Only a large firm can really afford to maintain a regular specialized training school. If a medium or small firm experiences little turnover in its sales force, it makes little economic sense for that firm to invest in a training school.

Larger firms that are constantly hiring new sales people tend to maintain specialized training programs. The need for these schools increases with the technology level of the industry. Firms in the electronics industry are noted for well-developed training schools. A new saleswoman in electronic business machines may be involved in four months of formal schoolroom training during her first year on the job. Surely this represents a substantial investment for the firm. Firms investing in this type of training are usually very careful in recruiting and screening applicants. An executive in this industry estimated that it takes up to two and a half years of normal performance by a salesperson for a company to break even on this formal training. There must be a special satisfaction to be derived from the realization that this investment is being made in you. The company is investing money on the expectation that you will be a valued employee. They are taking a risk that you will be able to perform as promised.

It would be in your best interest, in your sales manager's best interest, and in the best interest of the firm that your training be of great value in developing your potential. The third question you should ask in trying to understand your manager's task is "What is likely to interfere with the effectiveness of my training?" One of the possible answers is you.

A training period can be frustrating. If you joined the firm anxious to get out there and sell but find yourself spending day after day in a classroom, your enthusiasm can fizzle. Without enthusiasm it can be difficult to maintain a high level of attentiveness. You may find yourself suffering from a case of postemployment droop. There is always a degree of excitement which accompanies the process of seeking out a new job. There is a courtship which goes on between you and those interested in recruiting you.

If the reports on the interest in hiring women for industrial sales are even partially accurate, a qualified woman who expresses an interest in this career and who makes an effort to contact sales recruiters should generate a flattering amount of interest. The uncertainty which accompanies the decision to take a position with a particular firm is in itself exciting. Then the thrill of the chase is over. People who were particularly solicitous while endeavoring to entice you to accept their offer do not intend to take you for granted, but they necessarily turn their attentions to other pressing matters. Instead of being taken to lunch or dinner, you may be spending your evenings studying some sales manual. While you had experienced the thrill of receiving phone calls from important-sounding people, you may now find yourself calling home. During the first few days on the job there were lots of things to do, but then you may find yourself in limbo. You have yet to be stamped with a seal of approval as a fully trained, competent saleswoman. Being a trainee smacks of second-class citizenship. It is reminiscent of being in a cocoon. Training can be the least exciting stage of the metamorphosis from an ordinary human being into a saleswoman. But you do have an advantage over that would-be butterfly. You can envision what lies ahead of you. The question is whether you can draw upon those visions for energy when the postemployment droop hits.

The biggest danger in the postemployment droop is that you may feel that you're the only one who suffers from this condition. You may mistake it for an indication that you have made an error in choosing this career. If you recognize it for a normal condition, you will be better able to overcome its effects. It is more likely to strike those who venture into newer areas. A woman who suffers some mild depression during her student teaching in preparation for a career in education will receive adequate support from her associates and relatives. If your enthusiasm runs down a little during sales training, your friends and relatives might take it for a sign that you are coming to your senses. Even if they have been supportive, they may just have been reflecting your enthusiasm. This may well be their first experience with someone in sales, and they may not know what to expect.

If your droop is obvious, your sales manager or some experienced salesperson may come to your rescue by offering support. But what if you are a Closet Drooper? If you have had the feeling that you have had to fight for every inch of progress in your career, you may become slightly paranoid. You may believe that if you let down your guard for a moment, others will seize the opportunity to damage you. That may be true with others, but remember that you and your sales manager have a great deal of mutual interest in your success. You may find that this is just the time to call on your sales manager to perform the second of the three managerial functions—the care and feeding of your ego.

Have you ever seen one of those movies in which the officer yells, "Charge!" and the line of troops storms forward to meet the enemy? How about the close-up shot of the football team chanting its last minute "Go! Go! Go! Go! Go!" before taking the field for a big game. People who are being asked to take risks usually need a little extra encouragement. While the personal risk in selling can hardly be compared to charging into battle, one of your sales manager's responsibilities is keeping the sales force emotionally ready.

Imagine that every person has a little internal storehouse of ego energy which operates much like a bank account. In order to keep a healthy balance in that account, the deposits have to at least equal the withdrawals. In some types of work, people are seldom called upon to withdraw from their ego energy account. Their egos are somewhat protected. Because they make fewer withdrawals, they don't actually need as many deposits although it is always nice to increase the balance. In sales, the ego energy accounts are much more active. You may experience a big deposit one day only to face another day which drains energy from your account. One of the things your sales manager may be trying to accomplish is to keep your ego energy account at a productive level. This is more than simply making you a loan if your ego energy account drops to a critical level. It also involves providing you with a feeling of constant reinforcement which allows you to take emotional risks with some assurance that there will be someone to support you.

What tools and resources can your manager draw upon to provide these reinforcements? In one national sales organization which sells vacuum cleaners door-to-door, each sales manager actually leads the assembled salespeople in singing the company fight song every morning. While this is a bit extreme, there are some widespread forms of both individual and group reinforcements. Ask yourself what techniques your sales manager might use to keep your ego energy account at that most productive level. Many of these techniques build on either personal recognition or team spirit.

While increased compensation is one of the rewards of an improved sales performance, personal recognition is also an important form of reward. All of the organizations which distribute lists of top performers or establish special clubs such as the Million Dollar Round Table in the insurance industry are providing public recognition of outstanding performance. Sales contests through which you can win special prizes or trips are another vehicle through which you are encouraged to focus your efforts and increase your ego energy level. Indeed the prize is often less important than being named the winner.

Some of the ways in which your sales manager can provide personal recognition may be less visible. Being available as a concerned listener when you are frustrated or discouraged is actually a way to say that your individual well-being is important. Of course, this is a tool which can only be used with your permission. Informal personal comments on your performance are another extremely important form of ego energy deposit.

What can interfere with your sales manager's attempts to keep your ego energy account in healthy shape? The biggest constraint is that in being human just like you, your sales manager has some limits. There is only so much time and energy which can be devoted to stroking the sales force, and there are other people who have the same needs as you. Your sales manager is, in effect, priming your pump. If from that start you can build yourself up, the energy devoted to priming your pump was energy well spent. If you simply absorb the energy, the supply will be used up more rapidly. To continue to receive recognition, you must demonstrate a responsiveness to that recognition.

One type of recognition which people tend to view with some degree of anxiety is the performance evaluation. Part of the anxiety is a result of the way performance evaluations are often structured, part is because of the way some evaluations are handled. Almost all of the anxiety can be relieved by managing your manager. A performance evaluation is a formal review of your professional activities over a specified time. It may be unfortunate that it is called an evaluation. That only tells half the story. The evaluation is only the basis on which the important process of personal progress planning rests. Your manager is really interested in how you have done over the last period in order to predict something about your potential in subsequent periods. To hand out either rewards or punishment for past performance is not the primary managerial benefit of performance evaluations. Psychologists long ago established that the value of either punishment or reward is the greatest immediately following the incident. If your manager was to save up all the punishments and rewards for a yearly evaluation, it would be almost meaningless to you.

What does your manager expect to accomplish through performance reviews? Why do managers take the time to go through this process with each salesperson? In most organizations these reviews are a required part of the manager's job. Why do organizations decree that their managers should devote the time to reviews? Surely there are other ways to measure the productivity of the sales force. The fact that there are figures available which would indicate the productivity of the sales force emphasizes the real purpose of evaluations—to help you see yourself relative to the objectives of the firm. Then you can develop workable plans to improve your performance consistent with those objectives.

Your review should hold no surprises. You should be continually assessing your own performance through your follow-up procedures and should be interacting with your manager on a regular basis. Through this interaction you should have a fairly concrete opinion of your manager's opinion of your performance. The evaluation is only a formal time set aside for the two of you to make some specific plans regarding your progress.

What tools does your sales manager have to draw upon in the

evaluation process? Besides some type of form and the statistics on your sales performance over the time period, most managers must depend only on personal management skills. The form is basically a clerical device. The management skills make all the difference, both yours and your manager's.

The form defines the areas to be covered (see Exhibit 11-1). There are usually five. There is usually some space for the numbers which spell out your sales performance. The amount you actually sold may be compared to your quota, that is, the amount you were expected to sell. Second, there may be some rating system to evaluate your personal characteristics, such as dependability, cooperativeness, appearance, time management, customer relations, oral or written expression, and other qualities related to successful selling. In order to provide for improvement, most forms have a space for your weaknesses. It might be more palatible if those were called "Places for Improvement." These weaknesses are usually balanced with a space for a listing of your specific strengths. The fifth part of most evaluations is a space for suggestions regarding your developmental needs.

What might interfere with the achievement of the objectives of the performance evaluation? There are lots of possibilities. Some of them are clearly beyond your influence. The accepted form is the accepted form. The accepted time period is the accepted time period. You may be able to discuss your progress more frequently on an informal basis, but it is not likely that the evaluation period would be extended. There are, however, some potential problem areas where your actions might be useful.

If the most productive focus of the evaluation process would be the development of a plan to improve your performance, how can you quickly move the discussion to that topic and assure yourself that the time is well spent? Often the most comfortable, although least productive, use of the time allowed is to discuss the sales statistics, that is, the numbers which are supposed to represent your performance. This is usually an attempt to avoid the two biggest difficulties in evaluations—anxiety and defensiveness. It is not only the person being evaluated who can be anxious and defensive. The evaluator also suffers these uncomfortable feelings. To be placed in a situation of having to judge the performance of another can be anxiety producing. What if your evaluations are in error? There may be some undisclosed explanations. Your judgments may be chal-

EXHIBIT 11-1

DISTRIBUTION:
BRANCH - ORIGINAL AND DUPLICATE TO DISTRICT MANAGER.
TRIPLICATE, BRANCH FILE.
DISTRICT - REVIEW, INITIAL AND FORWARD ORIGINAL TO BMG
EMPLOYEE & INDUSTRIAL RELATIONS;
DUPLICATE, DISTRICT FILE.

PERFORMANCE REVIEW AND EVALUATION
NON-MANAGEMENT SALES PERSONNEL

REVIEW PERIOD:

FROM _____ TO _____

NAME	BRANCH	LOCATION

JOB TITLE	STATE OF HEALTH	MARITAL STATUS	AGES OF CHILDREN

AGE	DATE EMPLOYED	EFFECTIVE DATE OF PRESENT ASSIGNMENT

PREPARED AND DISCUSSED WITH EMPLOYEE BY:

ZONE/ACCOUNT/SA MANAGER _____ DATE _____

BRANCH MANAGER _____ DATE _____

REVIEWED BY: DISTRICT MANAGER _____ DATE _____

EMPLOYEE'S SIGNATURE _____ DATE _____

WHAT ARE THIS EMPLOYEE'S AMBITIONS AND DESIRES AS EXPRESSED IN THE INTERVIEW? _____

_____

	LINES OF BUSINESS	DATE TO BE TRAINED	TRAINED	EXPERI-ENCED	EXPERT (SPECIAL-IST)	COMMENTS
KNOWLEDGE BY LINES OF BUSINESS	FINANCIAL					
	GOVERNMENT					
	EDUCATIONAL					
	MEDICAL					
USE ADDITIONAL LINE FOR SPECIFIC APPLI-CATIONS BY LINES OF BUSINESS AS REQUIRED	TRANS., COMM., & PUBLIC UTILITY					
	MANUFACTURING					
	WHOLESALE					
	RETAIL					

*SALES RECORD YR-TO-DATE - - Month _____ 19 __

	PRODUCTS	DATE TO BE TRAINED	TRAINED	EXPERI-ENCED	EXPERT (SPECIAL-IST)	TOTAL ORDERS	QUOTA	UNITS SOLD
	GROUP I					$	%	
	GROUP II					$	%	
	GROUP III-S					$	%	
	TOTAL GP					$	%	
PRODUCT KNOWLEDGE						$	%	
	GROUP V					$	%	
	GROUP VI					$	%	
	GROUP VIII					$	%	
	TOTAL EDP					$	%	
	TOTAL SALES					$	%	

	YEAR	ASSIGNMENT	DATE ASSIGNED	TOTAL ORDERS	QUOTA	UNITS SOLD
SALES RECORD	PRIOR YEAR 19*			$	%	
	PRIOR YEAR 19			$	%	
	LAST YEAR 19			$	%	
	CURRENT YR 19 __ (__ MOS.)			$	%	

* FOR LAST YEAR, OR CURRENT YEAR IF REVIEW IS PREPARED AFTER FIRST QUARTER - - FROM ZONE SALES PERFORMANCE REPORT.

EXHIBIT 11-1 *(continued)*

THIS FORM IS DESIGNED TO HELP YOU APPRAISE EACH EMPLOYEE UNDER YOUR SUPERVISION WITH RESPECT TO SPECIFIC GOALS AND STANDARDS OF PER-
FORMANCE. IF EACH APPRAISAL IS CARRIED OUT IN A SYSTEMATIC MANNER, THE PROGRAM WILL ASSIST YOU IN MAINTAINING AN EFFECTIVE ORGANIZA-
TION THROUGH EMPLOYEE DEVELOPMENT AND IMPROVED JOB PERFORMANCE.

CHARACTERISTIC (PLEASE RATE THE PERSON ON THE FOLLOWING CHARACTERISTICS)		EXCEPTIONAL	VERY GOOD	SATISFACTORY	NEEDS IMPRV	UNSATISFACTORY	COMMENTS USE SEPARATE SHEET FOR ADDITIONAL COMMENTS
LEADERSHIP ABILITY	1						PERSONAL QUALITIES
WILLINGNESS TO ACCEPT RESPONSIBILITY	2						
DEPENDABILITY	3						
COOPERATIVENESS	4						
AGGRESSIVENESS, PERSEVERANCE, PERSUASIVENESS	5						
GENERAL APPEARANCE	6						
RELATIONS WITH SERVICE & OFFICE DEPARTMENTS	7						
LEARNING ABILITY	8						
WILLINGNESS TO ACCEPT AND TRY NEW IDEAS	9						
WILLINGNESS TO ACCEPT CONSTRUCTIVE CRITICISM	10						
CIVIC ACTIVITIES	11						
PLANNING AND MANAGEMENT OF TIME	12						TERRITORY OPERATION AND SALES ABILITY
THOROUGHNESS	13						
QUALITY OF INSTALLATIONS	14						
QUALITY OF DEMONSTRATIONS	15						
QUANTITY OF DEMONSTRATIONS	16						
ABILITY TO ANALYZE PROSPECTS NEEDS	17						
ABILITY TO CREATE INTEREST - ENTHUSIASM	18						
CLOSING ABILITY	19						
ABILITY AGAINST COMPETITION	20						
ABILITY TO HANDLE LARGE ACCOUNTS	21						
CUSTOMER RELATIONS	22						
ABILITY TO EXPRESS SELF IN WRITING	23						
ABILITY TO EXPRESS SELF IN SPEAKING	24						
COLLECTION RECORD	25						
SOFTWARE REVENUE	26						
EXPENSE CONTROL	27						
RESPONSIVENESS	28						

WHAT ARE THIS PERSON'S STRONG POINTS?   BE SPECIFIC. _____

_____

WHAT ARE WEAKNESSES?   BE SPECIFIC. _____

_____

COMMENT REGARDING THIS EMPLOYEE'S DEVELOPMENT NEEDS. _____

_____

_____

IS THIS EMPLOYEE WELL PLACED? _____   PROMOTABLE? _____
WHAT WOULD YOU RECOMMEND AS NEXT ASSIGNMENT?   COMMENT. _____

_____

_____

OVERALL PERFORMANCE APPRAISAL

EXCEPTIONAL	VERY GOOD	SATISFACTORY	NEEDS IMPROVEMENT	UNSATISFACTORY
Consistently does an excellent job. Performance approaches the best possible for the job. ☐	Exceeds requirements for satisfactory performance for the job. ☐	Meets all job requirements in a satisfactory manner. ☐	Performance must improve to meet job requirements. ☐	Performance does not warrant continuing in present assignment. ☐

HIS PERFORMANCE GENERALLY HAS _____ IMPROVED _____ NOT CHANGED _____ GONE BACK SINCE LAST REVIEW lenged. The situation could be ugly. The statistics are safe ground. The objective of the evaluation procedure may be distorted to getting through the process safely or simply to pass the evaluation.

Whether or not your manager is skilled in this process and comfortable in conducting reviews, your actions play a substantial part in the outcome. What kind of actions can you take to get the most benefits out of the process? A simple four-step process can be helpful.

1. Prepare before the evaluation.
2. Acknowledge the ratings.
3. Seek your manager's advice.
4. Suggest a plan for improving.

If you have been conscientious about your follow-up activities, you should have a clear picture of your performance. If you haven't, the scheduled evaluation should offer you an extra incentive to review your own performance. An evaluation is not something which is done to you or for you. It is an interaction. You must prepare your own evaluation of yourself. This evaluation must be prepared in terms of the organizational goals and standards. If your goals and standards are a great deal different from those of the organization, you might consider a different employer. As long as you are employed by this firm, its goals must be your goals.

To prepare effectively, you need three types of information. First, you need to fully understand the points to be covered in the evaluation. You might even ask your manager for a blank copy of the form. Second, you need information on your own performance. This includes not only the statistics on your sales but also subjective evaluations of your sales skills, work habits, and other job-related characteristics as indicated on the evaluation form. Third, you need some standard for comparison. There are really two relevant standards. One is the accepted performance level in the firm. This may not be readily available. The second standard is your previous performance. As you progress from evaluation to evaluation, keep records for comparison. Time spent in preparing for your evaluation can save valuable time during the evaluation.

The object of your preparation is not to counter the evaluation of your manager. Unless your manager's figures and ratings are wildly different from your own, the best thing may be to simply acknowledge them. Since they are only opinions anyway, to argue over them is to waste both time and energy. Your object is to move to the heart of the evaluation, that is, your plans for improvement.

To get the planning process started it is often wise to seek your manager's advice. "There seems to be some indication that I could improve in the area of demonstrations. Could you suggest some ways I might get started at that?" In soliciting suggestions you need not necessarily start with your lowest rated quality. There are two other approaches. One is to start with the quality where you feel your greatest potential lies. Perhaps at this point in your career you were rated lower on leadership potential than on any other quality.

If you believe that your leadership potential will improve with experience and maturity and that your efforts might be more productively devoted to some other area, you might seek advice on the other area first. Of course, some areas are always more crucial than others. You may begin with these. You may choose to use your time to seek advice on improving your closing abilities or abilities to analyze customer needs before turning to advice on civic activities. It is usually better to try to develop workable plans on one or two items than to attempt to incorporate all of the evaluation topics in your plan. If you try to do that, your plan will be little better than a simple statement: "I'm going to try to do better."

You should be prepared to suggest your plan for your own improvement. While your manager can advise you and suggest resources or techniques, only you can formulate your plan. A plan which is imposed upon you will be more difficult to implement. Plans imposed by others are often more restrictive than helpful. Your manager's overall objective is to be helpful, but you can only be helped if you are willing to help yourself.

All of the suggestions for helping your manager help you can be summarized in a simple question: "Am I behaving in a way I would want someone I managed to behave?"

Ask yourself what you would like to see in someone for whom you had responsibility as a manager? If you could describe that perfect person to manage, some of the characteristics on your list might refer to ability, intelligence, or skills. Sooner or later though, you would probably come to some questions of attitude. Ask yourself whether you would want to manage yourself.

12 You, too, can have role models and sponsors

Among the explanations which have been offered for the imbalance between men and women in professional sales is the absence of role models and sponsors for women. The idea is that one man will help another man succeed either through direct actions as a sponsor or through indirect actions as a role model. Because there have been few women in sales, it is supposed to follow that you will lack the benefits of appropriate role models and sponsors. This is supposed to mean that you will continually find yourself running into blind alleys, disoriented, without a sense of direction, or having to go it alone while men share their progress with each other.

That whole idea is nonsense. You too can have plenty of role models. There is no reason why you can't cultivate a sponsor. It is a question of how you define yourself. If you define yourself as a woman and see men as men, you're lost. If you see people as people, a whole new picture comes into focus. If you are a salesperson, there is no reason why observing any other successful salesperson shouldn't provide you with clues to appropriate behavior. If you are a competent per-

212

son with a great deal of potential, you may well be viewed as a protégée prospect by a possible sponsor. If you show a little flexibility and ability to adapt, there are lots of possible human resources for you to draw upon. If you take the attitude that unless the situation fits perfectly you aren't going to play, you will soon find yourself left out of the game.

Before going into some of the practical techniques and rules regarding the selection of role models and the cultivation of sponsors, let's take a look at what you stand to gain. After all, if you are going to put some effort into it, it is important to know that the returns will justify the investment.

ROLE MODELS

What is a role model? A role model is simply a person after whom you can pattern your behaviors as you play one of the many parts of your life. Each of us plays a variety of roles every day—friend, employee, wife, mother, lover, citizen, customer, and on and on. Others are playing those same roles, and some of them play the roles very well. Especially as you are facing a new role, there is a lot to be gained from observing veterans and imitating some of their more successful acts. If it is a new role and you really don't have any established patterns for it, why not start with some that seem to work? Your alternative is the trial-and-error approach. In many of the roles you are called upon to play, the world isn't willing to wait while you try and err and try again.

Role models can provide a balance between individuality and acceptability. Your objective is not to become a carbon copy of someone else. Indeed flagrant imitation can be offensive. Your objective is to behave in the accepted manner in situations in which you have no particular reason to act any other way. That should leave you with more freedom to vary from the normal patterns in situations where variance is justified. If you are generally well within the accepted range, you are usually allowed a few quirks. If you are always on the borderline, others will be less patient and understanding if you slip even a little.

To behave in accepted ways in no sense means that you should behave in a nondescript or unobtrusive manner. Perhaps you have heard expressions which imply that a low profile is the best profile. As long as you blend in you can't get in trouble. That may be true in the short run, but in the long run you may well encounter a different and more serious trouble. While a low profile may keep you out of the little spats, it will also keep you out of the running for the long-term rewards such as a management position.

You must be certain that you are noticed if you are ever going to succeed. The important point is that there is a big difference between good attention and bad attention. The observation of role models can help you to avoid bad attention. Bad attention can result either when you do something which is unacceptable or when you fail to do something which is considered to be an accepted part of business interaction. For example, an important part of a good personal impression in the business world is to be in control of yourself. Although everybody has moments when they are unsure, uncomfortable, or unprepared to act, the people who eventually succeed are the people who maintain control of themselves. One indication of a lack of control is nervous laughter. If you spend some time studying the people in positions of authority, you will see very little nervous laughter. To allow yourself to maintain such a habit is to do something which is unacceptable and can generate bad attention.

You can also generate bad attention by failing to do things which are acceptable. One accepted practice is shaking hands. When you get right down to it, there is probably no absolutely justifiable functional reason for shaking hands. It may even involve some health hazard, but it is an accepted business custom. Business people shake hands when they meet and they shake hands when they depart. If you were to fail to do so, it would generate bad attention. Of course, you must shake hands correctly. As silly as it may seem, little boys are taught to shake hands, and while it may be changing, little girls have been taught to kiss or smile politely. To shake hands limply may be worse than to skip it entirely. A firm handshake is apparently a sign of steadfastness, dependability, and other desirable business characteristics.

Other people pay attention to these signs even though they may not communicate that to you. They keep score silently. When you reach a certain point, the lights and buzzers go off and it is too late to make up for it. You can be making errors and no one will tell you. Have you ever been at the table when another person had a piece of food stuck on his chin but no one at the table would speak up? Everyone was worried that to point this out would have embarrassed the person and so they allowed him to continue to look silly. You could be continuing to do something which is making you look bad. Even though others are aware of it, no one will speak up. Remember, you are your own responsibility.

Checking your behaviors against various role models is one way to guard against this. If you look at what you are or are not doing and then observe the way that others are behaving and they don't match, you should ask yourself why. You may come up with a very good reason and continue to do it your way. You may, however, uncover a potential problem area. Role models may simply be a convenient vehicle for learning those important rules of the business game.

SPONSORS

Sponsors can also be an important source of information on the rules of the game, but there are some significant differences between the role model relationship and the sponsor relationship. A role model relationship is one-way. It does not require the cooperation of the role model. You simply watch the way this other person acts and borrow whatever behaviors you see as acceptable. Your role model was acting that way anyway. Your model didn't have to change. In fact, your role model may not even realize that you are alive.

A sponsor relationship, on the other hand, requires the active cooperation of both parties. A sponsor makes an investment in you and expects some return. A sponsor is a person who is in a position to provide you with opportunities. You will be selected by a sponsor if it appears that, in taking advantage of those opportunities, you will bring satisfaction to the sponsor. A sponsor relationship can truly be one of those rare win-win situations. If you perform well for your sponsor, both you and the sponsor benefit. You are exposed to additional opportunities which you would not be able to provide for yourself; your sponsor can be rewarded in several ways. Part of the credit for your accomplishments spills over onto your sponsor, and there is a certain satisfaction which comes from being able to help someone else.

Just because role models and sponsors are supposedly less available to women does not mean that they are any less valuable. In fact, these human resources may be even more important to women because their paths may be a bit less defined. A little more guidance might be required. The benefits of having role models and sponsors

216

are really not in dispute. The more difficult question is: How do you do it?

HOW DO YOU DO IT?

In making the most out of role models, you really have two concerns. The first is where to find them, and the second is what to do once you have. There are lots of role models, but the idea is to find ones that are valuable to you. If you look around your immediate environment, you may not see any. It depends on what you are looking for. If you are looking for a total picture that will serve as a guide for most of your actions, you have a good chance of being disappointed. It might be better to use the cut-and-paste method of role modeling. The idea is to build up a composite role model by drawing upon the strengths of several people. A very important point to remember is that your role model is not a standard against which you are measuring your own performance. If that was the case, you would be setting yourself up for that downward image spiral. You cannot hope to equal that strengths of a number of people. The composite role model is a learning device. It is an acknowledged collection of desirable behaviors. It is useful as a guide.

Where do you find the people from which you construct this overall model? There are many sources if you keep in mind that this is basically a one-way operation. Of course it is convenient if the people in your immediate environment demonstrate all the appropriate behaviors, but you need not be restricted to those you could reach out and touch. You see people on television, read about them in newspapers or magazines, or even read autobiographies of successful people. Add them to your model. The information is there, the only question is whether you are willing to accept and process it for your own good. Some people read a story about a successful person and react, "Isn't that interesting!" Other people can read that same story and ask themselves, "What can I learn from this?"

Sometimes learning from the behaviors of another person requires that you make an interpretation. Sometimes while the specific behavior is not directly transferable the idea has merit. For example, consider business clothing. There is an accepted business dress code for men. While this code is seldom written down, it pervades the atmosphere. There is a strong reason for the code. Clothing is highly visible and provides an excellent vehicle for a person to establish status. A man who wears a good quality navy blue, wool business suit with appropriate accessories will not likely be mistaken for an unskilled laborer. His clothing makes a statement about his position. That's where the interpretation comes in. You aren't going to go out and buy a good quality navy blue, wool man's business suit and have it altered to fit. You aren't expected to wear a man's shirt, tie, or shoes. That's not only silly, but it would be offensive. To interpret this potential role model impact you have to ask first, "Why does a man dress like this?" Then you have to ask what actions you could take to achieve the same objectives. Let's follow through on that example. One objective is obviously to establish identity. The blue suit is in effect a uniform which binds a man to his preferred peer group and separates him from other groups. Into your role model file goes the message "Dress like those with whom you wish to be associated." If you don't want to be mistaken for a typist, don't dress like one. In his book Michael Korda advises women to dress as though they had already succeeded.

Does that blue-suited businessman have other objectives? How about distractions? His attire is basic, not flashy or distracting. It probably isn't even fashionable in the high fashion sense. It isn't the newest or most exciting. It is probably best described as conservative. Why? One of his objectives is to establish a feeling of trust and confidence in his customers. There may even be more objectives, but at some point you must ask yourself, "What is the equivalent?" Your purpose is not necessarily to do as he does but rather to achieve the same objectives.[1]

Think of the advantages you have. A young man might blindly mock the behaviors of successful men never understanding the underlying significance. He might miss out on the opportunity to formulate behaviors which not only meet the requirements of the immediate situation but fit his personality as well. You have that opportunity to more fully understand the implications of the actions of role models. A young man may restrict his vision to a single role model who seems to fit and overlook some of the actions of others which might be even more helpful. Since you are not likely to find a single person after whom you can pattern your behaviors, you will have the opportunity to draw from a wider range of resources.

---

[1] For a well researched discussion of appropriate business clothing for women, see John T. Molloy, *Dress for Success for Women* (New York: Warner Books, 1978).

There is really no shortage of role models for you as a saleswoman. There isn't even a shortage of highly appropriate role models. All that is really required to bridge this apparent gap is a better understanding of the way to utilize the role models who are available. There are lots of people whose behaviors you could profitably observe. That is only the first step. To make use of the information requires some thought. You are like a detective who has uncovered the modus operandi, but now must understand the motives to solve the case. It is one thing to see what someone else is doing and to try to imitate it. But if you are to truly benefit, it is important to have some understanding of why that other person is successful. By understanding the whys, you can develop parallel actions in areas in which the exact imitation would be inappropriate. You can also avoid blind imitation of purposeless actions. Once you understand something, it becomes your own action rather than a borrowed action.

Your careful attention to role models can be important in developing appropriate business behaviors. This actually removes some of the barriers which might have interfered with the ability of others to estimate your potential. In their minds, proper behavior makes you more predictable. If you are playing their game, they are more comfortable dealing with you. This may even make it possible for you to experience the advantages of a sponsor relationship.

A sponsor can be very important to your career development. Sponsorship implies a public commitment. It is fear of this commitment that has often interfered with the establishment of sponsor relationships between men and women. Most of the people who have the personal positions to act as sponsors in business have been men. Men with the capacity and interest to act as sponsors have found it both more convenient and less risky to sponsor other men. There is much less likelihood that others would question the relationship. Many women have never even realized that they have been left out. They never understood why a man who seemed equal to them in most ways seemed to have an inside track. The normal behavior for most women has been to internalize the problem. They have tended to believe that there was something about them which was holding them back, not that the man had some particular advantage. That advantage might well have been a sponsor.

One woman recalls with mixed feelings her first exposure to the idea of sponsorship. It was in graduate school. She was assigned as a graduate assistant to the senior professor in the management school.

She felt she had done well in discharging her duties. She was even a little proud of herself. At the end of the year she was in the professor's office, and he began to speak of their relationship in terms of regret. He apologized for having been unable to show her the kinds of treatment he had bestowed on previous graduate assistants. "After all," he said, "if you had been a man we could have gotten together, had a few drinks, and talked about your future. I just couldn't do that with you. What would people have thought?" She was stricken. To this point she had not realized that she had been treated differently, but now she realized that she had been deprived of one of the most valuable facets of the professor-assistant relationship—the opportunity to experience a close professional relationship with a senior person who provided needed guidance. While she felt cheated, she was also lucky. Some people never have the opportunity to understand that this is either necessary or available. She had learned early.

There are really two forms of assistance which can be offered by a sponsor. Some sponsors open doors for you and others give you the keys to open your own doors. To open the doors for you involves greater risks for the sponsor. To take this kind of risk, a sponsor needs some assurance that you will live up to your potential. Sponsorship for women often takes the low-risk form.

Here's an example. It is not as uncommon as you might think for a woman who is already employed by the firm in some staff capacity to make the switch to sales. In most cases she finds that her experience on the inside is extremely useful when she is on the outside. The question is How does she make the switch? Many times she has a sponsor. In one incident a woman was working as a secretary. After repeatedly expressing interest in the activities of one of the salesmen, he finally gave her the advice and encouragement she needed. She had seen his work as interesting but did not realize that she had either the abilities or the opportunities to do the same thing. He had seen her as capable but had not realized that she was interested in sales. He was instrumental in helping her to put the pieces together and go after the job. He couldn't open the door, but he helped her to find the keys.

In the high-risk form, this person would have actually recommended the woman for the job. He would have used whatever influence he had with the sales manager to help this woman be considered for an opening in sales. As it is, his identity was protected.

The sales manager really didn't know why the secretary suddenly expressed strong interest in the job or how she seemed to know enough to be chosen over other candidates. But she did. Her silent sponsor had provided her with the keys. It was a cooperative effort, but had she not gotten the job, he would have been unsmudged.

In another silent partner incident, a saleswoman was concerned about her assignment. She felt that she was assigned to a low potential territory and wanted to move up. When she brought the idea up with her manager, he told her he would think about it, but there was no other territory open. Soon after that the manager approached a salesman in the office to discuss a territory which he expected to have available within the month. This salesman, who really didn't want to be reassigned, unwittingly discussed the matter with the woman who was so anxious to change territories. She didn't know what to do, so she actually sought out the advice of an experienced salesman who had been willing to talk with her in confidence about other issues. He was actually acting as a silent sponsor even though she had established the contact. She was feeling very neglected and considering quitting. He suggested that she try a little less disruptive tactic first. Instead of getting mad, she should assume that there is some logical explanation. In this more calm state of mind, she should stage it so that she could casually ask her manager about her request for a change of territory in front of someone else, preferably the young man who knew that a territory would soon be open. It worked. Again the advice opened up the opportunities although the advisor, the silent sponsor, remained in the shadows.

In the classical sponsorship, a senior person selects a younger person with potential. This senior person, who is usually a male, uses his influence to provide the younger person with opportunities. When the opportunities materialize, the sponsored person performs admirably. The credit for the accomplishments falls in part on the protégé and in part on the sponsor who was obviously wise enough to suggest this person for the assignment. Both partners are rewarded for the risks they have taken.

What are some of the questions you are going to have to consider if you are going to get anywhere near this ideal? The first is: How do you and your sponsor select each other? There may be several possible combinations. How can you tell which is the right one? For a highly visible woman there may be many candidates, and some may not be as good as they look. Sometimes the problem is recognizing a potential sponsor.

Obviously, one of the most important considerations is starting out with the best partner. It isn't simply a matter of being chosen. You have some say in the matter. It is better to have no sponsor at all than to have an inappropriate sponsor. One woman found that out the hard way. She was gullible enough to fall for the lines of a senior person who had really peaked out but was clever enough to recognize her potential. He had been hanging on and now saw her as a way to cover for his inadequacies. Under the guise of providing her with a chance to prove herself and to benefit from his contacts and experiences, he used her. While that was deliberate, there are other cases where the would-be sponsor who really intends to be helpful just doesn't have what it takes. Without influence or useful experience, good intentions are just good intentions.

You have to decide whether the relationship will be beneficial to you. That is the big test. It is fine that your sponsor will benefit, but your intention is not only to do someone else a favor. You must consider both your long-term and short-term benefits. You may be investing more now in order to collect at a later date. That's fine. Many fine opportunities have been wasted because people have been unable to take a longer look. What are you looking for?

You could ask yourself whether you would be proud to have your association with this person printed up on the business page of the morning newspaper. That covers a lot of ground. Even if you are anticipating a silent sponsorship, you must have some respect for the person. You could ask yourself if you will be able to live up to the expectations of the sponsor. If you don't think so though, ask yourself again. You may be taking a safe path but denying yourself important opportunities. One sales manager related his frustrations. He had quite honestly attempted to serve as a sponsor for one of his newer saleswomen. As a recent convert to equal opportunity, he wanted to assure her at least an even chance. He told her that the company was putting together a team of people to work on a special bid on a big state contract and that he thought it would be a good experience for her. While he thought she would jump at the chance, she turned him down. He was stunned. He had offered her a big opportunity, and she had rejected it. She said she did not feel she was ready for it. If he hadn't felt she was ready for it, he wouldn't have asked her. She not only cheated herself out of a big chance, but she contradicted his judgment. His confidence in her plummeted. Why should he have confidence in her if she lacked it in herself? She never got a second chance. Think twice before you reject opportunities. Second chances are rare. Try to think of your ultimate potential instead of your current capabilities.

Perhaps this woman would have reacted in her own best interests if she had recognized this opportunity as an initial sponsorship bid. You can't expect someone to come up with a clear statement: "I'd like to be your sponsor. I will explain what I expect from you and what I will be able to offer." Your potential sponsor may not even realize that this relationship could develop. In many cases, the most you could expect is an indication of some interest in your progress. It is your responsibility to reward that interest if you want to cultivate the sponsor.

Since many men are either reluctant to view women as a protégée or do not realize the potential benefits for both parties, it may be to your benefit to actively cultivate a sponsor. Carefully evaluate the senior people with whom you have contact. Select one or more potential sponsors. If you make a point of seeking their advice on your legitimate professional concerns, you could be establishing the basis for a sponsor relationship.

After you have found a sponsor, you must consider your responsibilities to each other. How do you make sure that this arrangement produces the benefits that should be expected? There may well be a point where you have to deal with the question of a defunct sponsorship. What do you do if the arrangement is no longer viable? Sponsoring is an ongoing relationship. There is a mutual commitment. It is a professional marriage. There are great benefits to be gained from handling it well and a high price can result from handling it poorly.

As you move into this relationship, what are your responsibilities? The basic rule is performance. In days of old, rulers might settle affairs of state by sending their champions into the arena. What do you suppose was the fate of the champion who failed to defend his ruler's honor? When you are selected as a champion, you have an obligation to defend your sponsor's honor. You have an obligation to make your sponsor proud of you.

There is also a matter of discretion. Being sponsored is a privilege. It is earned, but it is still a privilege. Any individual sponsor can only extend this privilege so far. Not everyone is given those same opportunities. It can be thrilling. You may be exposed to opportunities and experiences which you would want others to appreciate. If you go about bragging, even quietly, you could find those benefits cut off. Your sponsor may brag about you, but it is not acceptable for you to brag about your sponsor. You have one responsibility—to give your sponsor something to brag about.

What do you do if it all falls down? To dissolve a sponsorship is not unlike a divorce. It can be painful. Once you and your sponsor have teamed up, your destinies are interrelated. You can't walk away from it as if it never happened. Several things can bring about the end. Some sponsors suffer a fall from grace and thereby lose their ability to hold up their end of the arrangement. If you are publicly associated with your sponsor and this happens, you may also be looking for another job. For one woman, this happened very early. She had interviewed for a sales position for which she lacked some of the specified qualifications. Following some of the tactics for selling herself, she had convinced the district sales manager that she was the right person for the job anyway. But between the time that he stamped his approval on her and the time she was to start on the job, he lost his job. She was swept out right along with him.

You may outgrow your sponsor. You will need different types of opportunities and experiences early in your career. A person who can provide those may not be able to provide a higher level of opportunity later on. Some people have made the mistake of carelessly discarding past sponsors. Be careful about how you treat people on your way up because you may see the same faces on your way down. Besides that, some sponsors might have been willing to help you because someone before you had left a good impression. Someone coming along behind you deserves the same chance.

Sometimes sponsors are threatened by the rate of progress of their protégés. What happens if you appear able to move into your sponsor's job before your sponsor is ready to move out? Some sponsors are happy to see you advance as long as your rate of progress does not exceed their rate. They would like to see the established order maintained.

Despite some of the difficulties which can occur, sponsors can help you to progress in a sales career. They can offer advice, guidance, encouragement, and opportunities. They can share experiences and contacts to help you get started. When you are ready to move into management, a sponsor could help you to open that next door.

But that very first door can be the hardest. If you are going to reach for any of the opportunities which await competent women, you are going to have to make the first move. You can't afford to sit back and wait to see if something happens. You have to make it happen. You have to go out there and seek opportunities.

Professional selling has been providing competent men with the opportunities to earn above-average incomes and to advance to management careers for a long time. More than ever before these same opportunities are now available to women. You have to make the effort to overcome any doubts, fears, or inadequacies which stand in your way. You can't expect to change the world, but you can make positive changes in yourself. You have to understand reality and make the most of your opportunities.

Index

A

Abuse, 90, 97-99
Accountability, 12-14
Achiever, 19
Alert avoidance, 94
American Marketing Association, 45
Appointments, 170-71
  sandwich approach, 171
Approach; see Sales call, approach
Assertiveness, 66-67
Attention, good and bad, 214

B

Backstabber, 88, 92
Bashful Backer, 88, 91
Bigot, 88, 92
Birddogging, 106
Blind ads, 42
Booster, 88, 91
Bridge; see Sponge techniques
Bulldozer, 18-19
Buyer behavior, 104, 114
Buyers' motives, 114-15
Buying states
  modified rebuy, 115-17
  new purchase, 117-18
  straight rebuy, 115-17

C

Card file, geographic, 170-71
Career planning, 43
Cautious Creepers, 28-29
Clothing, 216-17
Cold calls, 110
Communicating with customers, 31-33
Comparative advantage; see Theory of Comparative Advantage
Compliments, 71-75
Constructive communication, 193, 197-99
Contribution, measuring, 7-10
Customer relations, 181-85

D

Delegate; see Time management mechanisms
Deliberate misinterpretation; see Sponge techniques
Disruptions; see Sales call
Doormat, 17-18

E

Earnestness, 50, 54
Education, 50-51
Ego drive, 16-21, 24, 30-32
Ego energy account, 204-5
Eliminate; see Time management mechanisms
Empathy, 16-21, 30
Employers' needs, 46-47
Employment agencies, 43
Entertaining, 184
Enthusiasm, 50-53
Equal Employment Opportunities Commission (EEOC), 99
Executive search firms, 43
Expansible income, 13
Experience, 46, 50-53

F

Fair Employment Practices Commission, 99
Feminine charms, 181
Follow-through
  internal and external, 148
  to job interview, 62-63
  with nonbuyers, 144-46
  after sale, 147-50
Follow-up, 138-44

G-I

Generalists, 14-16
Harassment, 90, 92-97
Image spiral, 26-28
Imperfections, 54-55
Inadequacies, 54, 56-57

Industrial sales, 3
Inflexibilities, 54-56
Initiation option, 178
Interpersonal contacts, 77-78
Interviewing, 58-62
  bias in, 60-61
Intimacy
  mental, 190
  physical, 189
Intracompany sex, 181

J-L

Jealous Jabber, 28
Lakein, Alan, 155, 164-65
Law of Diminishing Returns, 154
Leprosy Syndrome, 68-69
Line positions, 11-15
Listening, 129-30
Lists, 164

M

Management, the benefits of effective, 193-95
Managing your manager, 193
Market, 107
Menace, 90, 96-97
Molloy, John T., 217

O

Objections
  handling, 126-30
    active techniques, 129-30
    anticipating, 129
    passive techniques, 128-29
    reduction to the ridiculous, 129-30
    types, 126-28
Organization; see Time management mechanisms

P

Paperwork, 138, 148
Parkinson's Law, 10
Peer group definition dilemma, 185-87
Performance evaluation, 206-11
Positive attitude, 193
Postemployment droop, 203-4
Pragmatic positivism, 84, 86-87, 182
Precall objective, 118, 140-41
Prime time, internal and external, 165-66
Professional sales, definition, 2
Prospecting
. for job leads, 40-46
  for qualified customers, 102-11
Provocation, 90-92
Psychology Today, 71
Purchasing agent, 114

Q-R

Qualifying, 107-8
Queen Bee Syndrome, 187
Regularity, 6-7
Rejection, handling, 80-82
Résumé, 57-58
Retail sales, 2-3
Revson, Charles, 112
Risk and opportunity, 22
Role models, 213-16
  the cut-and-paste method, 216
Rules of the game, 173-74

S

Sales call
  approach, 119-22
  close, 130-36, 142
    assumptive, 133
    positive choice, 134
    start big, 134
    start small, 134
    trial, 133
    urgency, 135
  presentation
    in job hunting
      making, 57-62
      preparing, 50-57
    for the sale
      canned, 111-12
      making, 119-22
      preparing, 111-19
Sales Manpower Foundation, 11
Sales and Marketing Management, 49, 195
Scanlon, Sally, 195
Selective thickskinnery, 59, 91
Self-esteem, 72
Self-image, 24-26
Sequential solutions, 97-99
Servants, 18
Sexual harassment; see Harassment
Shaking hands, 214
Simplify; see Time management mechanisms
Speaking out, 78-80
Specialization, the dangers of, 10-11
Spider Mites, 187-89
Sponge techniques, 182-83
Sponsors, 215-24
  classical, 220-21
  cultivating, 222
  dissolving the sponsorship, 224
  screening, 221
  silent, 219-20
Staff positions, 5-11
Standardizing; see Time management mechanisms

Statement qualification, 75-77
Substitute; *see* Time management mechanisms
Success image inhibitors, 24-30
Support assessment scale, 36

T

Telephone use, 58, 110
Theory of Comparative Advantage, 154-55
Tickler file, 146
Time budgeting, 167-68
Time demands, internal and external, 158-59
Time flexibility, 11-12
Time management mechanisms, 158-64

Time tag, ℋ, 157
Trade fair, 106
Trade sales, 3
Training, 196, 201-4
Travel, 175-80

U-W

Undermining, 65-66
Unevaluative acknowledgment; *see* Sponge techniques
Visual reminders, 37
The Wall Street Journal, 42
Weaknesses, 54-57
Wives of coworkers, 189-90